BLOOD TRYST

Jesse Cummings slipped on a pair of surgical gloves, opened the car door and pulled out the quivering Melissa. Her shaking hand tightly gripped in her uncle's, she was led down a dirt path to the silent empty place he had chosen.

Cummings ordered her to disrobe, then pulled the naked eleven-year-old close to him, her back against his chest.

"I wanta fool around 'fore I take you to your mama."

Cummings assaulted the girl once more, then with his right hand, pulled a hunting knife from the scabbard of the belt fastened around his coveralls. His left arm hugged Melissa's neck, gripping her tighter as he covered her mouth to stifle her screams.

She tensed at the first thrust of the knife, then slumped against her uncle as the knife entered her slight body again and again. The screams he expected never came. Even as she died, Melissa was too afraid of him to make a sound.

With icy indifference, Cummings placed the knife on the left side of her neck and deftly slit her throat.

BOOK YOUR PLACE ON OUR WEBSITE AND MAKE THE READING CONNECTION!

We've created a customized website just for our very special readers, where you can get the inside scoop on everything that's going on with Zebra, Pinnacle and Kensington books.

When you come online, you'll have the exciting opportunity to:

- View covers of upcoming books
- Read sample chapters
- Learn about our future publishing schedule (listed by publication month *and author*)
- Find out when your favorite authors will be visiting a city near you
- Search for and order backlist books from our online catalog
- Check out author bios and background information
- Send e-mail to your favorite authors
- Meet the Kensington staff online
- Join us in weekly chats with authors, readers and other guests
- Get writing guidelines
- AND MUCH MORE!

**Visit our website at
http://www.pinnaclebooks.com**

SUFFER THE LITTLE CHILDREN

Barbara Davis

Pinnacle Books
Kensington Publishing Corp.
http://www.pinnaclebooks.com

Some names have been changed to protect the privacy of individuals connected to this story.

PINNACLE BOOKS are published by

Kensington Publishing Corp.
850 Third Avenue
New York, NY 10022

Pinnacle and the P logo Reg. U.S. Pat. & TM Off.

First Printing: August, 1999
10 9

Printed in the United States of America

The personalities, events, actions and conversations portrayed within this story have been reconstructed from extensive interviews and research, utilizing court documents, letters, personal papers, press accounts, and the memories of participants. The trial testimony is taken from the author's recorded tapes obtained during the trial. In an effort to safeguard the privacy of certain individuals, not directly involved in the crime, some names and identifying characteristics have been altered. All minors have been renamed.

*To Leon, for your unwavering
belief in me.
I miss you my friend.*

PART ONE

"Suffer the little children to come unto me, and forbid them not: for of such is the Kingdom of God."
—*Mark 10:14*

Prologue

The citizens of Oklahoma patiently suffered through the summer's blazing temperatures waiting for the fall to bring in a welcome reprieve. The October weather in southeastern Oklahoma came to the rescue, carrying with it mild clouds that lifted the veil of heat the stifling September had left.

On October 16, 1991, the change of season nudged Choctaw County volunteer fireman Brian Wilkins to load his fishing gear into his truck and head toward Crystal Road's Twin Set Bridges, which crosses over Clear Boggy River just north of Boswell. Barely forty, a strapping all-American male, Wilkins perfectly fits the image of a fireman. Passing over the river, Wilkins pulled onto the gravel shoulder within a few feet of the bridge's end. Looking forward to a day of rest, he got out and strolled toward his favorite fishing hole, taking in the smell of the fresh country air with each step.

A stench began to waft along with the cool breeze. It stopped the fireman dead in his tracks. The sight and pungent smell smothered him as he battled to keep down the lunch he had eaten earlier. Putting down the tackle box and fishing pole, Wilkins peered past the metal railing of the bridge into the woods. Holding his breath, he searched for the cause of the odor.

He spotted a small trail leading deeper into the woods. Squinting into the bright sunlight, he examined the path more closely. The source of Wilkins's queasiness appeared to be a small decaying animal sprawled on the ground and partially covered by brush.

A sense of urgency quickened his pace as he hurried toward the object and came sliding to a halt. The bones only inches from his feet were now clearly identifiable. The sudden recognition shattered any hope that this was just an animal.

Although he was acquainted with tragedy in his capacity as a volunteer fireman, nothing could have prepared Wilkins to deal with the heartache lying scattered on the ground in front of him.

Releasing a deep sigh, he slowly bent over the body for a closer examination of the small skull covered by a few strands of long brunette hair.

The hide, once the baby-soft skin of a child's, had turned tough as leather from the unforgiving elements of the hot sun. Vermin had devoured the muscle tissue and organs not already evaporated by the harsh summer heat.

"Oh, my God." Wilkins whispered. Encircling the bones of the left wrist were four tiny friendship bracelets similar to ones he had seen his own daughter wear. Although scorched and tattered, the familiar bracelets woven by a child's innocent and playful hands were unmistakable to the father.

The veteran fought back tears as he stared in disbelief at the horrible vision that was stretched along the dusty path. Glancing around for a sign of clothing, Wilkins searched for a clue to the identity of the child, but found nothing. He realized the torn and ravaged corpse must have been nude whenever the monster who was responsible for the carnage left his prey out in the open to be exposed to the elements of the terrain.

Forcing his attention back to the body crumpled in the dirt, Wilkins scrutinized the horrible sight carefully. A knot formed in his throat when he spotted the only clue to be found, a small gold loop earring still attached to the toughened, sun-scorched right ear.

Eventually the tiny skeleton would be identified as that of a spirited, beautiful eleven-year-old girl. Her name was Melissa.

One

Jesse James Cummings was born November 19, 1955, on a freezing cold day in Modesto, California. His mother, Marie, had a difficult delivery, barely surviving her son's birth. Jesse's mother would be the first woman to suffer excruciating pain because of him. She would not be the last.

Marie Cummings and Jesse Samuel Cummings, Sr., married in 1951. Between them Marie and Jesse, Sr., brought five children into the marriage and had two children together. A boy, Jesse James, would be the first. After Jesse's difficult birth, three miscarriages followed. Then Marie successfully carried to full term a girl they named Debra Lee. Poor and with meager resources, the couple would struggle to survive as each conception and birth brought more hardship. As migrant workers the Cummingses traveled a lot, moving every couple of months, seldom putting roots down for very long in any one place, eking out a living the best they could.

Depending on where the family landed, they would do whatever manual labor was available, picking cotton and oranges, or sometimes hauling logs, wood, or junk iron. As their parents roamed for work, the kids switched schools with each move, never establishing stable or long-lasting friendships. It took its toll.

Cummings, Sr., though a little on the wild side and known to drink and run around on his wife at times, was kind in heart and good-naturedly tolerated the children's misbehavior. Marie

Cummings, who was quite unstable and at times resembled a full-blown schizophrenic, was known by her family to also be a raging alcoholic with a temper to match. Most thought it best to just stand clear of her.

From the beginning chaos entwined with violence was a normal part of the dysfunctional family's life. Cummings, Sr., wanting to avoid his wife's wrath, kept himself busy and left her to deal with the children as she saw fit. They rarely received hugs and kisses from their mother. Instead, daily and merciless beatings were administered, and Jesse seemed to provoke the ire of his mother more than anyone. Marie Cummings had a horsewhip that she used mostly on Jesse. As the skin was ripped from his back with each harsh lash, the little boy would stubbornly refuse to cry.

The harsh abuse of Jesse Cummings started when he was just a toddler. As he grew older, the abuse continued nonstop. By the time he could walk, he began to capture helpless animals and do to them the things done to him. It was vicious and always cruel.

Throughout his life Cummings would use his mother as a guide for his behavior, mimicking her ways, using the same harsh and cruel methods he would learn from her.

When the children were sick or disobedient, Marie administered homemade remedies comprised of awful-tasting concoctions. The medicine usually induced vomiting instead of promoting healing. Like his mother, Cummings would carry on the tradition of "Mama's Home Remedies" within his own family, making the children hate him as vehemently as he did his own mother.

As soon as the children could, they would leave home to escape her craziness, and they would stay away. All but Jesse.

Contributing to the family income was a main priority. Education was the last. During Jesse's early school years the family remained in Coalgate, Oklahoma, where they barely managed to scrape by. Cummings quit school at the age of twelve and began working with his father to help support them. The young boy's problems with the law started just shortly after he dropped out of school. With no more supervision and no real guidance, the boy promptly rebelled against anyone and anything in his path.

Within two years of dropping out of school, the youth ran away. He was barely fourteen years old.

Jesse Cummings's leaving home at such an early age left his younger sister to fend for herself against their mother's beatings. Up until that point Cummings had always taken Debra's side and tried to shield his little sister from the harsh, irrational punishments.

Although Cummings ran away from home, it was never for good. He merely took brief sabbaticals from his hell-raising mother. When he was away from home, he managed to get in even more trouble. Too young to have a driver's license, Cummings drove without one. One of the things he enjoyed most was taunting the police. Whenever Cummings saw a police car he would pull up beside the unit, gun his engine, then peel out; jumping canals once the police car gave chase.

The beginning of such willful disobedience, coupled with a long string of petty crimes, eventually caught up with Jesse Cummings. He was placed in a California juvenile facility, where he would serve fifteen months before being released.

Cummings had the uncanny ability to shelter a charming personality within an abusive one. The charming part of him imparted a false image to which many women were drawn as Cummings grew from a teenager to a man. His pattern, which began to emerge in 1973, consisted of using the charming part to pursue a young lady. When Cummings had her thoroughly under his thumb, his abusive personality would appear, and it would be the one that would stay throughout the relationship. In 1973, at the age of eighteen, Cummings ran off to Mexico to marry a fifteen-year-old girl he had met while in California. Margaret Hazel Yaws stood five feet tall, was heavyset, and had dark hair. She was the mirror image of Jesse's mother. When Marie and her new daughter-in-law stood with their backs to other people, the similarities were so great no one could tell who was who.

Cummings brought his young bride straight back to Coalgate, Oklahoma, and to the woman he despised. The newly married couple took up residence in an old, beat-up bus the color of mustard, which was parked in his parents' backyard.

With Jesse and Margaret Hazel entrenched in the broken-down bus just feet from Marie, Jesse was in close range for the torment his mother still loved to shove his way.

Cummings's new bride had been crippled since childhood by debilitating polio. A series of operations, which had little impact on the disabling disease, left her dependent. Margaret Hazel Cummings counted on three things to get around: her crutches, a leg brace, and Jesse.

Her husband took cruel advantage of his wife's condition, delighting in moving the crutches and brace beyond her grasp so she had no way of going anywhere unless she wanted to crawl.

The length of time he left her dependent on him hinged on his varying moods. Cummings would laugh and brag about the control it gave him over his wife. It was just the beginning of a paradigm of depraved behavior that would consume his life.

Margaret Hazel was a sweet, kind girl who never provoked her husband. At any given time she had bruises on her body that were inflicted by her abusive husband. Cummings instructed her to say she got them in a wreck or any other calamity she could quickly call to mind if anyone should inquire about them.

Margaret Hazel and her mother-in-law barely had a chance to get to know each other before the marriage broke up. But one thing was clear, Margaret Hazel was terrified of Marie, and Marie was not too fond of young Margaret Hazel, either.

Jesse Cummings came home one day to find that Margaret Hazel had simply packed her things and disappeared. Somehow, the crippled young woman had gathered the strength and courage to leave her husband and his cruel behavior behind. She knew that she had to get far away from him before his meanness evolved into a madness she could see simmering within him.

Cummings could not live without a woman. The urge came not from a need for love, but from his ever-growing compulsion to control everything around him. Upon finding the empty bus, Cummings went looking for another woman to replace the one who had gotten away. Janet Moore quickly entered his life when Cummings moved temporarily to Arkansas. Janet was twenty-four when she fell prey to Jesse's charms, and they married in 1978. Jesse Cummings was barely twenty-three years old.

For Cummings, the line between marriage and divorce was nonexistent. Having a wife never stopped him from trying to acquire another one, and he never bothered to get a divorce from Margaret Hazel.

Cummings returned with his new wife to the broken-down bus still parked in his parents' yard. Unlike her predecessor, Janet was close to five seven, thin, and possessed a thick, full mane of red hair.

As with the previous daughter-in-law, Marie made no real effort to try and get along with her. It was evident that neither Jesse's mother nor his wife could stand each other's company. And that suited him just fine.

Cummings treated Janet just as he had Margaret Hazel. As his second marriage precariously teetered along, he continued to date as though he were a free man, just as he had when he was married to Margaret Hazel.

Janet and Jesse returned every so often to visit relatives in Arkansas. Several years after their marriage, Cummings left his wife home and took his mother along with him on the trip instead.

Cummings met a young girl named Sherry at the family gathering he and Marie had traveled to. Sherry was very young, and had been born the year Jesse dropped out of school. Dark-haired, barely five feet tall, and heavyset, she resembled Marie as much as Margaret Hazel had.

Lahoma Yaws had brought her daughter Sherry with her to

the gathering to get her mind off her rocky, trouble-laden marriage. There was a large assembly of people in the house belonging to Slim and Maudie Moody, and Sherry knew few of them or their particular ties to her family.

The two Cummingses were there to visit Jesse's half sister and Marie's natural daughter, Judy. Judy was married to the Moodys' son, Tinky. Lahoma Yaws's ties to the family were rooted in her marriage to Charles Yaws, and she was visiting the Moodys, who were relatives of her husband. Charles was also the uncle of Margaret Hazel, who had been Jesse's first wife.

Itinerant workers, like gypsies, live off the bounty of the land and travel to the states that afford them the best opportunity to work year-round. Seasonal changes dictate the direction the band of workers head in.

Since most of the Cummingses, Yawses and Moodys were itinerant workers, they traveled constantly in a circle of three states: California, Arkansas, and Oklahoma. Never in one place for very long, fostering outside relationships was difficult, if not nearly impossible and familiarity and trust became exclusive within the family units. This way of life resulted in complicated unions peppering family trees.

These common familial relationships facilitated Jesse Cummings's and Sherry's first meeting in the Moody living room. Sherry's attention was immediately captured by the well-built young man, who looked to be twenty-six or twenty-seven years old.

He was flirting outrageously with every female in the room. Cummings had been showing off for them by wrestling with some of the people there and describing in a bold manner, as only he could, the finer points of the sport.

Sherry had broken her right wrist a few months prior, and although the cast was off, the wrist was still tender. Much to her surprise, Sherry found herself an unwilling participant in a wrestling match. Sherry's right arm was pulled behind her by

Cummings, and was twisted so far back that her right fingertips touched the top of her left shoulder.

The maneuver was excruciating, and Sherry asked the man holding her arm what his name was. He replied, "Jesse."

Young, but sassy and undaunted, Sherry started off nicely. She spoke to him in firm, measured words. "Let go of my arm, Jesse."

Cummings just laughed and popped off, "You can't do nothing 'bout it, little girl."

The pain was getting worse and niceties were put aside as the words "I said let go of me, motherfucker!" sprung from Sherry's mouth, surprising both participants in the arm lock.

Cummings let go, shoved her forward, and spit out, "You better leave 'fore my mama gets a hold of you, gal." As Sherry glanced over her shoulder, she noticed Cummings's mother had overheard the "motherfucker" remark. She might have been young, but the dirty look that came from Marie was not wasted on Sherry.

Unhappy over the push, and her arm still aching, Sherry headed toward the front door. She cast one more look in Cummings's direction and hurled parting words at him. "You stupid son of a bitch." That was twice Sherry had called Cummings a disparaging name and unintentionally managed to zing his mother, too.

Lahoma Yaws had known Cummings since he was barely thirteen and she eighteen. The two young people even shared the same birth date. They had met for the first time, ironically, when she was visiting Slim and Maudie years earlier. Sherry's mother had not seen the altercation between her daughter and Cummings, and it wasn't mentioned during or after the visit. But it would not have surprised her. She knew just how wild and irresponsible Cummings was.

Lahoma Yaws had known he was troubled, and she was aware that he had incorporated petty thefts into his life as far back as when she knew the boy of thirteen. Lahoma recalled, "Jesse was a juvenile delinquent. Every time I turned around, Jesse was in some kind of trouble. I knowed he'd been arrested as a juvenile for the first time in California."

Lahoma Yaws remembered a particular event that occurred when they all lived around Bakersfield, California, that was bizarre. "There was a plowed field by the Cummings house and we was going down the road minding our own business. We seen Jesse was running 'cross that plowed field followed by Margaret Hazel. Both was trying to get away from Jesse's mother who was shooting at 'em. We stopped the car on the highway and waited for him to run over there and quickly got him in the car with us. Then we sat there and waited for Margaret Hazel 'cause everybody was afraid to get outta the car 'cause of Marie popping shots out 'cross the field. She was drunk as hell. Margaret Hazel finally made it to the car, and she was just white as a ghost, hobbling across that field. I don't remember if she had her crutches or her brace, but she owned both at the time. We asked 'em what was the problem this time, and Margaret Hazel told us Marie got mad 'cause she wanted Jesse to go to town and get her some more beer, and he wouldn't do it."

Cummings's remark about the shooting incident was a simple "One of these days that woman's gonna kill me yet." Then he laughed.

Lahoma shook her head in astonishment at the memory. She had watched terrified as the bullets hit the dry dirt close behind the young couple's heels.

Lahoma recalled one con Cummings was exceptionally good at—getting automobiles illegally and turning a profit by selling them. She said, as soon as a buyer fell a payment behind, Cummings would pay them a visit. "He'd go over and say, 'Well, that car don't belong to me, and the persons come to me and they're gonna repossess it.' It wasn't nobody else's vehicle, it was his. But to keep him out of saying 'I want my money,' he'd lie and tell 'em this person is down on me and they want their money and I ain't got it, so you're gonna have to get it or they're coming to get the vehicle."

According to Lahoma, throughout his troubled youth and into his marriages, Cummings seldom held down a job, but preferred to pull cons like the one just described, to steal to make money, and to stay stoned. She remembered, especially, Cummings's heavy use of drugs. "I have no idea what he was on, but they [Cummings and Margaret Hazel] showed up at our house and it was late in the evening. He slept on our couch for five days, and didn't even know he was there. He was strung out bad on something.

"That five days he spent at our house," Lahoma remembered vividly, "Jesse woke up one morning and said, 'How in hell'd I get here?' And we told him he'd been there five days. This was normal behavior for Jesse. He wasn't a drinker as far's I know. It was drugs he was mainly on."

Lahoma Mitchell had given birth to Sherry in Jay, Oklahoma, on October 17, 1967. Sherry's father, Ernest Barnett, was Lahoma's stepbrother. From the day of Sherry's birth, Barnett denied her existence.

Shortly after Barnett fathered another child with Lahoma, a boy whose existence he also denied, the teenage mother and her two children returned to Bakersfield, California.

Sherry was barely five years old when her mother told her who her real father was. Until that point Lahoma had let Sherry and her brother believe that Charles Yaws was their real father.

The little girl dreamed of meeting her father someday. At the age of fifteen she talked an older friend into driving her a city away to meet this man named Barnett. Mindful of the fact that her father was married with several children, she did not want to insert herself into his life. She just wanted to meet him.

Sherry nervously sat in the passenger seat while her friend went to the door to tell Barnett his daughter was in the car and would like to see him.

The two visitors were dispatched to the house of Ernest Barnett's sister-in-law, where Sherry was told to wait for her father to arrive.

After two anxiety-filled hours of nerve-wracking waiting,

Sherry suffered humiliating disappointment when her father's wife was sent with a message for the young girl. The woman told Sherry she had no business looking up her father. The weeping girl was told to go away and leave them alone. Feeling betrayed and dejected, Sherry returned home to flee the dream that had turned into an awful nightmare. No matter how far she ran, it would happen to her over and over. There would be no "happily ever after" for Sherry.

Two

As an adolescent in California, Sherry had forged a friendship with Jesse's half sister Judy Moody. Sherry went to school with Judy Moody's children and frequently played over at Judy's house.

While Sherry struggled to get an education, she also tried to fend off the sexual advances of a relative staying in her home. Later she would recount her confrontations with the abusive relative: "This man kept trying to come in my room, and I didn't think Mom'd believe me." It didn't take long for the young girl to decide the best solution to her problem was to drop out of school and get married. "So I found someone who'd marry me, and soon as he ask, I said yes." She sighed and continued, "I was all grown-up when I was still just a kid."

On April 12, 1982, at the tender age of fourteen, Sherry married a young man by the name of Kenneth Fagin. Sherry and her new husband followed her family as they returned to Arkansas.

At a very young age Sherry learned the type of treatment to expect at the hands of a man. Never educated about birth control, it didn't take the child bride long to get pregnant. The pregnancy promptly ended in a miscarriage, her young body not ready to accept the burden of carrying a child. A second miscarriage quickly followed the first. Sherry suffered her third miscarriage shortly after the second. This loss would devastate Sherry, and she would never forget it.

Sherry was excited that she had gotten pregnant so soon after the second miscarriage. When she found out, she did not tell anyone. In her childish way she reasoned that if no one knew the first two months, she would successfully carry this one to term. She badly wanted a child to love, and be loved by in return.

Kenneth and Sherry shared a little apartment with an elderly, retired couple, Joyce and Lloyd White.

Joyce had been told the news of the baby, and Sherry shared with her that she was excited about telling her husband he was going to be a father. Sherry planned a romantic dinner for Kenneth to orchestrate the mood.

The Whites volunteered to eat out and catch a movie to give the expectant parents some time alone. Sherry excitedly bustled around the kitchen cooking Kenneth's favorite meal. She quickly set the table, then changed into a nice dress and primped for her husband's arrival.

The food grew cold, and Sherry became anxious as time passed and no husband arrived. Finally, hours after he should have been home, Kenneth burst through the apartment door drunk, furious from a fight at work. He spotted the now cold and inedible food arranged on the red-checkered tablecloth and sent it crashing and flying across the room.

Sherry had seen Kenneth upset before, but never like this. She didn't experience immediate fear, because her husband had never physically abused her. She was flabbergasted over the turn of events.

Shaken, she fled to the bedroom to seek solace. Ranting and raving, Kenneth followed her. Sitting on the bed, hands folded over her lap, Sherry hoped the storm would quickly pass. When Kenneth kept yelling in her ear, she decided it would be better to leave him alone to work out his anger. She jumped off the bed. Kenneth slammed the door as he left.

As Sherry cleaned the kitchen, her abdomen started cramping, and the upper part of her legs began to ache. The last of the broken dishes clanked against other broken debris as Sherry deposited them in the trash container.

In the middle of the kitchen, a tired Sherry wiped her hands with a dish towel. She was relieved to have finished cleaning up the mess before the Whites came home.

Moments later the door opened and Sherry glanced up. As blood started running down both of her legs, the teenager took a step away from the trash can. She heard a plop as a congealed clot of blood landed on the floor between her feet. In shock, and now embarrassed, Sherry reached down with the hand towel and quickly scooped up the bloody mound. The Whites looked on in horror.

Joyce White hurried over and took the hand towel enclosing the aborted fetus out of Sherry's trembling hands.

The silver-haired woman shook her head sadly as she instructed Sherry to get in the bathtub and take a hot bath. Sherry did what she always did—exactly what she was told, without question. She ran a hot bath. Eyes closed, she immersed her whole body in the steaming liquid.

Although she was upset and crying, relaxation began to course through her body, slowly calming her.

The water in the tub eventually turned crimson. Sherry pulled the stopper out and watched the red liquid swirl down the drain. She stood up, turned the shower head down, then eased back into the tub letting the warm water spray across her body.

When thirty minutes had passed, Joyce White ventured into the bathroom to see what could possibly be taking the girl so long. She asked Sherry why she was still in the tub. Still dazed and confused, Sherry answered she didn't know. Mrs. White helped her out of the tub and began toweling off the shivering girl.

With the towel wrapped around her, Sherry went into her room and sat on the bed. Joyce followed, wanting to know what had happened. Mortified, Sherry told her.

The older woman ordered her to get dressed so they could take Sherry to the hospital.

In the living room Lloyd White sat on the couch, his fingers buried in his thick white hair. He wept quietly.

On the drive to the hospital, Joyce White gingerly approached Sherry. "You don't realize what you picked up tonight, do you child?"

So much had happened so quickly, the confused girl answered back, "I promise I'll replace all the broken dishes I put in the trash can." Assuring Sherry she wasn't concerned about the dishes, she delicately began to explain to Sherry what had happened. Sherry listened in horror. The reason for the trip to the hospital was now completely clear; the young girl dissolved into sobs that broke the older couple's hearts.

Sherry never got the romantic dinner she had so carefully planned. She never even got the chance to get the words "We're gonna have a baby" out of her mouth before it was no longer true.

Mrs. White wanted to know where Kenneth was. The shaking and crying wife answered she had no idea where her husband had gone after he stormed out of the apartment.

At the hospital the doctor performed a D & C on Sherry. No one volunteered to the doctor how this happened, and he didn't ask. Before the teenager was released, a nurse talked to Sherry about birth control. It was the first time the subject had been broached with the young girl. The nurse instructed her to get on the pills she was handing her and stay on them.

Strict bed rest for the next three days was ordered. Kenneth meekly returned home after two days. The minute the young husband walked through the door, Mrs. White pushed him into the older couple's bedroom, loudly lashing out at him for his behavior.

Having never seen or heard a woman stand up to a man, Sherry listened in amazement as Mrs. White's voice carried through the wall.

Sherry had grown up being taught a woman should stay in her place. You did what your husband told you; had kids, kept house, and waited on him because he was your responsibility.

That attitude would foster the tragedy Sherry would encounter as she tried simply to follow what she thought were the rules.

Kenneth made his way into their bedroom. He apologized profusely to Sherry for his behavior.

But the die had been cast. Trouble was nurtured too quickly in the young marriage. Struggling to save it, Sherry asked Kenneth to take her to Arkansas for a short rest and to visit with family.

He agreed and drove Sherry to the wooded, lush state. When Sherry realized that Judy Moody lived in the vicinity of some of her relatives, the couple stopped over to see her. Judy, always ready to extend a helping hand, invited them to stay with her as long as they were in town.

Delighted at the invitation, Sherry quickly accepted. Kenneth told his wife that she could stay, but he had to return to his parents' home in Colorado to pick up a car. As he left, Kenneth told Sherry he'd be gone about two weeks, then return and get her. In the meantime he wanted her to rest and have fun.

Judy and Tinky Moody had eight children, always a full house when Sherry saw them in California. At times she had even attended school with the Moody children that were her age. It seemed so quiet. Where was everyone? Sherry asked her friend.

Judy told Sherry that while she and Tinky were in California they were reported to Child Protective Services. An extensive investigation by the state was launched and resulted in the removal of all their children from the home. The reason given for the drastic measure was ongoing sexual and physical abuse attributed to the children's father. Sherry listened raptly as Judy relayed the story, her head held in shame over her husband's reprehensible behavior. She ended the story by saying that Tinky had recently died of tuberculosis.

Sherry looked up just in time to see a beautiful, little girl toddle up to her mother sitting at the kitchen table. The little girl flashed a big smile at the visitor.

One more child had been born to the Moodys before Tinky's

death. Judy and Tinky had managed to escape the wrath of Child Protective Services by simply moving from California to Arkansas before Judy gave birth. On March 7, 1980, Melissa Marie Moody was born. Judy named her last child, at Jesse's insistence, after their common parent.

Sherry lifted Melissa onto her lap. She played with the little girl for hours, delighted at her friendliness with a perfect stranger.

Judy Moody was a large woman weighing almost three hundred fifty pounds. Her size affected her health and ability to work. Disability checks had been recently awarded on that basis. She also received widow's benefits from Tinky's death. Judy managed to take care of herself and Melissa with the government aid.

Buried in his grave, Tinky Moody no longer was a threat to his last child. Deeply buried within the bosom of Melissa's own family, however, remained a terrifying danger so sinister not even the mighty and far-reaching arms of California's Child Protective Services would be able to save her from it.

Three

A month passed and there was no word from Kenneth. Sherry was worried. She didn't know what to do. Since the couple had married, Sherry had always been snubbed by Kenneth's mother. The Fagins had more money than Sherry's family. Mrs. Fagin unhesitatingly told Sherry from the beginning of the marriage that Kenneth had married beneath him.

Finally working up enough courage, Sherry called the mother-in-law who loathed her.

Anxiously twisting the telephone cord and waiting as the phone rang, Sherry anticipated what she would say to Mrs. Fagin. A stern voice clipped through Sherry's thoughts. She caught her breath, then explained nervously to the older woman that Kenneth was supposed to get a car and return for her, but it had been over a month and she hadn't heard from him. She wondered if she might know where Kenneth was, please, if it was not too much trouble to ask. After the verbal account spewed out, Sherry took a second breath.

The callous voice on the other end of the phone responded, "Oh, you don't know?"

A chill coursed through Sherry's body as she asked, "Know what?"

Mrs. Fagin responded to her daughter-in-law's question detachedly and acridly. "Kenneth died in a car wreck."

Sherry started sobbing and shaking uncontrollably. A click could be heard as Mrs. Fagin hung up. Devastated, Sherry dropped the receiver and collapsed on the floor. As the shock began to lessen, Sherry realized she needed to call someone to come and get her. She couldn't stay with Judy Moody forever. Sherry picked up the phone and, still trembling, dialed her mother's number.

Lahoma tried to soothe her daughter and told her she would send money for Sherry to return home, which was now Afton, Oklahoma. Staggered, Sherry packed her clothes and went home to live with her mother.

Sherry started drinking away her sorrow over her losses: her father, her childhood, her Kenneth, and her babies. Despondent, Sherry drank so much she didn't know and didn't care what day it was. She only knew that the alcohol anesthetized her pain.

Sherry had been home less than a month when, in a drunken stupor, she watched her dead husband walk into her room. Crouched in a corner, Sherry thought she was talking to a ghost when she heard Kenneth calling her name.

After a long, cold shower and some sleep, Sherry was sober enough to realize that Kenneth wasn't an apparition. He explained to his wife that when he got home his mother swore she would rid their family of the not-good-enough thorn in her side. If Sherry ever called she would be told Kenneth had died. Kenneth argued that he didn't know that his mother actually went through with the charade and had no hand in it.

Pleading, Kenneth begged for his wife's forgiveness. After begging for the better part of an hour, he convinced Sherry to take him back. Too much had happened too soon to the weary teenager, but she forgave him anyway.

After all of Kenneth Fagin's posturing, only three months would pass before he confronted his wife saying they needed to talk. He sat on the bed with Sherry and told her he would always love her but he had fallen in love with someone else.

Kenneth explained to his wife, a crushed woman who had forgiven him so many times, that he was in love with her cousin, Linda Bean.

The announcement took Sherry by complete surprise. Her

mind could barely comprehend the words she was hearing. After all they had been through together, how could he?

Sherry recalled, "I just got my husband back from the dead and he's standing here telling me he doesn't want me. I knew I couldn't go stay with Mama much longer. All I could think of was, who's gonna take care of me now?"

Reluctantly Sherry stepped aside and agreed to give him a divorce. Having no place else to go, she switched places with her rival, moving in with her cousin's parents while Linda moved in with Kenneth.

Linda turned out to be quite fickle. After Kenneth and Linda had a son together, she bolted from the relationship with the child. Kenneth, tail tucked between his legs, moved back to Colorado to live with his parents.

At their invitation, Sherry continued to live with Linda's parents. She was now divorced and only sixteen years old.

As migrant workers searched for ways to feed their families, the change in seasons directed them to Arkansas. It was here that Jesse Cummings's family returned to work, and it was here that Sherry would meet him for a second time.

After their brief and unpleasant first meeting, Cummings and his father had been arrested and extradited from Arkansas to California for the murder of a police officer.

They were in custody for eighteen months before a jury acquitted both father and son of the murder. After he was set free, Jesse bragged to friends that he had gotten away with murder. Out of custody, the Cummingses moved back to Arkansas.

Sherry's uncle Henry watched as his niece went farther into a shell with each passing day. Trying to cheer her, he introduced Sherry for the second time to Jesse at a family gathering. Though Sherry remembered the immature stunt Cummings had pulled years ago at Judy Moody's house, her uncle's encouragement was enough to gently nudge her to give him another chance. Cummings was twelve years older than Sherry, and that gave her pause. A man of twenty-eight surely had ties to a woman somewhere. Maybe a girlfriend, or perhaps even a wife.

But her uncle had said nothing about a wife, and he was the one encouraging her to see Cummings.

Hungry for a person to be connected to, Sherry put the thought aside and decided to cautiously give Cummings another chance.

The Jesse Cummings that the emotionally wounded teen was reintroduced to that night was completely different from the rough, mouthy man who had held her arm pinned against her back years before. This man was a sweet, caring, and gentle person. This Jesse was mature. He took things slow and deliberate, careful not to push too far like guys her age inevitably did. Cummings was exactly the type of warm, tender man Sherry needed to commandeer her shipwrecked life.

The first night they went out, Cummings casually asked Sherry her middle name. When she answered "Marie," he smiled.

Learning of Sherry's marital desertion, Cummings pulled Sherry into each conversation in an attempt to comfort her from her recent and devastating losses. If Cummings possessed no other skills, he had impeccable timing.

For weeks they would go riding around the lake or just walk hand in hand downtown. Cummings told Sherry that he had a job as a security guard working for a salvage yard. He went into great detail about his importance to impress the teenage girl. It worked.

Through all the many walks and talks, Cummings failed to mention to the young woman he was so fervently courting that he was married, or that he was a bigamist because he had never bothered to divorce Margaret Hazel before he took Janet as his bride.

Sherry never asked. She continued to reason with herself that if another woman was prominent in Jesse's life, he would have told her by now.

Cummings could be as charming as he needed to be. He would take advantage of the tragedies in Sherry's marriage to explain to her that not all guys were jerks.

Catering to her likes and dislikes, Cummings was smooth. Confidently he assured Sherry that she would soon find her "white knight in shining armor."

One month after Cummings started taking Sherry out, he finally asked for permission to kiss her. Impressed he had waited this long and had asked permission first, Sherry eagerly told him he could. Slowly and skillfully Cummings led Sherry through the dance of seduction until he had permission to bed her.

Whether caught up in the moment or too scared to pursue the subject, Sherry waited until they had consummated their relationship before asking him if there was another woman in his life.

Her heart pounded as she held her breath waiting between the long pause and Cummings's answer, "Well, I'm married but we're separated." Sherry wasn't pleased with the answer, but he had been honest; he got points for that. She decided to ask no further questions.

That warm, sultry night solidified their relationship and Sherry became pregnant once more.

Sherry turned seventeen in October. She told her mother that she had been dating a man by the name of Jesse. Lahoma warned her daughter that she was messing with a married man.

The mother and daughter argued loudly over that point, with Sherry vehemently defending Cummings and informing Lahoma he was separated from his wife.

Tired of arguing with her daughter, Lahoma told Sherry, "Well, if this is the Jesse I think it is, I know him and he knows me, and he's definitely married and living with his wife."

Sherry was falling in love with this man. Terrified her mother was right, but praying she wasn't, Sherry arranged for her mother and Cummings to meet at Lahoma's house. The moment he walked in, Lahoma recognized the young man she had stopped to pick up years ago in the field as his mother took potshots at him.

Lahoma grilled Cummings to see if he would wilt under the

barrage of questions and finally admit that he knew her. He didn't. If he was nervous, he didn't show it. Within thirty minutes he was ready to go, said goodbye, and grabbed Sherry's hand and walked out of Lahoma's house.

When Sherry returned to talk to her mother the next day, Lahoma emphatically told her stubborn child, "Listen, I hate to burst your little bubble, but this is the same Jesse I knew. He's not only married, little gal, he's still living with his wife, just like I said."

Still trying to convince the trembling girl that she knew Jesse, Lahoma informed her daughter that Jesse was Judy Moody's half brother. The same Judy Moody that Sherry grew up knowing in California and had recently visited. The Moodys and Cummingses were such a large family, it was hard to remember who everyone was.

By this time Sherry and Cummings's relationship had forged tightly as she was carrying Jesse's child. What more could Lahoma say? She knew her daughter was going to do what she wanted to. It was that simple.

Several months after Sherry and Cummings had become intimate, Janet Moore Cummings called Sherry on the phone and asked if she could come by and visit the teenager.

Sherry steeled herself that no matter what the woman said, she was not about to let the father of her child go. Sherry agreed to meet her rival at Lahoma's house. The meeting was not the confrontational one she had expected.

Janet sat beside Sherry and started talking softly. Cummings's wife told her husband's girlfriend, "Listen, Jesse don't know I'm here, and I wish you wouldn't tell him."

The remark prompted Sherry to respond defensively, "If this has to do with Jesse, I'm not discussing the subject, so you might as well leave."

Janet quickly assured Sherry that she did not come over to pick a fight. Over a cup of coffee Janet explained to Sherry that she and Jesse were moving back to Oklahoma, Jesse's birth state.

Sherry fought hard to suppress the surge of nausea beginning to churn in her belly. Jesse had never even hinted he might move. Panicked, Sherry thought if Janet was telling the truth, Jesse was going to leave her stranded in Arkansas with a baby to take care of.

As the expectant mother's heart hammered in her chest, she was amazed as Janet calmly continued. "It's gonna be harder for Jesse to get to see you when we leave. So I was thinking, why don't you just move away with us?"

Astonished, Sherry stammered searching for words, then told Janet she had to think the proposition over before she could give an answer.

After Janet left, Cummings called to test the emotional waters. He asked if he could come over and see Sherry later that evening. The love-stricken girl told him he could.

Cummings would become a master at getting his wives and girlfriends to pick up other women for him.

When Cummings arrived that afternoon, cornered by a pregnant and emotional girl, he confessed that he was still married. Then he began to make a direct plea to her. "Sherry, I love you. But I'm moving to Oklahoma and I'm taking my family with me. I want you to come, too. But you need to know we'll have to live with Janet until we all get jobs. I don't want it that way, but that's the way it's gotta be."

Cummings was so smooth that within minutes, Sherry was admiring him for being a decent enough man to stay on friendly terms with his wife, even though divorce papers had been filed.

Of course, no divorce had been filed, and no divorce was going to be filed. The age-old ruse of "We're not in love anymore, we're just staying together until we can get a divorce" worked for Cummings, just like it had worked for men throughout centuries.

The constant feuding and fighting that went on between Cummings and Janet made their relationship anything but amicable. For years Cummings had forced her to prostitute herself for him.

Cummings had spoken one truth to Sherry. He was not in love with Janet. He just didn't want to lose the potential to make money off her body. Their alliance was like a balloon with Cummings pumping more and more air inside of it, testing to see just how far he could stretch it before it burst into tiny pieces.

Sherry was relieved that Cummings was not going to desert her and their unborn baby. She was happy he asked her to go with or without Janet. She would have gone under any circumstances.

He was aware that Sherry and Lahoma had been feuding over him, and he wanted to separate the closeness the two shared. A move to Oklahoma would accomplish that.

It took Sherry less than two weeks to tell Cummings she would go away with him. After he told Sherry that Judy Moody and her daughter Melissa were also moving with them, it made Sherry feel even more certain she was doing the right thing. She had known Judy for a long time and felt comfortable around her.

Cummings successfully moved his family, including wife and expectant girlfriend, back to Oklahoma. However, the operation didn't go as placidly as he had planned. Sherry's stubborn mother followed. Not only would he have Lahoma to deal with, he would have to put up with Janet's mother, who lived in nearby Calvin. One ranted and raved at her daughter, wondering how she could tolerate a husband messing around right under her nose; while the other one was arguing that he was a lying, no-good, cheating son of a bitch who would treat her like a dog.

The emotional turmoil from the women in his life swirled around him like a fierce Oklahoma tornado in spring. Cummings ignored the turbulence surrounding him and continued to do as he pleased. Reared on chaos, Cummings now thrived on it.

The old battered bus he had lived in with Margaret Hazel before she fled, had also housed Cummings and Janet. The bus clanked and sputtered as he drove it around to the back side of the property rented by Sherry's mother. Lahoma's place seemed the best solution to the problem of where Cummings could park the old bus. She wouldn't ask him to pay her any money, and he could use her utilities for free.

Sherry, Janet, and Cummings used this stopgap house as their temporary home. The sleeping arrangements were dictated by Cummings. He and Sherry would sleep in the front of the bus in a makeshift bedroom. Janet would be relegated to the back of the bus.

As Cummings's baby grew inside Sherry, Janet remained a silent partner in Jesse and Sherry's union. Humiliated, she deferred to Sherry as Cummings's partner and continued to sell herself to whomever, whenever he told her to. Sherry had no idea that the man she loved was nothing more than a low-life pimp.

After Sherry had been in Oklahoma a month, she cautiously set out to visit Jesse's mother. Jesse Cummings, Sr., and Marie had moved into a little house not far away. Sherry had heard talk of the violent behavior between mother and son but had never witnessed it. Her love for Jesse was worth the risk to get to know Marie.

Marie sat Sherry down at the kitchen table. She started talking to the young woman, advising her how bad it looked that Jesse was living with two women. Marie tried to reason with Sherry. "How can you live with a man that's got a wife already?"

Patiently Sherry listened to Marie, who came across as genuinely concerned about the situation. She didn't have an answer for Marie, except to say that she loved Jesse and did not intend to leave him.

As the discussion continued, Sherry started shifting in her chair uncomfortably. If his mother was so upset about the situation, she thought, then it probably did look pretty bad to other people.

Cummings walked into the house and overheard a snippet of his mother and Sherry's conversation. Promptly he advised his mother to butt out of his life. The two argued back and forth until Sherry's head was swirling.

Whenever Marie and Cummings were around each other, a hateful air surrounded the two. Affection between them was nonexistent, and pretenses were never made.

Part of Marie's eccentric behavior was her habit of constantly carrying an old coffee can full of knives with her wherever she went. She sat at the table holding the can as she and her son argued. Sherry could tell how angry Marie was getting.

When Marie really got mad at Cummings, she would do several things to unnerve him. First, she would call Jesse by the name "James." The matter was between the two, and no one else understood why the name incited Cummings so. But it did. Marie started goading her son by throwing out the word "James" whenever he took a breath from railing against her. Sherry watched Cummings become hotter every time his mother threw the name in his direction.

The discussion continued to escalate and Marie stood up and did the second thing she knew would get to him. With the coffee can full of knives tucked in the hollow of her left arm, she truculently told her son just exactly what she thought of his living arrangements. She topped her opinion off by taunting her son a final time, spitting the word "James" out like bitter medicine.

Cummings had had enough of the old bitch. Furious with his mother and acting like a little boy, he walked over to her and thumped her on the nose very hard. Marie's nose had been broken several times in drunken brawls and falls. The thump was all it took. Out of control, she went berserk chasing Cummings around the kitchen screaming, "James, you no-good son of a bitch, get the hell outta my house!"

As always, Cummings met this type of behavior with contempt and laughter. Even more infuriated, Marie reached into the coffee can and hurled knife after knife in the direction of her son as he ducked and danced to avoid getting stabbed.

Sherry watched in horror. Marie continued to throw the knives until the can was empty.

After the temper tantrum was over, Cummings collected Sherry and took her back to the bus. Sherry would never forget the incident and promised herself to avoid being caught in the middle of any more rifts between the two of them.

Cummings's behavior was almost always predictable with the women in his life. When he decided enough time had passed, he ordered Sherry and Janet to sit down on the stained, smelly, cold metal floor of the bus for a talk. He announced, "Okay, this is the way it's gonna be." Then looking directly at Sherry, he told her there would be no divorce from Janet and she "wadn't going nowheres." The three would be a "couple" from then on. The unexpected revelation left Sherry reeling and sickened. Years of abuse from Cummings had numbed Janet's emotions. For her, the revelation meant nothing. There wasn't much that did anymore.

While Cummings was married to Janet and sleeping with Sherry, he intentionally convinced Sherry that they had an exclusive relationship. However, Cummings had not slowed his dating habits in the slightest. Behind Sherry's back he started seeing Sherry's own cousin Amy Lennon, among many others.

One woman Cummings was sleeping with was Dorothy Louise Brown. Sherry knew how much Dorothy Louise slept around, and she thought the woman was nothing but a tramp. For that fact alone, Sherry despised her.

Dorothy Louise and Cummings flirted outrageously with each other in the presence of Sherry, making the young woman hate her even more.

With all this going on under her gullible nose, Sherry still believed Cummings would never be unfaithful to her. There was no doubt that he was a flirt, but it ended there, or so she thought.

One day Dorothy Louise gave Cummings the gift that keeps on giving: gonorrhea. Cummings had slept with so many women over the past few months that the Public Health Department in Independence County ordered him to make a list of each of his conquests. A promise was elicited from Cummings to bring every sexual partner in for treatment.

Faithful to his guarantee, Cummings brought fifty-seven women in for treatment. And he seemed proud of the staggering number. He decided it would be safer if he brought Sherry to the health center last. Cummings explained to her that they had to be treated for a minor infection they were passing back and forth during intercourse.

The only nurse on staff at the clinic had been overwhelmed by the steady stream of women Cummings kept bringing in. The last day he came to the clinic was a Friday, and the exhausted nurse was more than ready for the weekend break. When Cummings pulled open the glass doors of the clinic with Sherry in tow, the tired nurse let out an audible groan. Shaking her head, she handed Cummings the now familiar stack of papers that had to be filled out and asked in disgust, "Jesse, is there *any* woman in Independence County you *haven't* slept with?"

The nurse's proclamation went right over Sherry's naive, young head.

Relating the account from prison, one of his wives summed up Cummings's repulsive behavior, "When it came to sex, it didn't matter how old, how young, how big, how small, how clean, or how dirty his sex partner was. If it was female, he was with it." She shook her head and exclaimed, "Jesse could talk a nun out of her habit!"

Five months into her pregnancy, Sherry began experiencing light activity from the baby. She had never carried a fetus past the first trimester until now, and she relished even the slightest stirring inside her. Her favorite pastime consisted of resting her hand on her rapidly swelling belly awaiting any movement from a ripple to a hardy kick. Every time she felt the baby move, she would giggle with utter delight. Happier than she had ever been, Sherry was savoring the tranquility surrounding her. The serenity was briefly shattered on a warm spring night.

Cummings knew about the miscarriages that Sherry had suffered. He sheltered the mother-to-be from anything he thought might upset her. This was his baby Sherry was carrying and he wanted to make damn sure it was born healthy and perfect. To that end, he tried to keep stressful situations away from Sherry.

Janet and Cummings had been arguing the better part of the day. They had so far managed to wage their battles outside of Sherry's hearing.

When night fell, Cummings and Sherry went to bed, as usual, in the front of the bus. For what would be the last time, Janet was relegated to the back of the bus. She was relieved that she did not have to have sex with Cummings, but she abhorred the way he made her feel, now that another woman was present.

While the expectant father's concern for the baby was the reason he wanted to keep Sherry away from stress, he had no qualms with her tending to his needs. Sherry was sound asleep when Cummings nudged her awake. He told her to get up and get him a glass of water from her mother's kitchen.

Taught that women waited on their menfolk, Sherry obediently got up, slipped on a robe, and quietly tiptoed into her mother's kitchen to fetch the water.

When Sherry stepped back out into the dead of night, she could hear terrifying sounds coming from inside the bus. Piercing screams and scathing voices yelling at a deafening volume exploded the calm of the night. Sherry heard the sickening sound of Cummings's fists slamming against Janet's body. Glass shattered as items were hurled inside the bus. Cummings's and Janet's voices kept getting louder. The screams were horrible. Sherry stood paralyzed listening in disbelief. The battle going on inside the bus was unlike anything she had ever heard. Her hand shook uncontrollably, spilling water out of the glass she held.

Even if her trembling legs had allowed her to, she was not about to walk into the middle of the violent confrontation. Sherry eased her shaking body down and sat on the porch until only silence filled the night air.

Sherry waited a few more minutes before standing up. Steadying herself, she apprehensively walked toward the bus clutching Jesse's glass of water. Other than the one time Kenneth had hit her, Sherry had never encountered violence. She certainly was not prepared for the extent of the brutality that had gone on in her absence.

Cautiously Sherry boarded the bus. She was horrified at what she saw. Janet and Cummings were both drenched in blood. A pair of blood-smeared scissors lay on the floor resting between the two adversaries. Janet eased her badly battered body to her feet and stumbled toward the back of the bus.

Cummings raised his left arm and attempted to wipe away the blood covering his forehead and flowing down his face. Sherry stood riveted with her mouth agape. Her shaking hand extended the glass of water to him as he sat cross-legged on the floor. He gulped down what was left of the cool water. He placed the empty glass beside him on the bus floor, then stood up and told the bewildered woman that Janet had flipped out and snuck up on him as he lay in bed. According to Cummings, she had a pair of scissors in her hand and started lashing out at him trying to stab him. "That goddamn crazy bitch tried to kill me!" Cummings's attempt to explain the violence that transpired while Sherry was gone was short and to the point. Then he told her that none of this concerned her and ended by telling her to get back in bed.

Sherry, still in shock, slipped quietly between the sheets and lay beside Cummings quivering. She didn't fall back to sleep that night—she didn't dare.

Early the next morning Cummings got up, quietly dressed, and left. As was his habit, he didn't bother to account to anyone regarding his whereabouts.

Janet emerged from the back of the bus bruised and swollen. She limped out of the bus and headed for the nearest telephone. Her right hand shook as she dialed her parents' phone number. Less than fifteen minutes had passed when Janet returned. Sherry watched as the battered and bruised woman quickly packed what few belongings she had.

On last night's violent note, the eight-year marriage was finally over. That evening Janet's parents collected their daughter and took her home. Mr. Moore left a terse note for Cummings ordering him to be up and ready to leave by ten o'clock the next morning. The note informed Cummings he was going to be driven to the courthouse, where the marriage would be ended. Cummings didn't do what other people told him to, but the tone of the note was enough to get him out of bed and dressed as instructed.

The next morning Mr. and Mrs. Moore, with Janet in tow, pulled up beside the bus. Moore ordered his son-in-law into the car. The Moores drove downtown and escorted Cummings and their daughter into the courthouse, where a "shotgun divorce" was obtained.

Cummings had controlled Janet for eight years despite constant philandering on his part and his frequent physical abuse. There were no children born of this marriage, although Janet had suffered three miscarriages.

Cummings was delivered back home. As the tires on the Moores' car peeled out, Sherry remembered the brief conversation with Janet before her parents came to rescue their daughter. As she hurriedly packed, Janet had glanced back at Sherry and sternly advised her, "I'm divorcing that no-good son of a bitch! I'll try to check on you if I can, but if I were you, I wouldn't stick around here too long. He'll do the same things to you he done to me. Jesse ain't never gonna change!"

Heading for the door of the bus, Janet turned toward Sherry. Haunted, empty eyes looked straight into Sherry's. "I'm telling you, get out while you still can!"

Cummings had never raised his hand to her, Sherry silently rationalized as she watched Janet disappear. She couldn't afford to believe that Jesse would ever turn on her.

The warning was immediately tucked away in the recesses of Sherry's mind, securely squeezed into an alcove carved out by a sobbing child in the backseat of Lloyd White's car, where it would join other events too painful to remember. Sherry made the decision to ignore Janet's grave warning. It would be the biggest mistake of her life.

Four

Sherry began to spend more time with Marie, careful to choose a time whenever Jesse was not around. She probably got to know Marie Cummings as well as anyone would ever know the woman. "She could be the meanest bitch on earth, but I kinda liked her anyway." When Marie became ill and was hospitalized, Sherry faithfully accompanied Jesse Cummings to see his mom. Two weeks after Marie entered the hospital, she was sent home to die. Sherry never quite knew what had made the woman fall ill so fast. Neither did anyone else.

On January 24, 1986, Marie Cummings died in her bed at home in Tupelo, Oklahoma. She was only sixty-five.

The enigmatic Jesse seemed shattered by his mother's death. He took her passing like a distressed, devoted son who felt only love and affection for his mother.

The duty that would have naturally fallen to Jesse, Sr., to see to the funeral arrangements was wrestled away by what appeared to be a grief-stricken son. His reason for assuming the responsibility was simple. He felt he was the only one that could give his mother the kind of funeral she deserved. The first thing Cummings did was to arrange to have his mother's body transported to Criswell's Funeral Home in Ada, Oklahoma. He thought it was one of the nicer funeral homes that would do his mother justice. Nothing less would do.

The Cummings's family pastor, Rev. Joe Lester, was approached by Jesse and agreed to preach at Marie's funeral.

Though money was a scarce commodity in the Cummings's lives, Jesse managed to scrape enough money together to purchase a nice casket for his mother's body to lie in. He ordered flowers from a local florist and surrounded the casket with beautiful, colorful sprays. The sweet fragrance filled the small room where Marie Cummings rested. One wreath placed near the coffin was draped with a yellow ribbon. Sparkling glitter sprinkled across it spelled out the words "Loving Mother."

A framed picture of Marie was placed on top of the closed casket. It showed Marie in her youth when she had been a breathtakingly beautiful woman.

Cummings traveled to the neighboring town of Lehigh, where he purchased a burial lot for his mother in Lehigh Cemetery. The cemetery known pfor its carefully clipped lawn held sentimental value for Cummings because his maternal grandfather was buried there. It was highly unusual for the stolid Cummings to show emotion or embrace fond memories of anyone, but this clearly was the exception. The grandson was proud of his grandfather, particularly taking glory in the fact that he had culminated a lengthy career in law enforcement by being elected marshal of the nearby town of Coalgate, where Marshal Garrett honorably served its citizens until his retirement.

As money for his mother's funeral was gathered and quickly spent, Cummings had one last purchase. He bought an expensive headstone of gray granite. Chiseled in stone were the words "Marie Cummings," underneath her name was printed "Feb. 28, 1920." Below that date was "Jan. 24, 1986." In larger lettering underneath the name and dates, Cummings, who had loathed his mother all of his life, commissioned the words "LOVING MOTHER" chiseled in the fine granite. A burnished vase for flowers was secured to the right of the monument.

The headstone was expensive under any circumstances, but was downright extravagant for the Cummings family. When Jesse would bury Jesse, Sr., next to his mother, he would search as fervently for his father's headstone as he had for his mother's, the exception being Jesse, Sr.'s, headstone was the cheapest he could find.

Marie may have died on a chilly morning in January, but her legacy would live on through Jesse as he embraced the torture his mother put him through, perfecting it. As bizarre as the mother and son's relationship had been, whatever hate and loathing had transpired between them, it actively ended the day Marie died.

From the day after Marie's funeral, Cummings never mentioned her again. But he would add his own sick twist to the Oedipal feelings he had toward his mother. The women in his life, and the ones to come into his life, would share two common traits with his mother: her looks and her name.

In the years to come, Cummings would become the epitome of a myopic man who substituted other women in his life in place of his mother, seeming oblivious to the difference.

Shortly after Marie's death, Jesse, Sr., approaching sixty-five, married his much younger lover, Joyce Denman. He had been committing adultery with her long before his wife's death. His father's infidelity had been known to Cummings for a long time. The only thing that aggravated the hell out of him about the situation was that he wanted Joyce for himself, and he was certain she would make a fine prostitute.

Immediately after the marriage Joyce became pregnant. The assumption that the baby could have belonged to either the father or the son was a reasonable one. Joyce had been the center of many physical confrontations between the two, both acting like dogs fighting over a bone.

When Joyce went into labor, Jesse, Sherry, and a midwife were present. According to Cummings's version of the story, Joyce was in advanced labor when the midwife left the room to gather up more clean cloths. The baby decided to make its entrance before she made it back. Cummings quickly positioned himself between Joyce's legs, and the baby girl, who would be named Shelly Marie, fell into his arms.

The gospel according to Jesse Cummings was that the midwife deferred to him when asked to sign the birth certificate. The old woman looked at Cummings and announced, "You delivered her. You sign it." The story would be embellished as the years passed, eventually ending with Cummings being allowed to sign the birth certificate and print the initials "MD" after his name.

The listeners to his tale were held in rapt attention and either believed or pretended to believe Cummings's doctoral debut. Whether true or not, the experience of the delivery started his obsession with drugs and doctoring.

In later years, as Cummings got more caught up in grandiose thoughts, he would fancy himself somewhat of a doctor in theory and practice, eagerly treating family members for everything from a cold to pelvic inflammations.

The one single encounter between Cummings and Janet was the only time Sherry had ever seen Jesse violent. In fact, a couple of weeks later, when Cummings awoke from a dream kicking and fighting, he had Sherry leave his bed. The expectant mother would sleep in a separate bed because Cummings was afraid he might accidentally hurt his baby.

Sherry would continue to sleep alone until the day their child was born.

Once Janet had left, Cummings abandoned the worn-out, trashed bus, leaving it parked in back of Lahoma's house. He rented a run-down shack for a few dollars and some change. Foremost in Cummings's mind was finding someone to replace Janet's services as a prostitute. With a baby on the way, they could use the extra income. Joyce was the logical choice. Cummings set about to convince his aging father to move Joyce and the baby in with him and Sherry.

It was agreed that the two Jesses, their wives, one with an infant, the other due to deliver in June, would share the old shack that looked like it would collapse if the Oklahoma wind blew just right.

Joyce remained a bone of contention between the two men. Fights between them escalated. Drinking and drugs fueled the long-standing feud between father and son. Not long after Jesse, Sr., moved in with his son, a shouting match intensified into a savage fight. In a vicious attack Cummings picked his father up and hurled the older man across the room.

He then walked over to his father lying on the floor of the shack and in a blind rage started hitting him. He beat his father until the sixty-five-year-old man was almost unrecognizable. The women waited for Cummings to leave, then rushed over to Jesse, Sr., and helped him into his room. They doctored him up as best they could and then let him sleep. It was a week before he could get out of bed and walk. Having had enough of his son's irrational violence, Jesse, Sr., packed up and moved his family out.

Within ten days Sheriff Bill Ward served Jesse Cummings with a protective order instructing him to stay away from his father. But a piece of paper meant nothing to Jesse. Cummings's violent temper was swift and deadly, and a piece of paper would never change that.

Jesse, Sr., and Joyce also fought constantly. He knew she was sneaking out and seeing Jesse, and he suspected his son was pimping Joyce and pocketing the money. Joyce was so dysfunctional she never knew from one day to the next if she wanted to be with the father or the son.

It was on June 9, 1987, a sweltering summer day, that Sherry went into labor and was rushed to the hospital in Atoka, Oklahoma. The couple had thoroughly discussed names for the baby. Sherry made it clear to Cummings she wanted to name the baby Jessica Ann, if it was a girl. Cummings acted like this was acceptable and the matter was settled.

Awakening from a drug-induced sleep, Sherry was told by the nurse adjusting her IV drip that she was the mother of a beautiful baby girl. Offhandedly the nurse remarked that Jessica Marie was a cute name. Sherry was livid. When Cummings walked into the room, she lit into her husband telling him that they had discussed the baby's name and it had been agreed between them that her name would be Jessica Ann. She reiter-

ated that she had always hated Marie as her middle name "and
he damn well knew it." She demanded an explanation as to why
he had put Marie on the birth certificate instead of Ann.

Cummings turned on his heel to leave and threw an aggravated look back in Sherry's direction. As he walked off, he
advised her, "Don't flatter yourself. I didn't name her after you.
I named her after my mama." And that was the end of the discussion. Cummings did as he wanted. Marie Cummings had
been dead a little over a year.

When Sherry and Jessica came home from the hospital,
Cummings appeared genuinely thrilled. He fussed over the little
girl and spent a lot of time with her. His obvious affection for
their baby softened Sherry's heart, and she soon forgave him
over the name.

Four months after Sherry gave birth, she got the wish she
had repeated over and over so many times she had lost count.
On October 8, 1987, Rev. Joe Lester married Jesse Cummings
to the mother of his child.

Although Cummings's attitude toward Sherry had changed
somewhat after their daughter's' birth, the most physical he had
gotten with her was an open-handed slap across her face. His
behavior would take a drastic turn after Jessica's birth.

Sherry had been busy learning how to care for her daughter
from the time she brought her home from the hospital. Although
young, Sherry was conscientious about mothering and tried
very hard to do the right thing. She even breast-fed little Jessica.
Mesmerized by the whole process of nursing, Sherry loved the
bond that formed with each feeding.

Her daughter was everything Sherry had always wanted.
Someone to love her unconditionally. No reason. No precon-
ceived plan. Someone to love her *just because.*

For the first time in her life, Sherry was truly happy.

Not only did she have the child she wanted so much, she
finally had Cummings all to herself. She was now a respectable
wife and mother.

The house the Cummingses lived in was run-down by all

standards and primitive, but it was a step-up from the broken-down, old bus they had shared with Janet.

Sherry never asked too many questions about what Cummings did with his time or how he managed to support his family. She knew the proper order of things. Men took care of the family, and women took care of them.

In an effort to put her best foot forward, Sherry learned to cook the things her new husband liked. Being poor also meant being creative and frugal at the same time, and Sherry was good at both.

Sherry deferred to Cummings in all matters. He was the king of his castle—no matter how dilapidated, it was still his castle. But Sherry was the kind of sweet-natured person that didn't require much to be content. And she was completely satisfied, until Jessica turned eighteen-months-old and Sherry would see a side of Cummings she would never have dreamed existed.

After Jessica's birth, Sherry, like most new mothers, had trouble losing the weight that she had gained during her pregnancy.

"Jesse screamed at me so bad I quit eating what I should've while I was nursing. When I did eat, it wadn't the right food. Jessica got where she was refusing to nurse 'cause what I was eating was affecting my milk. I tried everything to get back in shape. I'd stop eating. Then I'd take water pills. I'd eat breakfast, then skip lunch and eat hardly any dinner. But it didn't matter. Jesse'd bitch at me if I ate, and he'd bitch if I didn't. I couldn't win."

This new Jesse was nothing like the sweet guy she married. He was never happy. According to Cummings, his wife was perpetually unsuitable.

The baby was a little over a year old when Cummings's mood appeared to lighten and he suggested a night out for the beleaguered mom. Sherry quickly accepted his considerate offer to give her a break. Maybe he was turning back into the kind man she had fallen so deeply in love with.

Although she worshipped her daughter, Sherry was exhausted trying to keep up with everything and desperately needed a short respite. Cummings told her to get Jessica dressed. They were going to drop the baby off at his sister Debra's for the night.

Sherry excitedly dressed up and gathered Jessica's baby food, diapers, and clothes. She piled in the car with her husband, anxious for a night alone with him.

This would be the first night since Jessica had been born that she would not put her to bed. That saddened her some, but the feeling was soon abated by the chance to be alone with her husband. Perhaps renew his sweet side. Jesse had his shortcomings, but didn't all men?

The couple dropped their daughter off and Cummings told his sister they probably wouldn't be back for the baby until the next day. A wonderful mood washed over Sherry after hearing this.

It was early in the evening when they said their final good-byes to Jessica and left Debra's house. Traveling down the highway, Sherry felt her excitement increase when Cummings would not disclose plans for the night.

Small talk passed between husband and wife. Cummings gradually steered the conversation to a game of "what ifs." Like a diversion. The game started out light enough with silly things like "What if I asked you to do something for me, no matter how stupid, would you?" The pastime continued with Cummings coming up with various scenarios of "what ifs."

Sherry was enjoying the ride and was amused with Jesse's playfulness. His next "what if" was a bombshell. He started out hesitatingly, "Well, what if I asked you to have sex with Jimmie [Cummings's brother-in-law]?"

Sherry rolled her eyes at the silly man. She wasn't in the least offended or alarmed by the question. She assumed Cummings had just expanded on their game, turning it more risqué. She came back with, "Jesse, I'm not really all that much into sex. I mean, if I's a nympho I might go for it. But I'm not."

Ignoring the reply, Cummings continued with the "what if"

questions, naming off several friends in Atoka and Coalgate. Each time Sherry would respond she just was not that interested in sex. She wasn't lying.

Sherry had been taught that sex was an obligation a woman performed for her husband. It was a duty. The sexual act had never brought her enjoyment.

Undaunted, Cummings chided his wife, "Well, I'm just asking what if." Calmly he proceeded along the same line of questioning. Sherry was enjoying the scenery when his next hypothetical question popped out. "Well, what if I'd ask you to prostitute for me?"

This question offended and alarmed her. Trying to suppress her anger, she mentally reminded herself this was just a game. It wasn't worth ruining her first night out with her husband in a long time. Surely, Jesse would tire of this silliness any minute, she hoped. Sherry's voice betrayed her annoyance, "Jesse, I told you the only men I've been with are the men I been married to, and maybe one or two in between."

Concern spread across her young face as she watched her husband become visibly agitated with her last response. Cummings was silent for a few minutes, then finally changed the subject. Sherry breathed a sigh of relief that the stupid game was over.

As the car continued down the road, Cummings grew quiet or sullen, Sherry was not quite sure which. The uncomfortable silence in the car convinced Sherry to try and engage her husband in small talk. His icy silence persuaded her to stop. As they both stared straight ahead, the atmosphere changed rapidly from being just uncomfortable to one of strong tension.

Cummings removed his right hand from the steering wheel of the car and replaced it with his left one. Out of the corner of her eye, Sherry saw her husband's hand raised. Expecting him to slap her, she turned toward him to try and placate him. Cummings's right fist sharply connected with the left side of her jaw. The blow astounded her. She could taste the blood from the cut inside her mouth. Sherry raised her left hand and caressed her aching jaw in disbelief.

Another blow was delivered swiftly. When his fist crashed into her face the second time, a repulsive sound accompanied it as several of her teeth were fractured. Cummings had struck her with such fierce strength Sherry's jaw was shattered on impact.

Until now, when she had done something wrong, Cummings had slapped her with an open hand. It stung but she always figured she must have deserved it. But he had never hit her. Never! Turmoil infiltrated Sherry's mind as questions silently whirled like a funnel: What'd I do? What'd I say to make him so mad?

Sherry's subservient state of mind instinctively blamed herself for what her husband had just done to her. The internal interrogation continued: I can't believe he did that. What in hell did I do to set him off?

While Sherry played the blame game, an exasperated Cummings complained, "Goddamn it, I can't do this shit while I'm driving." He pulled off the highway that led to Coalgate and turned on to a paved back road. The paved road soon turned on to a dirt one.

Cummings slammed on the brakes throwing Sherry forward into the dashboard. She quickly exited the car. "I figured Jesse's stopping the car to make me walk home. 'Cause I knew whatever I'd done, it'd really pissed him off."

Standing contritely on the dirt road waiting for Jesse to order her off into the night, Sherry contemplated the long scary walk ahead of her in the darkness.

Turning off the engine, Cummings bolted from the driver's side of the car. The irate husband dashed over to where Sherry was standing. In the middle of the road, he started pummeling his wife with both fists so swiftly it was impossible for her to fend off the blows. He ruthlessly slammed his fists against his wife's body, with Sherry's ribs and stomach suffering most from the attack.

The sobbing woman cowered while Cummings continued to pound on her relentlessly. Terrified, she implored, "Jesse, I'm

sorry. What's the matter? What'd I do? I won't do it anymore,
I promise. Just stop, please!"

Sherry lost her balance, then fell backward. The onslaught of
blows pinned her to the ground. As she staggered to her feet, she
was knocked down again. The vicious flogging had gone on for
several minutes when Cummings heard a car turn down the dirt
road. Fearing detection, he ended the brutal assault.

Cummings roughly shoved the bleeding and bruised body of
his wife into the passenger side of the car. Sherry desperately
fought to stifle her sobs as he drove off, his tires flinging gravel.
He turned the car around and headed toward his sister's house.

As his fury was satiated, he began to compose himself. He
told Sherry she deserved the beating she got, and more. He then
calmly pointed out that he had avoided punching her in the
breast area because she was breast-feeding their daughter.
Wrapped in a perverted view of consideration, Cummings expected Brownie points for using such restraint.

Sherry's respite from motherhood had turned into a horrible
nightmare. Shuddering when recalling the incident, Sherry
would relate, "When Jesse completely calmed down later that
night, I got brave enough to ask him if he was sorry for beating
me like that."

Cummings had responded disdainfully, "Sorry's not in my
vocabulary."

When Jesse Cummings wanted something, he never failed
to get it. Every day he continuously harassed Sherry about prostituting for him. At first Sherry protested, screamed, and cried.
But Cummings was prepared for all contingencies. When he
had heard the last "no" he intended to receive, he resorted to
something stronger than the emerging violence in their marriage
to control Sherry. Cummings had found it and had just been
biding his time for the right moment to use it.

He asked her to recall the hospital visit when he told her he
had named the baby Jessica Marie. The task wasn't difficult,
she never would forget how angry she had gotten over his betrayal. The dumbfounded wife listened as Cummings told her

that his signature on the birth certificate automatically took away all her rights to Jessica and gave him full and permanent custody. If she ever tried to walk out on him, it would cost her Jessica. So from now on, the triumphant husband ordered, she would do what he said to do, when he said to do it. Cummings even managed to keep a straight face while repeating the brazen lie. Knowing no better, Sherry believed him.

Cummings had been seeking the method of ultimate control over Sherry from the day they married. Watching her face while nursing Jessica, he had immediately known what it would be. It was Jessica.

From now on, Sherry would prostitute herself or anything else Cummings told her to do. As much as she despised the thought of selling her body, she acquiesced and agreed to do the most despicable and degrading thing she could have ever imagined. The mother would have done anything, endured any humiliation and pain, to be with her child.

Cummings's short experience years ago as a trucker introduced him to the practice many truckers had of pulling into rest stops seeking sexual favors. Even those men who pulled into the area for nothing more than a few hours' sleep offered opportunity. Cummings immediately scheduled a series of rest stops for what he referred to as Sherry's "night work." As he had done with Janet, Cummings began to shamelessly market the woman's body he had promised to cherish and respect for the rest of his life. Promises were only words to Cummings. They meant nothing.

Cummings eventually became so well-known by the local law enforcement agencies in Oklahoma, that the pressure convinced him to leave the state temporarily until things cooled down. He made the decision to move his family.

Jesse Cummings headed toward Batesville, Arkansas. It would be an ill-fated move for his next bride-to-be, and a fatal one for Cummings.

Five

Juanita "Anita" Lewis was born on August 2, 1969. She grew up in Arkansas, in a privileged environment far away from the Cummingses, Yawses, and Moodys of the world.

Anita was born into a seemingly typical all-American family. Her father had retired from the military and taken a well-paying job as a machinist. Her mother was a registered nurse. The family was complete with one older brother, Jimmy, and a younger one, Harry, Jr.

The Lewises had lived in the same Arkansas town of Batesville all their lives. Middle-class stable, Louise and Harry Lewis strongly believed in the importance of education, not only high school but college, as well. The family was loving and for the most part supportive of their children. They both worked hard to give their children the finer things in life and provide them with the education they felt was so important to their children's future.

Anita, the only girl and the middle child, kept things from her parents in a childish effort to spare them additional worry. Anita would become skilled in the art of protecting her parents' feelings. Her coloring of the truth in a misguided effort would rob her of her parents' invaluable life experiences.

The young girl developed self-esteem problems at an early age. The "runt" in her family, Anita lagged behind her classmates and friends in height. No one had trouble picking Anita out of a school picture, she was always the kid on the end.

Anita remembered a vivid incident from her younger days in school that initially fostered her lack of self-esteem. "My third-grade teacher had unorthodox methods to deal with us kids. One boy was made to wear a diaper because he had an accident. Kids who talked wound up in the hall with paper towels stuffed inside their mouths. Degrading stuff like that. Me, I had really bad handwriting.

"She made me write a paper and take it to the fourth-grade teacher I would be getting the next year. I had to go in front of the class and ask this teacher if she wanted a student who wrote like me in her class next year. The fourth-grade teacher had a fit, the principal had a fit, and my handwriting still stinks. I was so embarrassed. That moment has always stuck with me."

Anita never told her parents about these humiliating incidents because her little girl's intuition warned her they would spank her. She shook he. head at a long-ago little girl's reasoning, "I can only remember receiving one spanking ever from them. I don't know why I thought my parents would spank me."

Physically more mature than her classmates, Anita was barely in the fifth grade when she started her period. The "lecture" given all girls in school did not take place until near the end of the year. Anita jumped the gun and was totally caught off guard by the event.

Anita remembered, "My mom was out of town and my cousin came over to visit. We decided to do our workout in the living room. I had a leotard on and was doing my 'Jane Fonda video' with Susie when I started cramping real bad. When I felt the blood running down my legs, I was terrified."

"Luckily, my cousin knew what was going on. She took me into the bathroom and explained what was happening to me. Hell, I was screaming, 'I'm dying. I'm dying,' because I thought I was. When you're ten years old, you don't expect to see blood leaking out of your body, anywhere, for any reason!

Directly thereafter, Anita's body, although still tiny in stature, betrayed her further. Her breasts developed almost overnight. The ten-year-old looked more like she was fourteen. Her top-heavy figure didn't escape the attention of the boys in her class, who would tease her unmercifully about it.

Anita's friends started sprouting up in height, while she remained four ten and weighed one hundred twenty pounds. A lot of the weight came from her huge breasts. The girls envied her. The boys thought they were simply magnificent. It didn't take long before the young girl was being asked out by older boys.

She recalled, "The older boys courted me, complimented me, and made me feel pretty. I was insecure, but this made me feel special."

Children have a malicious cruelty about them. Anita was teased about everything from being too short, too top heavy, for having a slight hearing problem that made her talk too loud, for wearing a temporary patch over a lazy eye, and finally, when they could think of nothing else, she was teased about her name. Schoolmates would follow her around chanting "Nita, Nita, peter eater." Her self-esteem plummeted.

Anita's brother Jimmy was six years older. Her younger brother, Harry, Jr., was six years younger. Anita was unhappily nestled between her brothers giving her the nondistinction of being the middle child.

She recounted with a laugh, "My family had the middle-kid syndrome down pat. Jimmy was a teenager just as I was starting school. His rebellion totally took the attention away from me.

"When Jimmy finally got married, I'm thinking, Okay, now it's my turn. Then fate strikes again and along came my little brother. It pulled the rug completely out from under me."

Despite the incessant teasing at school, Anita was bright and studied hard earning all A's and B's. But the way she physically perceived herself gave her great insecurity. "All my friends were talking about enrolling in Barbizon School, where they teach their students to model and put on makeup. I did it a couple of times and realized the place was just not for me.

"I'll never forget the day my mom heard me setting up the [Barbizon] interview over the phone. She took the phone away and told the lady, 'Listen, you don't understand. You don't realize this is a kid that's only four feet ten inches tall and weighs a hundred and forty pounds.' "

Anita sighed at the painful memory. "I know now my mom was only trying to protect me. But at the time all I thought was, 'Gee, Mom don't even think I can do anything.' " The bright, sweet, pretty, little girl's self-esteem took another plunge.

More resilient than she gave herself credit for, Anita entered Cushman High School, where she excelled scholastically. She also started her first romantic relationship with a handsome young boy named Eddie Miles.

Miles and Anita grew up together in the small town of Batesville. Caught up in romance, the two teenagers became serious quickly.

Miles showered Anita with attention, but he also had a quick temper. His impetuousness led to the first physical abuse Anita would suffer at the hands of a man.

Unlike Sherry, Anita had grown up in a home where men respected women. Marriage partnerships were equal and there was no physical violence. Anita's closest encounter with violence came when she plopped down in front of the television.

In the small town they lived in, there wasn't a whole lot to do on the weekend. So most of the teenagers drank and partied on Friday and Saturday nights.

One particular Friday night Miles and Anita had gone to the skating rink. A tailgate party was going on outside. Beer kegs were strategically placed for convenience. Miles's drinking started early and picked up through the night.

Through a window in the skating rink, Miles spotted Anita talking to a young man whom he particularly disliked. The drunken teenager went into a rage. He confronted Anita by ranting, raving, and waving his hands about. Anita advised him to stop acting like a four-year-old and stormed off. She retreated to Miles's car and promptly locked the doors.

Miles ran over to the car. As fast as he would unlock the

door with his key, Anita would relock it. She yelled at him, "I'm not letting you in till you calm down!"

Miles's little brother was there, too. Realizing Eddie was getting out of control, his brother decided to call their dad.

Momentarily distracted as Mr. Miles's car pulled into the parking lot, Anita took her attention away from locking the door. Eddie Miles started crawling into the driver's side of his car.

The next thing the teenager knew, he was being dragged out of the car by his father. Furious at the interference, Eddie hit his father, then headed to the passenger-side of the car after Anita. She jumped out of the car and ran around two parked pickups trying to get away from him. Her flight was halted because the next two pickups were parked tailgate to tailgate.

She felt herself flipping over the tailgates as Miles hit the side of her face with a closed fist. Anita landed hard against the ground. Before she could get up, Miles pounced on her and began choking her with both hands.

Mr. Miles pulled his son off the terrified girl. As he got his son under control, he lashed out at Anita, screaming and blaming her for not keeping a tighter rein on his son and allowing him to get so drunk. He hauled his boy up and roughly threw Eddie in the back of the car.

The young man Anita had been talking to inside the rink ran out and checked on the stunned teenager, helping her to her feet. The two got in his car and drove around the lake in an effort to calm down the angry, shaken girl.

Anita remembers why she was so mad. "I'd never seen a guy hit a girl. Here he'd hit me. Then his dad had the nerve to yell at me, blaming me for it all!"

Like the majority of abused women, Anita hid her bruises from the violent episode. She said she wasn't trying to protect Eddie, she just didn't want her parents to know what he had done to her. "There's no telling what my dad would have done." So she wore turtleneck sweaters when she was around her parents, until the black-and-blue marks faded.

After that night Anita broke up with Eddie Miles. Before

long she was deluged with pleas to go back with her abuser. Miles's mother, his teacher, his friends all told her he was drinking too much because of the breakup. According to the sources, Miles was going downhill fast, and Anita was rolling the barrel.

It didn't take too much haranguing before the message became ingrained in Anita's head. She was responsible for Miles's behavior and subsequent downfall.

Standing firm by her decision, she refused to give Eddie Miles the opportunity to ever hit her again. The way Anita was raised, boys did not hit girls, for any reason! Not ever! Miles was history.

Anita continued to excel at Cushman High School. She graduated with honors, winning awards in business, math, and leadership. Anita was the only female in her class to achieve the status.

On graduation day all the other female graduates wore white shoes to match the drape flowing down their black graduation gown. Anita wore black shoes to match the black honor cord draped across her white graduation gown, a privilege accorded honor students only.

The teenager loved to study mythology and planned to make that her major in college. She enrolled in the A.E.I.G.I.S. program to prepare herself for higher academic life. An excited Anita packed for her six-week preparatory course at Arkansas State College.

Once there, Anita showed a knack for writing and started working on the college newsletter. Tommy Bison, Anita's new boyfriend, pitched a fit from the day Anita started her studies at the university. She was neglecting him, Bison whined.

Anita was crazy over Bison. She made her first real mistake that would diminish her independence, perhaps more than anything ever would. Buckling under his continuous grousing, the promising young girl dropped out of the program. Her thanks for putting him first in her life came when she went to his apartment to surprise him with the news.

Bison had been more neglected than Anita had realized. She

looked in disbelief as a young woman, dripping wet, stepped out of the shower, then casually walked out of the bathroom wearing only a white towel. The romance was over, but the irreparable damage had already been done. Anita had made the mistake of putting a man before herself.

Years of insecurity created a yearning inside of her, and Anita soon became codependent on men. In the next relationship she forged, she became pregnant. Sam Weldon, the father of her baby, was in the service. When Anita told him about the baby, Weldon told her he had been restationed with immediate orders to ship out to Hawaii.

Anita quickly decided to go with him. Once there, Weldon started using drugs. Anita remained with him for two months before his erratic behavior convinced her to move back to Arkansas, leaving her baby fatherless.

Anita Lewis gave birth to a healthy, blond-haired boy on August 27, 1988. She named him Scottie. Scottie's father proved to be as unreliable as Anita had predicted. Back home with an infant to care for, and no child support, Anita was in a quandary. The Lewises stood firm, telling their daughter that Scottie was her responsibility. She made her choices, now she would have to deal with the consequences.

Determined to return to college and get her life back under control, Anita applied for a scholastic scholarship. She was notified that she was awarded a Dean's scholarship for North Arkansas University. But by the time the news arrived, the total financial and emotional responsibility of being a single parent had overwhelmed the new mother.

The young woman with such a bright future, "middle America's daughter" wound up on welfare, trying to support her son while raising him in public housing.

Anita knew her family and friends loved her, but in her heart she felt like a lost soul never quite fitting in. During this particularly dismal time Anita penned several poems expressing the depression that overshadowed her life.

The death of Anita's dream as a college graduate left her

aimless. She would later shake her head as she wondered how in the world she could have gone from what she used to be to what she had become. "My choices were bad. Bad choices is why I'm here [in prison]."

Anita's pattern of abusive relationships would continue and escalate. The next man in Anita's life was Danny Miller. The two started dating shortly after her return from Hawaii.

The couple soon moved in together. It didn't seem to matter that the companion Anita had chosen was unstable. She felt more secure just knowing another person was in her life to help take care of Scottie.

One night Miller came home drunk and brooding. He and Anita got in a screaming match when she saw the condition he was in. The argument culminated with Miller pounding Anita in the chest with both fists. The blow knocked her across the room. He ran out, and Anita went to bed crying.

The next morning Miller returned to their apartment. Far from sorry over his shameful behavior, he started picking on Anita the minute he walked in. The baby had kept Anita up all night. Little sleep coupled with the remembrance of Miller's reprehensible conduct from the night before, fashioned the hostility in the air.

They began to quarrel again. It turned into an altercation that quickly spun out of control. Miller hurled a five-pound iron weight directly at Anita. When the weight crashed into her body, Anita was knocked against the wall and fell to the floor. As she lay stunned and crumpled on the carpet, the out-of-control Miller jumped on the helpless woman. He jabbed one fist after the other into her body and the right side of her head. Anita tried to slap back, then wound up curled in a fetal position trying to fend off the furious blows.

His anger still not dissipated, Miller shoved the dresser on top of Anita, thereby pinning her underneath the heavy piece of furniture. She screamed for help.

Miller stormed over to the couch and plopped down. Anita managed to squeeze out from under the bureau. She wasn't about to let him get away with this. Defiantly she picked up the phone in the kitchen and called the police.

When the Batesville police showed up, they were confronted at the door by the bruised and bleeding woman. Blood dripped from her nose. The right side of her head caught most of Miller's punches. Her right eye and ear were beginning to swell. The eye quickly acquired the curious blend of blue-purple coloring that accompanied such battering. Anita's hearing loss caused at childhood sustained further damage in the attack. The ear throbbed with pain.

The police officers asked the young woman a few questions, took Miller out in the hall, then they left. Just like that, the police were gone. Anita watched incredulously as they disappeared. She had trusted the police to protect her, and they failed miserably. The experience would propel Anita into a lengthy history of distrusting law enforcement officials.

It took a few more incidents before Anita finally kicked the abusive man out of her apartment. She knew if she didn't, he might kill her one day. Embittered by the hand life had dealt her, Anita's behavior drastically changed. She started drinking and running around anytime she could find someone to sit with her son.

Miller's abusive behavior also cost Anita her job. The losses, coupled with trying to handle an inordinately hyper baby who suffered from Attention Deficit Disorder, resulted in Anita's physician putting her on Valium and recommending a local psychiatrist to counsel her.

Empty inside and depressed with the road her once promising life was taking, Anita kept spinning further out of control. The abuse began to carve notches into her sense of self-worth, and the crowds she soon hung around became even wilder.

Anita's oldest brother, Jimmy, knew Louis Covington, a prominent part of the wilder gang. One night Covington offered Anita a ride home. Jimmy spotted the car as it pulled into their driveway. Big brother was waiting for Anita when she walked through the door. Jimmy jumped all over his sister. "Anita, I won't allow you to associate with that asshole. He's bad news. You stay away from him!"

In typical teenage rebellious fashion, Anita minced no words as she informed Jimmy, "You're *not* my daddy, and you can't tell me what I *can* and *can't* do!"

Anita recalled her conduct. "I could carry a beer around, act stupid, and they all thought I was drunk. It was easy to fit in. Take a couple of hits off a joint, act like a fool, get totally plastered, and you'd fit right in." Fitting in was important to Anita and she always seemed to have trouble doing it. With the people she now surrounded herself with, it was no longer a problem.

Within one week Anita was dating the young man her brother had warned her against. Covington soon introduced Anita to his cousin Faye. Young and reckless, Faye drank a lot and seemed to answer to no parental authority.

One afternoon Faye was speeding down a back road in Batesville. When she checked her rearview mirror, she saw blue lights flashing on the car coming up behind her. She whispered "shit" as she pulled off the road. The impetuous girl quickly tilted the rearview mirror down, checked her lipstick, then hiked her pink skirt up, prepared to talk the officer out of the ticket. The uniformed man walked up to the car, bent down, and peered in at the short skirt and long legs. Uniform aside, the man wasn't a police officer at all. He just enjoyed using the blue light on top of his car to pull young, naive women over on back roads. The security guard uniform and the .38 pistol holstered in the gun belt wrapped around him helped convince them that he was a cop. His name was Jesse Cummings.

His goal was simple: Cummings got to play the cop that he so loved pretending to be and got sex in exchange for not writing the unsuspecting prey a ticket. Sometimes he would have to threaten the tearful girl that he would have to throw her in jail for an invented outstanding warrant if she didn't cooperate.

In this case not much of a threat was necessary, and a willing Faye rapidly complied. Faye liked Cummings enough that they began to date. She eagerly brought him into her circle of friends and introduced him around. Cummings would especially remember meeting her cousin Louis Covington because of the girl whose arm was wrapped around his. The cute, dark-haired Arkansan, barely standing four ten, reminded Cummings at once of his mother.

Not long after Cummings and Faye's romance began, the perpetually reckless girl pushed her luck too far. Drunk out of her mind, Faye lost control of her car on a back-country road. It careened off the road slamming into a nearby tree instantly killing her. The untimely demise of Cummings's girl would leave him looking for a replacement. Instantly he knew it would be the young girl hanging onto Louis Covington's arm.

Six

Jesse Cummings and Anita Lewis were two people who could not have been from more different worlds, with more different values and goals in life. The two paths that should never have crossed would forge into an ominous marriage, ending in mayhem and murder.

As always, Cummings's timing was impeccable when he strolled into the young, overwhelmed mother's life.

At the parties Anita had attended with Louis Covington and Faye, she and Cummings inevitably ran into each other. Cummings had decided against flirting with her too boldly. Covington was a pretty-good-size man, after all, but Cummings was friendly to her.

With the absence of an abusive man in her life and the help of Valium, Anita now had a job. She left Scottie with Courtney Kinney, a girlfriend of hers, while she was at work. Kinney and Anita ran with the same crowd.

Even though Cummings and Anita associated with mutual friends, they were not close enough to reveal too many details of their lives to each other. His wives had never slowed him down from dating, and Sherry was no different.

When Cummings was interested in someone, he made it his business to find out information he deemed necessary to know. He knew Anita was a single mother, and that she struggled to pay the rent.

He also harbored the suspicion that Anita might be an undercover cop. The white car Anita drove looked much like the undercover ones. And it had a sheriff's sticker on the front windshield courtesy of a cop Anita dated a couple of times.

With all the illegal activity Cummings was into, he felt it prudent to make sure he wasn't being watched by an undercover officer. Cummings never stopped to wonder why an undercover cop would display a sheriff's sticker in plain view.

Cummings had immediately been attracted to Anita the first time he met her. Anita perfectly fit the prototype female Cummings went bonkers over: dark-haired, short, and heavyset.

Cummings arranged to be over visiting at Courtney Kinney's house one day when Anita arrived to retrieve her son after work.

None of Anita's relationships ran very smoothly. She had been fighting with her current boyfriend, Doug Simpson, for the last week. The two had been arguing because he had taken an out-of-town trip with another girl, and Anita had found out. When she ran in to pick up Scottie, she took the opportunity to phone her boyfriend.

When she walked into Kinney's apartment, she saw Cummings sitting on the couch. They acknowledged each other, and Anita went into the bedroom to call Simpson.

The telephone call went as expected, both parties screeching at each other. Anita slammed the telephone receiver onto its cradle.

Knowing Anita would be on the phone railing at her boyfriend, Cummings used the opportunity to search Anita's car, rifling through her personal papers in the glove compartment. He found her car registration, insurance policy, welfare paperwork, and her and Scottie's birth certificates. He perused Anita's birth certificate searching for information he might be able to use. When his eyes focused on the middle name listed on the certificate, he smiled. It was Marie. Cummings tucked the papers back where he had found them.

He got back to the apartment in time to hear the echo of the phone being slammed down.

Anita was steaming over her boyfriend's philandering. She

began ranting about men. She'd had enough of them and she was just going to go out and get drunk. It was music to Cummings's ears.

He started teasing her. "Shit, you can't even buy liquor. You're too damn young."

The challenge had been issued. The heated debate took on a flirtatious tone. Anita retorted, "You men think y'all are so good and you know so much."

Hanging in there, egging Anita along, Cummings postured, "And y'all are so good, uh? Listen, I know you're pissed off, but you know not all men are alike." This was basically the same line he had used a year ago on Sherry.

That night Cummings and Anita went out together. He was in rare form—charmingly, patiently listening to Anita grumble about Simpson and putting down men in general. He was sweet and seemed to care.

He even took up Anita's rally cry, denouncing the errant boyfriend right along with her. He used the moment to ingratiate himself with the vulnerable woman. It worked.

The next week the two started spending time with each other. Cummings patiently listened to the young mother's problems. When she was vexed at something her parents had done, he would always support her position. Cummings assured her, "Anita, I love you and care about you. I think your mama and them are treating you wrong."

Cummings always knew an opportunity when he saw it. Before long he had successfully inserted himself into Anita's life.

Looking back, she reflected, "I was nineteen years old, a new mom, and not ready to settle down. Mom and Dad were saying, 'You got a kid now, 'Nita. That's your first priority. You need to get your life under control.' But I just saw them as constantly criticizing me without trying to help much." Shaking her head, she verbalized the thought she'd been thinking for so long. "Now I know just how right they were."

After so many abusive relationships in her life, Anita decided maybe she was wrong, maybe all men were not alike. Jesse

Cummings was unlike any man she had ever dated. Although he was not intelligent, he was kind, caring, and never so much as raised his voice to her.

Whenever they were together, the couple explored what the future held for each. Anita told Cummings she really liked him, but for now she just wanted to be friends. After her tumultuous relationships, Anita needed space and time to think.

Cummings seemed to have no problem with this request. He assured Anita he would be there for her and to protect her. He also promised he would not push her before she was ready. And he didn't. It was a unique experience for Anita.

As he had with Sherry, Cummings quickly established himself as her "white knight" who would protect her from the type of bad alliances she had been in.

Cummings had managed to introduce Anita into their lives by telling Sherry one day, "I've found someone I really like and she'll be around the house." He told his wife he would use the opportunity to get whatever he could out of the relationship, which Sherry understood to mean sex and money.

Anita was aware that Sherry was in Cummings's life. But he had carefully explained that he and Sherry used to be married and had a little girl together. He told Anita that he had custody of Jessica and allowed Sherry to take care of her so she could see more of her daughter.

To bolster the lie, Cummings arranged a date between Sherry and his friend Wade. Anita was invited to accompany Cummings on a double date with the couple. An order was issued to Sherry to sleep with Wade that night. Cummings didn't mind his women sleeping with other men. What was important to him, was that it had to be his idea, and usually he wanted to watch.

Cummings never gave reasons when he ordered Sherry to do his bidding, and she was too tired, too used, to ask anymore. But the reason was pretty clear. If Anita believed Wade and Sherry were a couple, it would eliminate any fear she had that

Jesse was lying to her. The deceit that encircled Cummings's life was massive. The ruse worked perfectly.

Predictably, Anita wound up in bed with Cummings that night. Anita, so used to being abused and sexually roughed up by inconsiderate boyfriends, found the gentle, considerate Jesse a pleasant change.

In a further effort to dupe Anita, Cummings took a job doing something besides pimping. He started working as a truck driver.

One afternoon Cummings had to make a short-haul run. He invited Anita to ride along. The two talked about life in general. Anita enjoyed riding along in the semi-truck with him.

Calculatingly Cummings started helping the struggling mother with her bills. A motive was always present whenever Cummings did anything, especially if it was something nice. Besides driving a semi, he had started doing work for Sam Weatherford, a local bounty hunter in Batesville. With the money from pimping, driving the truck, and doing bounty work, Cummings could easily afford to take care of Sherry, Jessica, and his new girlfriend and her little boy.

A couple of weeks after they had been intimate, Cummings asked Anita to accompany him on a run that would take only a few hours. She left Scottie with her mom and happily jumped into the rig. As the truck approached an underpass, Cummings miscalculated the height of the rig. The truck became stuck. By the time the rig was free, night had passed into morning.

Anita was frantic because she had missed work. Cummings gently calmed her down. He told her not to worry. "Look, 'Nita, I'll start paying your bills. Just ride with me and keep me awake."

Not a bad-sounding proposition to an anxious and beleaguered single mother. Arrangements were made for Cummings to take care of Anita's car payment, insurance, and her other bills. Maybe her bad luck with men was finally changing, Anita reflected.

The most important quality Anita had found in Cummings

was the way he cared for and took time to play with Scottie. So far, he had been the only man she had dated who had done that. He seemed a natural at fathering, and that pleased her more than anything else about him.

Things were moving along in the direction Cummings wanted, but he felt Anita was not falling into step as quickly as he preferred. He wanted the two of them married, but he had to be judicious and clever, so he set about to speed things up. Kenneth Hale, a friend of Jesse's, was drafted to make sure Jesse did indeed get what he wanted. Hale and Anita lived in the same junkie-laden, low-life apartments.

Cummings told Hale what he needed him to do. A few days after the two men hatched their plan, Hale approached Anita's apartment and knocked. Seeming to be concerned, Hale told Anita, "Look, I know you're hurting for money since you lost your job. I'm really busy today and I gotta get this package over to a guy's house or he'll have my ass. If you'll deliver it for me, I'll give you money to get diapers and whatever else you need."

Since Cummings would be out of town for several weeks on a delivery, Anita had no immediate money for Scottie's diapers and groceries. She saw no harm in the arrangement and delivered the package.

Three weeks later, Cummings returned. When he saw Anita the first night back, he had concern etched across his face. Cummings divulged that friends of his on the police force had alerted him that there was a warrant out for Anita's arrest.

Anita freaked. She had never been in trouble with the law in her life. Cummings saw real fear in Anita's eyes. The expression changed to terror as he continued. " 'Nita, there was drugs in that package Hale asked you to deliver for him. How could you be so stupid?" Anita broke down in sobs.

Her tears appeared to weaken Cummings. He took his hand and gently brushed the wet drops from Anita's cheeks, saying, "I'll think of something. Look, I have pull with the department. I'll talk to a friend of mine down there and see what I can do to get you outta this mess." As he hugged her, he whispered in her ear, "Don't worry. It'll be all right."

Tired of Anita's vacillation over marrying him, Cummings was sure by the time he got through with her, she would do whatever he wanted her to.

He left the anxiety-filled woman to sweat for several days. When he returned to see Anita, he made sure that a look of distress filled his eyes as he spoke with urgency. "My buddy at the department warned me that 'cause of your warrant, Child Welfare's been contacted. Honey, I hate to tell you but they're gonna take Scottie away from you."

This had the effect Cummings knew it would. It sent the devoted mother wailing in misery and whimpering, "I can't lose Scottie! Oh God, Jesse, what am I gonna do?"

Cummings knew how much she loved her son and he also knew she would do anything to get herself out of this mess to keep from losing him.

His arms encircled Anita. As he held her, he hushed her sobs away. As she began to calm down, Cummings said, "Didn't I tell you I'd take care of things? My friend at the department called in some favors for me. The department agreed to drop all charges against you."

Anita looked at Cummings in awe, with no reason to distrust what he was saying. He continued telling her they had made welfare back down, on the condition that she leave the state. Cummings told the scared-to-death teenager, "Look, just marry me. We'll leave, and this nightmare will be over." Everything was jumbled in her brain, crowding out her common sense. Quickly weighing her options, Anita made a decision and nodded her head. She would have agreed to anything to extricate herself from the situation she thought she was entangled in.

Because a blood test prior to marriage is not required in Arkansas, couples can walk into the county courthouse, get a marriage license, and be married within fifteen minutes by the local justice of the peace.

Before Anita had time to mull it over, Cummings had deftly

guided her out the door and pulled her into the car. When she looked up, they were in the courthouse parking lot in Batesville. The couple went inside and hurriedly obtained a marriage license.

Anita ran to a phone, called her mom, and asked, "You wanta go to a wedding?"

The surprised mother asked her daughter whose; to which Anita excitedly responded, "Mine."

Louise Lewis knew her daughter was dating Jesse Cummings. But she also knew he had a child by Sherry and that Sherry lived with him. Louise cautiously inquired, "What about the Sherry situation?"

Anita quelled her mother's fears by answering, "Sherry is dating Wade. She stays with Jesse to take care of her little girl. Mom, there is no Sherry situation, okay?"

Knowing she could not dissuade her hardheaded daughter, Louise agreed to call their minister. Anita and Cummings went back to his and Sherry's house to get dressed. When Cummings and Anita pulled into the driveway, Anita excitedly ran into the house and grabbed Sherry, "You wanta come to a wedding?"

The glance between Sherry and Cummings confirmed the sick feeling in Sherry's stomach as the excited Anita told her to come on. Sherry knew Cummings had an evil side to him, but this was something beyond evil.

By moving Sherry back to Arkansas, Cummings had successfully alienated her from any family support, leaving Lahoma back in Oklahoma. Years later Sherry would find out that every letter she wrote to her mother and every letter that had been written by her mother had been confiscated and hidden by Cummings.

Cummings, Sherry, and Anita arrived at the Lewis house. Louise and Harry Lewis, together with a few friends, watched as Jesse Cummings repeated wedding vows to his fourth wife on June 14, 1989. He was now "legally" married to three women.

Less than two years had passed since he stood with Sherry

in front of a minister to take the same vows. Sherry was paralyzed. She had done everything to try and make Jesse happy. She had degraded herself by prostituting her body for him; had slept with his friends for him. Sherry had demeaned herself in every manner possible just to try and keep her marriage going.

The only comfort and dignity Sherry clung to was her status as Jesse's one and only wife and the mother of his child. In stunned silence Sherry stood and watched as Cummings stripped that from her, too.

Sherry later said, "I stood in Anita's house, humiliated as I watched my husband marry another woman. I felt lower than dirt, like I was nothing, and that's exactly how Jesse wanted me to feel."

For Sherry, if you loved someone and believed in them, you trusted them. It had taken awhile but she was beginning to determine the things Jesse Cummings presented to her as truths were nothing more than lies.

Seven

Sherry never believed Jesse Cummings capable of such betrayal. She was as angry with Anita as she was with Jesse. Sherry was unaware he had been lying to Anita, too.

Always Cummings sought to minimize his misdeeds. After the marriage ceremony he took Anita aside and gently told her she would have to be patient, because Sherry would have to stay with the newlyweds for a while.

Explaining that since he was pulling up stakes for her sake in order to get her out of the drug-dealing jam she had gotten into, the move would separate Jessica from her mother. He told Anita he would not punish Sherry by taking Jessica away from her. Only Cummings would have the temerity to blame the situation on both his wives.

Sherry would move to Oklahoma with the couple and stay with them until she could get a job and a place to stay on her own. Same song, second verse. Cummings didn't have to think up new lines. The old ones continued to work just fine.

So relieved was Anita to have the dogs called off, she was tolerant of this minor drawback. After all, Jesse had managed to keep welfare from taking away Scottie and had gotten all charges against her dropped. She could afford to be tolerant.

Cummings's steady job as a truck driver had fulfilled its purpose of keeping up the pretense that he was a hardworking man who dutifully supported his family. The day he married Anita, he quit.

Cummings had always possessed a strong sexual appetite. But other than the frequency of sexual intercourse and the variety of partners, his sexual activities never involved sexual intercourse with more than one partner at the same time, but he had been thinking about it more frequently.

From the moment he married Anita, the wheels started turning as to how he could arrange a willing ménage à trois starring himself and his two wives.

Cummings carefully planned the event. Less than a week after he married Anita, he arranged to have sex with her when he knew Sherry would be at home. Leaving the bedroom door open, he hoped she would walk in on them. And she did.

Sherry explained, "I was already hurt by Jesse's betrayal. To top that off, here I walk in on them and I was so embarrassed." As she turned to leave, Cummings, not missing a beat, patted the bed and told her to sit down so he could discuss something with her.

Trying to avert her eyes from the two people in bed, Sherry sat down. The room was so small the only other place to look was in the mirror. It reflected the very sight she was trying to avoid. Cummings didn't want to talk, he just wanted to gauge Sherry's and Anita's reactions to the three being in the same bed together.

Anita felt awkward, Sherry was embarrassed to death, and Cummings was simply amused.

The next time Cummings would broach the three-in-a-bed theme, he became a little more sinister, dropping sleeping pills into a soft drink of Anita's. Grogginess overcame Anita and she went into the bedroom and fell fast asleep. Cummings persuaded Sherry to get into bed with him and have sex. He assured the nervous woman Anita was sound asleep.

As the two began having sex, Anita was stirred awake from the movement and sexual moans. Mortified, she decided to pretend to be asleep.

Both women found their own justification for putting up with this degrading behavior. For Anita, it was "All men cheat anyway, at least mine does it out in the open." Sherry's was basically the same premise.

The first time Cummings managed to have both women awake in bed with him was less than three weeks after his wedding to Anita. A predatory man, Cummings would use whatever he could to get what he wanted.

Anita had received a phone call earlier in the day that her cousin had been decapitated in a horrible car wreck. "Dr. Jesse" prescribed Valium for her and quickly fetched two pills. The shaken woman immediately downed them.

Anita's real doctor had prescribed a dosage of one Valium followed by another after six hours. Unused to the effect of a double dosage, she became slightly euphoric. Cummings put her to bed, then went to have a chat with Sherry.

By this time Sherry had little will or self-respect left. If Cummings wanted the ménage à trois to happen, it would. She joined him in the bedroom, where they stripped naked and climbed in bed. Cummings nestled between his two wives.

Still subtle and taking advantage of Anita's diminished capacity, Cummings slowly brought the two women together. As an orchestra leader would do, Cummings choreographed the women's movements. He placed Anita's hand on Sherry's body and then did the same with Sherry.

This was just the beginning of the degradation the two women would share in common over their many years with Cummings.

After the wedding Cummings, Sherry, Jessica, Anita, and Scottie started preparations to leave for Oklahoma. Anita would not only be leaving her imaginary legal hassles behind, she would be leaving her entire life's history.

She had grown up in Batesville, Arkansas. All her family was there. She cried as she hugged her mother, father, and brothers goodbye, but she knew because Kenneth Hale had underhandedly used her in a drug deal, it was for the best. The young woman took solace in the fact that holidays and other occasions would reunite her with her family.

On August 31, 1989, Jesse Cummings returned with his enlarged family to Tupelo, Oklahoma. They moved in temporarily with his sister Debra, until Jesse had time to locate living quarters. By now, little Jessica was almost two years old. Scottie was nearly a year old.

Within two days of their stay in Debra's home, Anita overheard a conversation taking place between Cummings and his sister. He was showing his marriage license to Debra. She didn't approve of Jesse having two wives and told him he couldn't do that. He laughed and told her not only could he do it, but he had done it. As Anita listened in the doorway, she grew sicker and sicker in her stomach. She thought she had made every attempt to find a man who was decent and loving.

Later that night Anita angrily confronted Cummings with her newfound knowledge. This time he told the truth; after all, he had Anita where he wanted her, so why not.

Surprised by his candor, and even more astonished he had no intentions of doing anything about his bigamy, Anita stood reeling from the revelation. He didn't see a problem, so he reasoned why should she. Furious, Anita screamed and threatened to leave him and return to Arkansas.

Prepared for this contingency, Cummings announced to his new bride she would not be going anywhere. Matter-of-factly he reminded Anita of his friends on the police force in Arkansas. He shoved the fact that the notorious bondsman Sam Weatherford was also a close friend. Weatherford was known for his seediness and it was rumored his services as a hit man could be bought cheaply.

Anita would stay right where she was or Cummings was prepared to turn her over to Weatherford, then God help her. Horrified, Anita ran sobbing into the other room and grabbed up Scottie, hugging him tightly to her. She sat rocking on the bed, saying over and over, "What have I done? My God, what have I gotten myself into?"

There was nothing much she could do about the situation and Anita was well aware of the fact. She had gotten herself into this mess, trusting a man she never should have. She reasoned she'd just have to figure how to get out of it.

When Anita was rebelling, running around, and drinking, she had picked up the habit of smoking. Cummings detested women who smoked. He had managed to put up with Sherry smoking but strictly limited her to daytime smoking only. Before Sherry was allowed to go to bed, she had to bathe and wash her hair to get rid of the smell. Sherry's auburn hair was long and lush. She would later get around this time-consuming ritual by spraying perfume in her hair instead.

Debra saw the dejected Anita sitting on the bed rocking her son. Trying to be helpful, she pulled out a bag of marijuana and carefully rolled a cigarette. She held the cigarette out for Anita to take, but she politely declined. Debra shrugged and placed it in a drawer, telling Anita she knew where it was if she should change her mind.

After Cummings deemed enough time had gone by for Anita to come to grips about the bigamy issue, he asked her to take a ride out in the country so the two could clear the air.

They left in their 1969 station wagon and headed in the direction of one of many country roads in the area. Tired of hearing the bitching he was getting, Cummings stopped the car and got out. He walked down the road, leaving Anita by herself in the car.

Anita reached in her pocket and took out the marijuana cigarette she had gotten out of Debra's drawer prior to her departure. Stressed out over this incredible mess, she figured she might need it to pacify herself. The joint was lit using the car's cigarette lighter. The mellow edges of the marijuana lulled Anita, slowly easing tension in her neck.

When she noticed Cummings heading back to the car, she quickly rolled down the window and frantically waved the smoke out. As he opened the driver's side of the car and got in, he looked over at Anita, sniffed his nose, and inquired, "What the fuck are you doing? I can't believe you, you stupid bitch!"

Before Anita could offer a word of apology, Cummings

grabbed Anita by the hair and slammed her face over and over into the metal steering wheel until he was exhausted. By the time he had finished the vicious beating, Anita's jaw was broken along the chin line, and her upper lip was split in two. One of her teeth had been knocked out.

Salty tears began to roll down Anita's cheeks on the drive home, rudely stinging when they reached her raw, splintered mouth. When a hand wiped the offenders away, others quickly replaced them. The rest of the way home Anita held her aching blood-covered face in her hands and wept. Anita jumped out of the car as soon as Cummings put his foot on the brake. She ran into the house and rushed toward the bedroom. People in the house stared at her as she ran for cover. Once in the bedroom she fell across the bed wailing from a combination of the pain, humiliation, and consternation.

No one ever called Cummings's hand when they knew he was abusing a woman. They were too scared of him to do anything but turn the other way. Debra came into the bedroom with a wet cloth and soothingly bathed Anita's face. Then Debra hightailed it to avoid drawing the ire of her brother.

The arrangement in Debra's house had Jesse, Sherry, Anita, and the two children staying in one tiny bedroom. Because the space was so small, all their belongings, except for a few items of clothing for each of them, were in Debra's shed, which was situated in the back of the house.

The bleeding eventually stopped and the aching had quelled somewhat. Anita continued to lie on the bed too nervous to get up. Her mind was numb. After an hour Anita finally got off the bed and went outside, sitting down on the back-porch steps. What little joy she now had in her life came from Scottie. The mother silently watched her son play as she waited for the pain and debasement she felt to subside.

Little Scottie was still in diapers. Too poor to buy disposable ones, he wore the more cumbersome cloth versions. The one he wore while playing was beginning to get dirt on it from the ground.

Inside Debra's house a messy diaper and a dirty towel and washrag had been wadded up and thrown into the corner of the bedroom where Jesse's family stayed.

A man never satisfied when things were calm, Cummings decided to stir things up a bit and further punish Anita's willfulness.

He went and got Sherry and brought her to the bedroom. He helpfully pointed out the items balled up on the floor, then demanded to know why they were there.

When Sherry told him she had no idea, he barked back. " 'Nita told me you put 'em there!" Knowing she hadn't, Sherry stood with her hands planted firmly on her hips and fumed. Cummings headed in the direction of the back porch to attend to the second phase of his plan.

He accused Anita of the deed and demanded to know why she had left the mess, adding Sherry had told him she was the guilty party. Still smarting from the earlier thrashing, Anita simply denied the accusation, not even bothering to look at her husband.

Neither woman knew what the hell Cummings was talking about. The truth, in fact, was Cummings himself had placed the items there to start the whole ruckus. He bounced back and forth between the two women, carrying on and on about the mess, seeking to incite a small fracas.

His efforts were not proving too successful, so in an attempt to prompt Sherry into action, he defiantly demanded, "If you ain't gonna do nothing about this shit, then I'll just go tell Debbie 'cause it's her house and both you bitches'll get in trouble." Disgusted, he marched off to report the incident to his sister.

Sherry had put up with Cummings's back-and-forth haranguing most of the afternoon and was beginning to get really angry. Already hurt and jealous over Anita, the last remark set her into the action that Cummings had been trying to spark most of the afternoon.

The antiquated house had no indoor plumbing. A rotted outhouse sufficiently served the family's needs. Bathing was accomplished in an old stained tub. It was positioned by the well, where it could be filled with well water. After the summer sun had heated the water up, one by one baths were taken.

Anita, her body still aching and sore, began to tire with Cummings's little game. Standing and stretching her bruised body, Anita headed for the shed to retrieve a change of clothes and take a bath. The caked-on blood needed to be scrubbed off, and hopefully, the warm water would ease the soreness coursing through her.

Cummings had worked Sherry into a frenzy. By the time she located Anita searching for a change of clothes in the shed, she was boiling mad and ready for a confrontation. Without thinking, Sherry grabbed Anita's arm and yanked her around. The two women exchanged heated words.

As the shouting grew louder, everyone poured out onto the porch to watch the ruckus. They began to egg Sherry on, yelling, "Get her, Sherry! Whup her ass, girl!" The most prominent voice crying out was Jesse's.

The fight between the women, such as it was, began. From the start Anita didn't have much of a chance in the match. Barely able to move from the earlier flogging, the added armful of clothes gave her no chance of defending herself.

Earlier Sherry had seen Anita's battered face and she was pretty sure how it had happened. Cummings had told everyone who witnessed Anita jumping out of the car that she had been in a car wreck. The last few years with Cummings had taught her automobile accidents were one of his favorite things to blame injuries on. She was pretty sure Anita had been beaten by him that day. She also had seen Anita's face and knew that her mouth had taken the brunt of the injury.

When your own pain gets bad enough, you begin to ignore the pain of those around you. The years of anger and frustration coiled tightly inside of Sherry began to loosen up.

Instinctively Sherry went straight for the part of Anita that would hurt the most. As she flung her rival around, she threw a punch that contacted against the badly mauled mouth. The single blow left Anita sprawled unconscious in the dirt as blood spilled from her wounded injury mixing curious patterns in the dirt as they blended.

Reprehensible and cruel behavior were two traits Cummings had learned at the knee of his mother—only he had perfected them to a fine art. Observing the anarchy he had created with little effort, Cummings turned around with a smile on his face and walked back into the house.

Stunned at her own violence, Sherry was left to pick Anita up, dust her off, and inspect the damage. When Sherry examined the abused inside of Anita's mouth, she saw that a tooth was missing. It looked to her like the dislodged tooth was imbedded in the roof of Anita's mouth. Apologizing for her appalling behavior, Sherry loaded Anita into the car and drove her to the nearest dentist. The tooth had been knocked loose when Anita's face had been repeatedly smashed into the metal wheel and she had swallowed it.

Although Sherry had found it cathartic to lash out with the full force of her pent-up outrage, she was terribly ashamed she had done so.

The pattern that emerged that day would go on for years with Cummings constantly pitting his wives against each other. When things appeared to be going too smoothly between the women, he would quickly think of something to start a fight. The last thing Jesse Cummings wanted was a bond of trust and friendship to forge between Anita and Sherry.

Cummings quickly outstayed his welcome and moved his family out of Debra's house. With no place else to go and no money, he used his old station wagon as a temporary home until he could find something else. At night blankets and pillows would be placed on the back floor, where three adults and two children would huddle and fall asleep. Anita could not believe what she was doing.

Cummings finally located an old house in Stonewall, Oklahoma, that was so dilapidated the owner charged Cummings next to nothing in rent, and that seemed excessive. For Cummings, anything that cost him at all was too much. It didn't matter, though, he had already started looking for something else. This house was not nearly isolated enough. He would have to find one where neighbors and their prying ears were far and few between, unable to hear the things he had begun planning.

With the women at home taking care of the children, Cummings continued dating. With the dissension still strong between the wives, he told Anita he was out working or looking for work. With Sherry an explanation was not necessary nor proffered. She knew where he was going. One night he met a girl named Mildred Tucker at one of the many street dances the small town held. The two would flitter toward each other like moths to a flame. Mildred Tucker, like all women drawn to Cummings, was a truly pathetic young woman. Made fun of all her life, the heavyset teenager ate for comfort until she was overweight. Mildred's plain looks and the loneliness that consumed her eyes gave away her feelings of being unloved. Cummings had become an expert at spotting those traits in young girls. He walked over and struck up a conversation with her.

The lonely woman who wandered around the street dance was looking for hope, companionship, closeness, and love, or if she was lucky, tonight she might find someone who cared enough to just speak to her. Mildred was a sitting duck as Cummings spotted the awkward teenager who stood alone. He easily recognized the desirable trait of desperation written across her.

Mildred Tucker provided the perfect target for Cummings. Mildred wanted so much for somebody to care for her that she was immediately infatuated with him. He spent time with the teenager, valuable time, heaping attention and compliments on the sad girl. Cummings took her to the Stonewall house the same night he had plucked her up off the street to have sex with her.

Cummings made sure to grab a cheap bottle of whiskey off the kitchen counter, telling Mildred it was "moonshine." He was pretty certain he would need the fortification. He led Mildred to the part of the old house farthest from his bedroom.

Anita was not primed enough to hear another sexual encounter just yet. Pressing his finger to his lips, he indicated for Mildred to stay quiet as they tiptoed through the house. Looking for a place safe enough from Anita's semivirgin ears—just in case the enamored girl couldn't keep her mouth shut—and not finding one, he led Mildred out the back door and into the field behind the house. Mildred had already started to giggle quietly at the intrigue of it all. She had been desperate that night as she milled around lost in the crowd. There were so many people around her, yet she was totally isolated from any of them. She had prayed just for one of them to speak to her. She hadn't dared dream of anything as exciting as intrigue.

Lying in a neighbor's field, among the barnyard animals that proliferated the property, Cummings had sex with the disbelieving, thrilled girl. He had been right about the liquor, it had come in handy. He used the alcohol as a sex prop accidentally spilling some on her. Then he proceeded to lick it off Mildred's body to the delighted teenager's squeals. By the time he was through, the bottle was empty. Mildred would recall it as the most memorable sexual encounter in her life.

She would become one of many sex partners and friends that wandered in and out of Jesse's house and life on a regular basis to serve him. Eventually it would be Cummings who would wind up totally dependent on someone else for the rest of his life. It turned out to be Mildred. After that night the nineteen-year-old started following Cummings around like a puppy ready to do whatever he asked of her. It would place Mildred within his close reach, allowing him yet another person on which to vent the uncontrollable rage rapidly growing inside of him.

PART TWO

"The family is where the least respectable and most ridiculous things go on."

—Ugo Beiti

PART TWO

Eight

In December 1989 Jesse Cummings finally found the house he had been looking for in Phillips, Oklahoma. The house was right in line with the other shacks he had used to shelter his family. This house was so shabby and run-down it rented for twenty-five dollars a month. But it had lots of room and a huge field where various farm animals roamed. It would suit Cummings's needs perfectly and it would be the only house he would ever need. Everything he had dreamed of accomplishing could be done right here.

Cummings was quick to furnish the bedroom first. The old rusted metal posted bed and urine-stained mattress obtained from the nearest dump was placed in the center of the tiny room. What Cummings lacked in intelligence, he more than made up for in ego. Rummaging inside the box of meager belongings placed next to the wall, he found the two marriage licenses he was searching for, promptly nailed one on each side of the bed and declared to his wives that they would sleep under their names. Of course, Cummings always the center of attention, would sleep in the middle.

After the move from Debra's and the confining nature of the station wagon and the house at Stonewall, it would be the Phillips house and the distance away from the children that would allow him to set up the rules for sleeping. The three of them would sleep in the nude. Since Cummings had secured a nail and old string to the door he did not have to worry about any of the children wandering in. When he decreed it was time to sleep, he would pen down the women on both sides of him so he could get some sleep. If they could get to sleep that way, it was fine with him. If they could not, even better!

"He had Anita on one side and me on the other," Sherry explained. "One of his legs was wrapped around me and the other leg was wrapped around Anita. If he turned over, there was a hand on me and a hand on her. If he turned over my way, he had his legs on me."

Anita added, "He would take our arms and put them around him so if we moved, even the least bit, he was awake. The man slept lighter than me. He was constantly aware of any movement by us."

Up until that point Cummings always had a reason for his irrational violence and would justify the assaults on his wives to them and others who actually saw him in action. But now Cummings was settled into his own home—the one place that would protect him against outsiders and the one place secluded enough to provide him the opportunity to start using violence without any explanation. Cummings enjoyed waiting until the women had fallen to sleep, then he would wake them with a well-placed elbow in their stomach or throat. At first he would offer the explanation he had accidentally done it during a nightmare. Later his reaction would be to simply laugh, turn over, and go soundly to sleep.

A few days after their move, Cummings was eager to introduce Anita into one of his most satisfying sexual activities. It would also serve to ingrain into Anita, subtly at first, his superior control and will. It would make it harder for her to fight back at his increasing control, will, and demand for salacious things from her.

One morning while Sherry, Anita, and Cummings were lying in bed, he told Sherry to jump up and instructed Anita to lie spread-eagle across the bed. Cummings handcuffed his new wife to the bed, while Sherry, without need for instruction, carefully tied her to the bed with rope, then tightly wrapped the twine around Anita's feet and legs.

"He made it sound like it was gonna be fun. He told me, 'Try it. If you don't like it, we'll quit.' We didn't have a headboard so the rope was tied down and around the mattress springs. My hands were tied around the metal pole at the head of the bed."

As soon as Sherry completed the task, Cummings told Anita he was taking everybody out so they wouldn't be in the way. He closed the bedroom door leaving Anita bound and alone, but now it seemed strangely special just to be alone with him. Hope springs eternal, and it was still alive in Anita. The kids and Sherry were loaded in the car and left. Anita expected Cummings to come right back.

Anita had been tied up for over an hour, when she heard Jesse Cummings, Sr., like Jesse's other followers, he would come in and out of his son's life like a revolving door, usually when he and Joyce were in one of their many separations. He was living at the house when Anita heard her father-in-law open the old screen door and shut the door to his bedroom.

Still sure Cummings would show up any minute, Anita tossed away any idea of calling out to Jesse Cummings, Sr., who could have easily heard her in the run-down shack. She had no intentions of letting him find her naked and bound, even if she had to lie there until Christmas.

The hours slowly ticked by. After eight hours of leaving his wife helplessly tied up, Cummings returned. Anita recalled, "I was very mad. I asked him just what in hell he meant by leaving me like that."

Almost as if the matter was inconsequential, he explained that he got detained at his sister's. "I only meant to drop 'em off and come right back." Anita didn't dare pursue the matter. After the brief explanation Cummings had sex with the bound woman for the next hour. When he was through with Anita, he untied her and told her to get dressed so they could go pick up Sherry and the kids.

The Cummingses still had no basic amenities. There was no indoor plumbing. An outhouse beside a barely standing barn serviced the adults. A children's porta-potty was placed on the back porch for the children to use.

As for water, there was a well a short distance from the house. The women would haul well water in by a bucket. On many occasions when the bucket was hoisted and reached topside, snakes coiled inside the bucket poked their heads out at the rude disturbance. The women would scream, drop the bucket back down in its hiding place, and flee.

The house was wired for electricity, but there were few outlets and the wiring was frayed and dangerous. Cummings scoured the local dumping ground and came up with two old lamps that he rigged up to provide lighting at night.

He also managed to find a discarded television set that still worked. When he wanted to, Jesse Cummings could scrounge up just about anything. It took more looking, but he eventually found an old VCR that had been thrown away. It was perched on top of the stained and worn cabinet of the television, which remained on constantly. Cummings even managed to round up a few old discarded pornographic movies carefully secreted from small prying eyes to be enjoyed later. A Polaroid camera proved more of a challenge for Cummings, who eventually bought one at a Goodwill store nearby. To him, it was worth its weight in gold as it captured hundreds of sexual activities over the years. The photographs carefully arranged by him were placed in a picture album providing him with years of entertainment.

As with everything else in their lives, Anita and Sherry had no say in what program would be watched on the television. The only one who seemed to have a vote on anything was Cummings.

The dilapidated house was overrun with rats. Cummings would sit in the kitchen, aim his pistol at the rodents as they scurried about, and fire away. He consistently managed to pick off several defenseless cans of beans. Sometimes he would get a rat, but more often than not, he just shot the place up.

One day a squirrel that had landed on top of the roof kept running back and forth. The noise was beginning to irritate Cummings. He retrieved his pistol and promptly shot several holes in the ceiling. It never worried him that one of the children could get hit by a stray bullet.

Cummings liked shooting the gun that always stayed in his back pocket. The main reason he had selected the old, falling-down house in Phillips was its perfect location and the large field behind it. The house was set back from the main road and there was only one other house in the vicinity. He could make as much noise and do whatever he wanted without fear of the police paying him a visit or nosy neighbors prying into his business.

Two decades prior to moving into the house at Phillips, Oklahoma, an event occurred that stunned the nation. Americans listened and watched in horror as the news of two separate massacres in an upscale neighborhood in California during the summer of 1969 unfolded. The atrocious nature of the slayings had people everywhere terrified. The bloodbaths would become known as the notorious Tate-LaBianca murders. Later that year a young man by the name of Charles Manson would be arrested, eventually tried, and then convicted of the crime. People were riveted and repulsed by Charles Manson, who was revealed as the mastermind behind the horrific murders.

Although Jesse Cummings was only fifteen when Manson became infamous for his deeds, he would begin to pattern his life after the man, using his hero's philosophies to guide him in every aspect of his life. Manson soon became a household word, and Cummings was fascinated by the man people were calling the anti-Christ. He admired the man he had intensely connected with. Over the years the nearly illiterate Cummings would read every article or book he could get his hands on about the icon, struggling for days at a time to read just a few pages. Cummings found himself amazed at how much the two were alike. Manson and Cummings were eerily similar. Both came from California. Both hated black people. Neither felt love for their family. Both lived with numerous women at one time in a run-down commune, in buses, and in cars. They lived among squalor, filth, and chaos. They prostituted the naive, innocent women around them. They both understood the value of isolating those under their control from their families. They instilled blind obedience of those around them with terror and brainwashing. Cummings even credited Manson's penchant for drugs and tattoos as the reason for the rather plain one he sported on his left forearm. During his marriage to Margaret Hazel Cummings, in a weak or perhaps an intoxicated state, Cummings had the initials of the crippled woman he had so coldly and cruelly tortured seared into his skin. He would boast to anyone who would listen that "MHC" stood for marijuana, heroin, and cocaine.

Manson and Cummings both shared the same apocalyptic vision. The forthcoming apocalypse was the deciding factor that Charles Manson had used in training his own army for the occasion.

It would be two decades later in Phillips, Oklahoma, where those philosophies and plans would come to fruition starting with survival training. Following his leader, Cummings used Manson's reasoning when he insisted that every man, woman, and child in his extended family go through extensive survival training.

The women and children were trained how to fight hard, hit fast, and protect their body from the enemies' blows. Weapons were also used in training. When Cummings first married Sherry, he would load the truck up with guns and plenty of ammunition.

Sherry remembered, "Our training started with how to take a punch and progressed to 'I want you to shoot this gun. Here's how you load and here's how you shoot it.' Then he'd hand us the gun."

Scared and apprehensive about weapons, neither Sherry nor

Anita had ever held a gun before Cummings handed her one. The first gun he handed Sherry was a .25 automatic pistol. Sherry squeezed off a few rounds and became a little more comfortable with the weapon.

Next he handed her a .16-gauge shotgun. He didn't bother to explain to her how to hold it. And he didn't prepare her for the kick. Sherry recalled, "He told me to put the gun on my shoulder and shoot. I asked him prior to shootin' does it kick, and he said 'naw.' Well, I believed him and I shot the double-barrel shotgun and fell back into a tire behind me and hit my head on the rim. My whole shoulder and chest was black and blue the next day. Jesse just laughed at me."

Cummings told his wives they needed to learn how to protect themselves. In truth, he was conditioning them to obey orders without question, like soldiers training for war. He was regimenting them to be killing machines, just as Manson had done so successfully.

As part of Cummings's survival training, he would walk up behind his wives and try to catch them off guard. He would put a sleeper hold on them until they passed out and collapsed to the floor. One day he did this to Sherry while she was preparing a meal. As she slid to the floor, he casually took the pan off the flame so the food wouldn't burn.

After she had regained consciousness, he chastised her because she had let down her guard.

Cummings knew the one thing that would set Anita off was to touch her face. One day when there had been no arguing or fighting, he took Anita by surprise. She was taken to the ground, then Cummings straddled her and sat with most of his weight on her stomach and chest.

For the next three hours he would slap her face back and forth in his hands, alternating between his left and right hand. When she screamed at him to get off, he would answer, "You gotta learn control, little girl. You gotta learn control." When he finished, Anita's face was badly swollen.

Cummings explained that he was doing this for her own

good. As she looked at the man in amazement, he told her, "If you ever get in a real fight and lose your temper, you're a dead woman."

As soon as Jesse and Sherry's daughter, Jessica, became old enough to hold a gun, the father started training her, too. By the time she started walking, Cummings started training her how to fight. By the age of seven she could shoot better than most grown men.

With Jessica, his goal was to instill undying love and loyalty in her. When Jessica was barely old enough to walk, he started her survival training. It was not uncommon for Cummings to take his daughter off in the truck and stay gone for hours. The feeling of being special assured Jessica's silence about their time alone. Cummings knew it would also assure him she would unquestioningly follow any order he gave her as he built her sense of loyalty toward him.

Sherry suspected that he was molesting the little girl, but she couldn't prove it. She knew Jessica had become so loyal to her father that she would never tell if he was molesting her. Sherry said that by now she was too tired to dwell on things she could not change, so she would simply deny they were happening. Every time they drove off and stayed gone for hours, Sherry would keep telling herself over and over that he couldn't be violating his own child.

Cummings's constant beatings and mental abuse of the women out in the open, instead of behind locked doors, taught the children and the hangers-on in his life his favorite Manson survival-training technique. It didn't matter what they did or how well they did it, everyone under his roof was under his complete control. Still, out of an abundance of caution and having learned from his mother the difference between fear and hate—Cummings knew not to teach the males around him—children or adults—skilled fighting or proficiency with weapons.

Cummings liked to brag to his friends that he had trained his wives so well that they could take a vicious beating and never shed a tear. "I've trained 'em to the point they can't feel pain."

"But I could always feel the pain no matter what Jesse said." Sherry shuddered at the memory as she stared vacantly ahead.

Anita spoke angrily when remembering her schooling at the hands of Jesse. "He'd tell us, 'Ya got to learn control. The world's falling apart and you never know who you're gonna be up against!' It turned out the only one we was up against was Jesse."

Charles Manson and Jesse Cummings were connected by their inherent capacity to do evil. They possessed no conscience, no morality, no human compassion. Sometimes monsters are born that way; sometimes they evolve. In Manson's and Cummings's cases, both methods applied. Jesse Cummings *was* Charles Manson, just a decade younger.

Nine

Life in the Cummings house was dismal and bleak. It was comparable to being dumped back into the nineteenth century. The bright, young, and pretty girl from Arkansas who had once lived with her parents in a seventy-thousand-dollar home filled with every convenience one could think of, now existed in a shack renting for twenty-five dollars a month. Anita learned to do things that she never dreamed she would. The women scrubbed clothes on a washboard in a five-gallon bucket. Sometimes they had to use the water trough, which was meant for the farm animals, to wash their clothes in. The articles were wrung out, then hung on a rigged-up clothesline to dry.

Cummings located a stained and rusted porcelain claw bathtub. It was huge, heavy, and deep. Once a week the family would get a bath. The women had to drag the burdensome tub into the house, then haul in buckets of water to fill it. Cummings had decreed the pecking order in which baths would be taken. Sherry and Jessica were first, followed by Anita and Scottie.

Cummings took his bath last. When their bathing was finished, the women had to empty the huge tub by scooping out the water with the bucket, and then carrying it out back where it was dumped. Then they were required to refill the tub with clean water for Cummings's bath. Only Cummings was allowed to have hot water. The women would haul the buckets of water indoors and heat them on the old wood stove in the kitchen. Bucket after bucket of water was heated until the tub was filled to Cummings's satisfaction. It was a tedious, backbreaking chore, but neither woman, who had been forced along with her child to tolerate the cold water, dared to complain about bathing herself or her child in the murky, cold water.

When time was a concern, Cummings ordered the women and children to hose themselves off in the backyard. Once a week the women and children were allowed to hose themselves down. The children danced around, their teeth chattering as the cold water hit their bodies.

Even cooking proved to be backbreaking work. In her life back in Batesville, when it was time for supper, the Lewises would reach into the freezer for some meat, toss it in the microwave to defrost, then sit down to a hot meal. If everyone was too tired to cook, then fast food was ordered or, especially on the weekends, the Lewis family went out to eat in a nice restaurant. But Phillips, Oklahoma, was a lifetime away from the life Anita had grown up accustomed to. Cummings controlled all the grocery shopping. To make the food stamps he managed to collect go as far as possible, he bought in bulk. Items like potatoes and flour were just a few of the things he would stock up on.

Anita was introduced to an entirely new way of cooking. Cummings demanded the food be made from scratch. This meant cheaper, and yet more backbreaking work for the women.

At first the urban girl wasn't even sure she knew what scratch meant. But she learned quick. Around Cummings slow learners were punished sometimes verbally, sometimes physically, whichever served its purpose best. Cummings used Anita's lack of country cooking as an opportunity to put her down on a continual basis. He frequently used the remark, "You're supposed to be so damn smart, little Miss Honor Student. Hell, you don't even know how to cook." Cummings hated the fact that Anita was so smart and independent. She would certainly issue more of a challenge to him. It would take much more to break this one, he thought.

Quietly seething inside, Anita took the insults hurled her way.

As he rambled on she would try to focus on the things she knew to be true, attempting to salvage the tiny parts of self-esteem still fighting to remain a part of her. "I knew how to cook, just not the things Jesse liked. Growing up, I'd never made biscuits from scratch. In our house biscuits came from a can."

Cummings liked meat and was partial to dishes such as chicken and dumplings, and squirrel with dumplings. Meat taken from the freezer had no microwave to thaw in. Since Cummings didn't want flies getting on the meat as it sat out to thaw, the women would have to struggle and strain taking turns cutting up the nearly frozen meat.

Cummings had stopped Sherry from wearing makeup early in their marriage. Anita was a tad harder to convince. "We'd go out in the woods to work, and he wouldn't give me time to get ready. He'd come in and wake me up and say, 'Get dressed. Let's go.' I'd start getting dressed. One day I hadn't been out of bed maybe ten minutes. Jesse drove off and left me. When he got home that night I got the hell beaten out of me 'cause I hadn't gotten up and gotten ready in time to get in that truck. I know many times me and Sherry were putting on tennis shoes and running for the truck to go work out in the woods. You learned not to take time to put makeup on. Then it got where the few times we had time to put it on, he'd get so pissed off I just quit."

Cummings's erratic behavior had Anita under so much stress she stopped eating. In less than six months from her marriage to Cummings, she had lost over fifty pounds. At four ten and weighing ninety-five pounds, Anita was shrinking away before everyone's eyes. When Anita tried to force the food down, the stress she was under would make the food knot up in her throat, making it impossible to swallow.

It wasn't long before Cummings began to notice Anita eating less and less and losing weight on a daily basis. The few times Anita could manage to swallow her food, she still wouldn't gain because of the manual labor Cummings had her and Sherry doing.

He worked the women steadily like workhorses. They would be in the woods from daylight until dark. The work they performed was manual and backbreaking.

As Anita grew thinner, Cummings would toss a barrage of contradictory insults her way, from "You're still a fat cow!" to "You're so skinny your titties and ass are gone. You look like a damn kid."

Cummings finally got fed up with Anita's food remaining untouched on her plate. Like a parent gone mad chastising a child, he got out his bullwhip and began hitting Anita with it. As each crack of the whip contacted with Anita's body, he'd scream at the recalcitrant, terrified woman, "Eat, goddamn you. Eat!"

Once he had battered Anita into submission and she would begin to eat again, he would start complaining profusely about her gaining weight. He was never satisfied, and Anita couldn't win.

One of the items Cummings bought in bulk was huge bottles of laxatives. He had Anita so distressed, she would jump up from the table after a meal and down the laxative. Instead of food digesting and dispersing properly through her body, it would go straight through her. Thus began Anita's horrible journey down the path of anorexia nervosa. Another problem in her life she did not need to tackle.

The once vivacious Anita, who was known to rattle on about things, soon quit talking. She gave one-sentence answers. Cummings continued to put her down. "Either that I talked too much, telling me it was stuff nobody wanted to hear. His favorite words for me were, 'stupid'—that was a big one; and 'ignorant.' He'd say things like, 'Do I gotta draw a picture for you. Females are so fuckin' stupid.'"

Anita's past was a forbidden topic. Cummings hated her talking about anything that didn't involve him. "I wadn't allowed to do it. According to him, my life began the day I married him and I wadn't allowed to talk about anything prior."

The few times Anita slipped and brought up something from

her past, Cummings would yell, "If you want that life you should've stayed there." Anita thought, Can I go back, please? But she didn't dare say it out loud. Anita Cummings was ready to return to the life she had in Batesville, Arkansas, no matter how bad she once thought it was. Now she was ready to crawl into the reality of anyone else's life but hers.

Anita would look back on her life with Jesse Cummings and shake her head. "I can't believe where I came from and what I became in such a short period of time. My life was a nightmare."

When Cummings moved back to Oklahoma, his sister Judy and her daughter Melissa followed shortly thereafter. Though Judy knew her brother and his temperament well, she tried to tolerate his tirades as much as possible. She wanted Melissa to grow up around family, and in Oklahoma she had two grown sons, her half sister Debra, and Jesse.

Mother and daughter settled into a little shotgun house in Tushka, a town so small that if you blinked your eyes you could easily miss it. Small towns were the best places to bring children up the right way, Judy thought. Now in her forties, the mother had made a vow that she would not repeat past mistakes. She would not mess up with Melissa. She intended to work hard to hang onto the little girl and raise her the best she could. Her determination to be a good parent could have been fueled by the mellowing of age or simply because she had lost everyone but Melissa.

Melissa Moody was just a slip of a girl, beautiful and vibrant. Long brown hair containing a hint of auburn spilled down her back. Tiny freckles scattered randomly across her pert nose. Immense chestnut eyes completed the features that made the little girl's face close to perfect.

Fortunately, Melissa did not seem to suffer from the periodic instability offered by her mother's frequent moves. Melissa's personality was as lovely as her face. Basically a carefree, happy child, Melissa's only angst came from a slight learning disability that slurred her speech.

Tushka was less than a twenty-minute drive from the Cummings house in Phillips. Frequently Judy would take Melissa over to play with Jessica and Scottie. Due to the conditions they lived under, coupled with Jesse's abuse and demand for isolation, the children had no playmates. Melissa's presence was welcomed by them. Outsiders were kept away. Cummings was aware that Child Protective Services was already watching him and he deplored their interference in his life.

The trio enjoyed each other's company, and with Melissa there, Cummings toned down the violence. The little girl was aware that Jesse handcuffed the kids. She had seen him do it. It terrified her. In the Cummings household a handcuffed child was perfectly normal, and even though Melissa knew this, it still terrified her.

Judy Moody's house had a cellar in back of the tiny home. In Oklahoma, the king of tornado country, every house, no matter how run-down, has its own cellar. The cellar at the Cummings house was located just a few feet from the back door.

The house, its field in back, and the cellar were the places that afforded Cummings a playground for his ever-growing maniacal behavior. The dark and dank cellar was particularly ideal. An old, heavy wooden door that had blown off the cellar's hinges stayed propped up against the entrance. Most of the time the cellar held a foot or so of standing water in it from rainwater blown in through holes above ground. Snakes frequently slithered in and out of the two large concrete holes seeking the dark, cool environment. Cummings found this environment perfect for punishing the children. When a child had done something Cummings deemed worthy of penance, he would banish the offender from the house. It was of no significance to him whether it was sweltering or freezing outside. The child was sent to repent in the scary dungeon. The doors to the house were locked to prevent the child from sneaking back in after everyone had fallen asleep.

At a minimum, the imprisoned child spent hours in the turbid cellar, screaming and begging to be let back in the house. When Cummings was really angry at the transgressor, the child would spend all night in the unlit, filthy hole. As if the cellar and its conditions weren't terrifying enough, Cummings enjoyed sneaking out of the house to howl like a wild, ravenous wolf looking for a meal.

Other times he would run around the sides of the upper mound that housed the cellar beneath it, hitting the sides so fast and furious the tiny troublemaker was unable to anticipate which direction the sounds were coming from. The unknown entity lurked like a shadow in the darkness for whichever child was being punished and would serve to prevent escape into the haven of a mother's arms. Cummings relished thinking of ways to enhance those fears, savoring every second of the delicious terror he was responsible for. He became a master at it in no time.

Ten

Scottie had celebrated his first birthday a few months before Cummings moved them into the house in Phillips. Anita never got over the change in Cummings and never accepted her husband's bigamy, but she found herself so paralyzed by her surroundings she felt she had no way out.

From the abusive relationships of the past to the deliberate lie Cummings pulled her into, Anita made up her mind that "Men are gonna cheat; men are gonna hit. This was the way it was." She would just have to learn to live with it.

In order to keep from having a complete nervous breakdown, Anita decided to concentrate on Scottie and on being a good mother to him. After all, he was really all she had left.

Cummings, Sherry, and Anita had lived in Phillips a couple of months when Cummings started harping on prostitution again. Sherry had long ago learned to accept her fate and no longer protested against selling her body to other men.

Anita, on the other hand, was a different story. She thought what Sherry did for Jesse was a private matter between the two of them and she staunchly vowed to never get involved.

That delusion was soon put to rest. One afternoon the door slammed as Cummings got home from scrapping junk iron for some quick cash. He found Anita in the bedroom. He pulled some clothes out of the brown shopping bag in his hand and threw them at Anita, instructing her, "Get dressed, you're going out tonight." It was almost two months to the day from when they had gotten married.

Anita couldn't believe what she was hearing. She stood up to him and said, "There ain't no way in hell I'm putting this shit on and hooking for you!" Cummings backhanded his insolent wife and told her to "Get your ass dressed."

Anita put on the clothes Cummings had especially purchased for her night on the town. She decided she would let him waste his time taking her to the rest stop. But unlike Sherry, he would find she would not cooperate, no matter how many times he beat her. Anita rationalized that sooner or later he was bound to get tired of arguing over the issue and let her alone.

Accustomed to always getting what he wanted, Cummings was determined this night would be Anita's initiation as a hooker. During the ride Anita flat out told her husband there was no way she would ever sell her body. "I'm not gonna do it. I have no need to do it, and I'm not gonna do it; so you're wasting your time!"

Cummings continued driving, paying the fuss no mind. He knew if he wanted Anita to do it, he would find a way to make it happen. But, damn, he hated her insolence.

When they pulled into the rest stop, Anita just sat in the car, arms folded defiantly across her chest. She refused to budge. Cummings got out and passed in front of the shining headlights. He returned to the car and threatened the stubborn woman with every calamity he could call to mind. She still didn't budge. His patience running out, Cummings began screaming at her, calling her every name in the book. She still didn't budge.

Exasperated at her defiance, he did what always worked for him, he threatened to beat the living shit out of Anita right then and there if she didn't get out of the car. She still didn't budge.

Infuriated, Cummings got back in the car, roughly gunned the engine, and peeled out of the rest stop leaving behind a trail of black skid marks. The whole ride home, Cummings yelled at Anita. She listened to his nonstop vituperation in stony silence. Anita's mind was made up. There was nothing he could say and nothing he could do to make her sell her body—nothing! She had sunk as low as she would allow herself to go. This wasn't going to happen, even if he killed her!

Cummings pulled into the gravel driveway and switched off the lights. Sherry had obediently put the kids to bed and was watching television. Jessica slept on a child's dirty, urine-stained mattress near the foot of the bed in the master bedroom. Scottie was soundly asleep in the front room in a bassinet.

Anita, still fuming over the whole incident, sat in the car and refused to get out. Cummings came around, jerked open the car door, and yelled at the obstinate woman, "Get the fuck in the house. Now!"

Anita had no doubt he would beat her for this, but she didn't care. If a beating was what she would have to endure to keep from degrading herself, then a beating it would be. She steadied herself for his wrath as she crawled out of the car and calmly walked into the house.

Cummings hated Anita's impertinence. He saw a defiance shining in her eyes that he knew would not go away with a mere beating. Instantly he realized how he could convince his wife to go along and prostitute herself for him.

Anita stood in the front room, hands on her hips, bracing herself for the beating she knew she was about to receive. She stood firm as Cummings unbuckled his belt and jerked it from the loops of his pants.

Always one step ahead of everyone, Cummings had a surprise Anita could never have imagined. Instead of heading in her direction, he walked straight to the bassinet where Scottie was sound asleep. Petrified, Anita watched as Cummings roughly pulled the infant out of the crib and laid him on the floor. He raised the belt over his head and aimed it right at the little boy, now crying from being awakened.

Before one blow connected, Anita screamed, "Jesse, don't!"

Her husband just looked at her, then as hard as he could brought the full force of the belt down like a whip across the infant's body. The baby wailed from the pain.

As the belt came down again across the infant's body, Anita howled, "Jesse, stop it! I'll do it! I'll do anything you say! Just stop! Please, stop!"

Ignoring the mantra, Cummings continued to beat the baby while Anita begged and screamed over and over and over she would do whatever he wanted her to, if he would just stop hitting her child, whose body was writhing with each blow. As her pleas fell on deaf ears, Anita fell to her knees. The sound of a wounded animal—part moan, part sob, part shriek—escaped from her soul as she pleaded with Cummings to stop.

The baby's body, covered with blood and welts swelling up from head to toe, began to twist in convulsions on the floor. Cummings finally stopped.

One of Cummings's rules set out in the very beginning of their new life in Phillips, Oklahoma, concerned what he called correcting the children. If a child who belonged to one particular mother was corrected, that mother was forbidden to comfort the child. If the rule was broken, the child and the mother would get in trouble over the incident, and for good measure the child would be corrected once more. It had seemed a harmless rule when Anita had first heard it. But she never dreamed that correcting a child in Jesse's mind amounted to beating a baby into convulsions.

Anita understood for the first real time just what Cummings was capable of. She did not dare break his rule tonight, no matter how desperately she wanted. Unable to comfort and aid her baby, and unable to bear to look at the convulsing child she had put in this position, Anita ran sobbing into the bedroom. Sherry, who had watched the barbaric act in total disbelief, ran to the baby. Scottie had lost consciousness. Sherry carefully picked the tiny baby up and cradled him in her arms, rocking and shushing the infant.

Her hands shook as she ran some water over a washcloth and gingerly bathed the tiny face. She thought she had seen everything, but she had *never* seen Cummings beat a child. Looking with disgust at the cowering woman desperately tending to Scottie, Cummings turned around and walked out of the room.

That night Sherry never left Scottie's side. She wanted to somehow try to comfort the innocent victim of the deranged man she was married to. The closer she was to the baby, the more chance she stood of quieting the baby. There was no doubt in her mind that if the baby's crying woke up Jesse, Cummings would get up and severely beat both of them. Sherry knew the little boy would not be able to survive another attack.

Anita lay in the bedroom in such a deep state of shock she looked dead. Her tears had subsided and she was physically unable to cry anymore. Sleep was out of the question, so she just stared in a trance at the ceiling.

Drained from no sleep and constant sobbing, Anita slipped out of bed several hours before dawn to check on her son. She sat quietly wrapped up in a blanket in a chair staring at her horribly bruised baby asleep on the floor with Sherry by his side. She carefully watched the clock and listened for any hint Cummings was up. Anita crept back in bed so he wouldn't know she had gotten up.

When Cummings walked into the front room, Anita went over to him and, cautious to hide her contempt, asked in a controlled voice, "I told you I'd do it. Why did you keep hitting him?"

Cummings coolly informed her, "I wanted to make my point. I wanted you to know, if you don't do what I want, he's the one that'll suffer the consequences. Don't you *never* forget that. You hear me woman? *Never!*"

It proved to be the perfect weapon Cummings had been searching for to control the headstrong, impertinent woman. With Sherry, he had quickly figured out that mentally abusing Jessica would accomplish the same thing he had just learned would be accomplished by physically abusing Scottie.

After the horrible beating of her defenseless child, Anita knew her marriage to Cummings was nothing more than a sham, and she joined the silent ranks of prostitutes Jesse pimped. Anita never slipped into the life of prostitution as had Sherry, who had been able to master the art of divorcing her feelings from the act, thereby making it tolerable for her. Anita was never able to do so. Every time Cummings took her out to sell her body, she would not dare say no, but he had to drag her out of the house. He would tell her, "Hell, 'Nita, what's the big deal? We're all whores, we just got different prices." This was the consolation he offered to his wife for selling her body to a stranger.

Cummings had Sherry accompany Anita when she went out for the first time. Sherry was to teach Anita what to do. After this lesson Anita was on her own.

Selling his wives was bad enough, but his sexual inclinations would begin to escalate in more degrading behavior aimed directly at Anita and Sherry. He had used women all of his life without conscience and would continue to do so.

Cummings had forewarned the women, if they ever tried to run off with one of their tricks or ask him to rescue her, if he saw the truck pull out and they were still in it, he would run his vehicle up under the truck.

Anita would later remark, "Hell, if I'd known it would've killed him, I would've encouraged the john to go. But he wouldn't have done that. He'd have headed straight to the house for Scottie and Jessica." Cummings's ultimate control over the women was a mother's love for her child.

Cummings had worked out a routine for the working girls to follow. Although he seldom took Anita and Sherry out to hook together, he chose to dress them identically. One of his favorite outfits for the women to wear was a half shirt, sporting a little bow on the front, dark blue with padded shoulders.

He wanted the women to wear jeans because in his opinion it highlighted their legs in the trucker's lights as they approached a potential john.

Another favorite outfit of Cummings's consisted of solid black nylon pants with a nylonlike jogging windbreaker. The women were instructed to wear silk panties and bras underneath their clothes.

When Cummings decided that they were going hooking, he would pick which woman he wanted to accompany him that night. The other woman would sigh with relief and thank God she got to stay with the children.

Although Cummings never allowed either woman to fix her hair or wear makeup, these nights out were an exception. They were even allowed to wear perfume.

Cummings favored rest stops because he knew quick and easy money could be had there. Horny truckers were his best customers. He had a CB radio installed in his car just to solicit potential customers.

Cummings had talked to the women and set up rules for them to follow. They were strict and to be adhered to until he told the women different. The violation of a rule would wreak havoc in their lives, and they would be severely punished for the error.

Under Cummings's system oral sex, which he referred to as "BJs," should take no longer than fifteen minutes. If the man hadn't climaxed within that amount of time, the women were to accuse him of doing drugs and get out of there. For sexual intercourse, the women were told to get it done in thirty minutes. Cummings timed the women when they were with a trick.

For whatever crazy reasons, Cummings had two different standards when the women would hook. Sherry was told to try and talk the john into wearing a condom. If he protested too much, she was to go ahead and have sex without one.

Anita was told never, under any circumstances, to have sex without a condom. This double standard would create constant jealousy, mistrust, and feuding between the women. Just as Cummings knew it would. He was a staunch believer in the theory of conquer and divide.

Another of Cummings's main rules was that the women were to always pretend to climax, because in his opinion, the john would feel he got his money's worth.

Both women would later express the exact same sentiment,

"Faking an orgasm wasn't hard to do. Jesse didn't know nothing when it came to sexually exciting a woman. If we didn't climax when Jesse had sex with us, he'd beat the living shit out of us." It didn't take long for both of them to get the hang of pretending.

When the truckers were heading toward a rest stop, they would get on their CBs to inquire if there were any "cats" or "ladies" available. Most of the truckers were likable guys, and most of them treated Anita and Sherry friendly enough.

Anita recalled what it was like, "Some of 'em treated you with a lot of respect, and others treated you like you were the scum of the earth. Sherry and I already hated what we did, and when we got one that felt like that, it just made matters worse. There was no way to explain to these men why we were doing what we were. The whole situation we found ourselves in was so sad."

As much as she detested selling her body, Sherry would later recall her single most satisfying sexual experience, both emotionally and physically, happened to her while she was prostituting.

She elaborated, "As much as I hated hooking, the one thing I got from it was a sexual experience I'll never forget." The particular night Sherry was talking about, Cummings had taken her to one of their regular truck stops to hook.

A man with the sweetest face peered out of his rig and beckoned her toward him. He was older than most of the truckers she dealt with, perhaps in his early sixties. The man seemed shy and even a little embarrassed about what he was doing.

Sherry explained the thirty-minute rule. The older man wanted to know who was the guy watching them. Sherry told him it was her husband, and that he was the one who made her do this.

The man did not try to hide his shock. Sherry told him Cummings had her on a tight chain and she could only spend thirty minutes with him. The man excused himself and walked over to negotiate with Cummings. When he came back to the rig, he smiled and told Sherry, "I gotcha for four hours." Sherry was amazed. For Jesse to allow this, the guy must have given him a lot of money.

The two crawled into the sleeping compartment of the rig. For hours they sat fully dressed and just talked about everything. The man's face emanated kindness. He actually listened while Sherry talked.

Sherry recalled, "He treated me like a human being, instead of a dog, and that hadn't happened in a long time."

A look of incredible sadness crossed the man's face when Sherry explained why she let her husband do this to her. She confided to him that the only reason she was there was because if she didn't do what her husband said, he would beat her into submission.

The man stunned Sherry when he responded, "I lost my wife last year. Why don't we just take off . . . right now. We'll just drive away. Get you away from that man. It'll be that simple."

Nothing surrounding Sherry's life with Cummings was simple. She began to explain to the man the things her husband was capable of if she ever tried anything like that. He would kill her before he'd ever allow that to happen.

The pair continued to talk about all manners of topics. But after a short while, the man brought the subject of leaving up again.

Sherry politely declined, "I've got a little girl at home. If I pulled something like this, he'd kill her just to spite me."

The gentle expression on the man's face changed at this statement. "That sonuvabitch. What right does he have to make you do this? If you lived with me I'd take care of you and your little girl. I sure wouldn't force you to have sex. Just as long as you were with me, that'd be enough."

The offer was so tempting and the man so caring, Sherry let the thought linger a few minutes longer than she should have, but she soon dismissed the foolish idea. She just wouldn't chance something happening to Jessica.

The last hour Sherry spent with the man, he touched her face and caressed her hair. His gentleness momentarily took her away from the nightmare she lived daily. Sherry was used to men always taking, never giving. This man knew how to give. Sherry had never known such tenderness at the hands of a man, and it felt incredible to her.

When the man's four hours were up, Sherry didn't want to leave. The stranger had done a great thing. He had treated her like a person, a decent human being, something that was foreign to the young woman. She knew if she spent one minute past what had been paid for she'd get a severe beating.

Reluctantly she kissed the man goodbye on the cheek. He hugged her and told her to take care of herself.

As she exited the sleeper compartment, the man took Sherry's hand. With compassion written across his face, he pressed four one-hundred-dollar bills into her palm, saying, "Don't tell him. You keep this."

The relayed memory prompted Anita to share the most satisfying sexual experience she had ever had. "I was working the truck stops one night with Jesse, and one of the truckers called me over and handed Jesse money."

Anita's experience was close to Sherry's, only the man was in his early thirties. He was from Alaska, and was one of the most gentle and kind men Anita had ever come across. He took his time with her, doing the most important thing a man can do in a sexual relationship. He put her needs first. Anita didn't feel like the man had sex with her that night, but actually made love to her.

Trying to maintain a sense of humor, Anita explained how deeply the experience affected her. "By the time my feet hit the ground, I was tempted to turn around and give the man his money back." Shaking her head woefully, she added, "One of the saddest parts of my whole life is that emotionally and physically the best sex I ever had was with a trick."

Two and a half hours flew by while Anita was with the man from Alaska. Mesmerized by his kindness, gentleness, and expertise, Anita had lost all track of time. She would pay for it with one of the worst beatings of her life. She took the beating and considered it a fair price to pay because that night she was treated like a worthwhile person. Of all the things Cummings did to them, the prostitution beat the women so far down that neither one thought she possessed worth anymore. Even a severe beating was worth having someone remind her she still did.

Anita would never get over the feeling of anxiety as it welled inside her when Cummings ordered her to solicit a trucker. "When you're hooking, your heart pounds, and you dread having to climb up in the sleeper compartment. But after what Jesse did to Scottie, I'd never take a chance with his life ever again."

That night burned into Anita's mind an indelible lesson. Even worse, it sliced deeper through the frazzled, thin thread of independence Anita was precariously hanging on by.

Eleven

Tushka Elementary, which was not far from Judy Moody's house, would be Melissa's academic home until she graduated into secondary school. It was at Tushka Elementary where Melissa would find a friend she would grow to love and cherish. Although Melissa's disability had caused her to fall behind a grade, she became fast friends with a young girl the next grade up, Lisa Cathy. Melissa was shy and in the past had very few friends. Judy had met Lisa and was thrilled Melissa had found a friend so quickly. The two young girls almost immediately became inseparable. Both liked many of the same things, and their personalities meshed perfectly.

The two girls thought alike, dressed alike, and sometimes even finished each other's sentences. A bond seemed to exist between Melissa and Lisa, unlike any either had ever known with any other friend. It was almost as if the two little girls were soul mates from another time.

The welfare, disability check, and widow's benefits Judy Moody collected didn't make living in Tushka any more profitable than anywhere else. Moody still struggled to make ends meet and scavenged to earn extra income. Judy knew Lisa Cathy's house was just a block away. Venturing out on a short walk, she passed by the house.

Moody had spied some junk in Lisa's backyard and was considering asking permission to haul it off. She hesitatingly knocked on the Cathys' door and nervously waited for it to open. Pat Cathy, Lisa's mother, fondly recalled their first meeting. "When she knocked on my door and I opened it, that's the first time I'd met her. Lisa'd brought Melissa over and I really liked the little girl. So I was glad to get the chance to meet her mother." Pat readily agreed to Judy's request. "I told her 'That's fine with me. It's no problem, 'cause it's just sitting there rusting.' I'll never forget what she said to me. Judy looked me in the eye and said, 'You don't know how much I appreciate that.' You know it was only junk, but she genuinely did appreciate the extra money it would give her. We became fast friends right after that."

The fact that Tushka was a small town suited Judy fine for another reason. Because Judy never got out much, Pat was just about her only friend. Like her mother, Marie, Judy stood barely five feet tall. As her weight eased past three hundred fifty pounds, she would slip into depression. While in a fit of depression, Judy would experiment with her hair color dying it back and forth from dark to light.

Jesse Cummings treated her just like all the women in his life, berating her and demeaning her large size. Judy's self-esteem was nonexistent, and her half brother's put-downs sent her spiraling into deep depression. The depression predictably called for a change in hair color. Before long Judy turned into a blonde.

Melissa wanted everyone to like her, including her uncle. Finally one day she just quit trying to please him. Despite her many attributes she was unable to work her way into Jesse's heart. It seemed no one could break through the pervasive armor wrapped around him. But observing the way he was treating her mother was making her hate him.

As Melissa celebrated her tenth birthday, her friendship with Lisa continued to blossom, and so did the attachment between their respective mothers. Pat was petite like her daughter and friendly and outgoing. Judy found her to be hardworking and honest. The two women began to spend a lot of time together. Pat Cathy would become a valued and loyal friend to Judy.

* * *

Cummings would hide several mini-recorders throughout the house before he left. When he returned, he would gather the devices up, go off, listen to the recordings, then confront Anita and Sherry about things they had said and done in his absence. The women were perplexed about how he knew what went on while he was gone. One afternoon Anita was in the children's room and heard something that sounded like her own voice. "I went into the living room and Jesse was listening to a tape he'd recorded earlier that day." Anita's face registered shock. Cummings snootily remarked, "Yeah, you think when I'm not here you bitches can do whatcha want, doncha?" One of Anita's misdeeds captured on tape was loving her child.

Cummings was always in control whether he was at the house or not. He made that very clear to the women with the recorders. Another method was by turning the phone off at the outside box anytime he had to leave. Whether he really was going someplace, or just lying so he could hide and see if they disobeyed him, neither was brave enough to try and sneak out to turn it back on.

However the ultimate method Cummings used to control the women when he was gone was through their children. He would take one wife with him and leave the other at home. The one that went with him brought the other one's child along while her child stayed with the one at home. If Anita went with him, they would take Jessica and leave Scottie with Sherry. He had taken them aside and told each the same thing, if they were disobedient or thought about running off, their child would be forfeited. Anita and Sherry's failure to communicate, and Cummings's skill at keeping them pitted against each other, assured total obedience on both their parts. It truly was an ingenious plan. But most of all, it worked like a charm for Cummings.

Darren Cooper, known as "Coop" to all his friends, had known Cummings since his move to Phillips and was frequently over at the Cummings house. Never one to fancy himself as anyone special, Coop was of medium build, possessed a wealth of curly black hair, and had traces of a potential mustache.

Cooper, who was harmless enough, first struck up a friendship with Cummings within days of meeting the man who was quite unlike anyone he had ever known in his life. The low-key, unobtrusive, young man desperately wanted to be somebody, and he straightaway joined the ranks of Cummings's army of "hangers-on." A friend to Cummings translated into flunky. He considered the words just a matter of semantics.

By the summer Cooper found himself inexplicably drawn to Cummings, fascinated by the power and control he wielded over those around him. The unassuming man rapidly became sucked into Cummings's way of life along with the other "disciples of Jesse," and in short order was obeying Cummings without question or hesitation, unable to extract himself from Cummings's intense presence, and with no urge to try.

He was very anxious to please Cummings. Soon, Cooper would be his number one flunky, around him more than the others. Whatever Cummings wanted done, Cooper could not do it fast enough. In short order his constant presence facilitated Cummings's plan to bring the unsuspecting man into a seduction scenario involving Anita and Sherry, with Jesse being the voyeur. Anita and Sherry were directed to start an affair with Cooper and make it appear that the affair was taking place behind Cummings's back. The women began a flirtation with Cooper outside of Cummings's presence. One thing Cummings told the women to do was to make Cooper think he was getting away with a sexual liaison and Cummings would be none the wiser. While the couple performed sex in Cummings's bed, he would watch through a hole he had drilled in the attic to satisfy his Peeping Tom tendencies. When Cummings was through watching, he would quietly place a board across the hole until his next trip back. As with everything in Cummings's life, when boredom set in he would devise another situation. The women were told to tell Cooper to be quiet, to take his hand and lead him into the bedroom where Cummings was pretending to be asleep, and to have sex next to him. The game afforded him an opportunity to assert total control and be sexually aroused at the same time.

Sex was of primary importance in Cummings's life. He began keeping a diary of all sexual activity that occurred in the house. His reasoning was threefold. If the women caught a sexual disease, he was sure he could trace it back to the culprit. If one of the women became pregnant, he would know who the father was. And if one of the hundreds of sex partners he had had accused him of fathering a child, he could count on the diary to absolve him as the guilty party. Sherry was in charge of keeping the daily diary, and Cummings made it clear that he wanted the sexual encounters written down no later than the next day. Failure to do so would result in severe punishment.

Melissa was now dreading going to the Cummings's farm. Although Melissa lived in a tiny shotgun house, at least it was bearable. Unlike the Cummings house, clutter surrounded Melissa's home, not chaos; roaches, not rats; and her mother gave her love, not hate. As the girls' friendship grew, Melissa would sometimes ask Lisa to come along. The deplorable conditions at the house coupled with Cummings's ever increasing sullen attitude embarrassed his niece in front of her friend.

Like it or not, in the summer Judy Moody had to depend on being able to let Melissa go to the farm. Pat Cathy worked and Judy baby-sat Lisa to earn money. She needed the money, and every time Cummings offered her a way to make it, she had to do it. When Judy was sent to do whatever Cummings was having her do, the girls were sometimes taken to his house for longer extended periods of time. Now older, playing with the younger children had lost its appeal. The entire summer, when Lisa and Melissa visited the Cummings house, both girls would busy themselves outside. Melissa's love of animals began in her home with her frisky little Chihuahua, Tippy, and extended to the farm animals behind the Cummings house. As soon as she and Lisa arrived there, they would head for the pasture. That way Melissa could avoid her uncle and play with the goats, horses, and other assorted menagerie.

Cummings began going out late at night to burglarize homes. The main thing he was interested in stealing was medicine. He would take any medication he could find, be it prescription or over-the-counter. Anita recounted in an interview, "He had this huge black bag filled with ever' kind of pill you could imagine." When Cummings would get home with his cache of drugs, the first thing he did was go through each bottle, look it up in his *Physician's Desk Reference,* and if he could not find the drug listed, he would make one of the women call a pharmacy. The druggist would be given the name of the drug on the bottle and told that a child had swallowed one. As with everything else in Cummings's life, he had a purpose for doing it.

Other than the *Physician's Desk Reference,* Cummings's favorite medical reference book was one on home remedies, however most of the remedies given the children came straight from Jesse's mother. If they complained about an ailment, he would use his stolen medicines to treat them. When he was feeling particularly mean-spirited, he would force his mother's home remedy of onion tea on the children. Onion tea is simply an onion boiled until the liquid is clear. The tea smells terrible and tastes worse. The children would gag and try to suppress the urge to vomit. At times that would be impossible, and as their stomachs twisted, they would throw it back up. When that happened, Cummings would yell at them that they were a bunch of sissies, then make them drink more. Anita recalled how "Jesse'd also make 'em eat soap. The whole bar. I don't know how many times my son had to eat a bar of soap. Sometimes Scottie gagged on it, other times he threw up."

Sherry remembered other items Cummings would use to hurt the children. "He would cut off the two straps underneath a saddle and use those. He'd whip their hands with it or their butt or legs. And Jesse had a wooden paddle, and of course he used the belt, too."

Cummings wasn't particular about his weapon. It didn't matter if it was the garden hose or a leather strap. It just had to hurt.

Cummings had a firm and ironclad rule. When one of the children was in trouble, he or she had "lovin's" taken away. Anita explained the term as follows: "We couldn't hold them, speak to them, anything. Basically, no one was allowed to comfort or love on the disobedient child. When Jesse would leave, I'd let Scottie slide 'cause I didn't feel he should have been punished in the first place. Because Scottie had ADD, he could be punished and ten minutes later it wouldn't matter. A week later when Scottie was still being punished for something he'd done, he wouldn't understand why." When Cummings was safely out of sight, the mothers would rush to their children and hug and hold them.

Meanwhile, Mildred Tucker was head over heels in love with Cummings, and he knew it. He spared her no indignities, calling her names and making fun of her at every opportunity. One of the most self-depreciating things Cummings did to Tucker was to make her earn the privilege of sleeping with him. The only way Cummings would allow her to have sex with him was as a reward. If she found a woman who was willing to come to the house and have sex with Cummings, and she delivered the woman, then Tucker got time with him. Mildred needed love so direly that she was willing to settle for it at any price. Cummings always picked overweight, plain, young women to bring into his entourage for that very reason.

Because of Cummings's hurled and biting insults about her weight, Tucker never wanted to eat when she was at his house. The young woman had fought her weight problem all her life. She would go on noneating binges for days, sometimes weeks. But her body never seemed to respond when she tried to lose weight. When Tucker was around Cummings, she would barely pick at her food, knowing the insults Cummings would throw her way. Sherry remembered his cruelty was especially vicious where Mildred was concerned. "Jesse would make her eat, beat her with the bullwhip till she actually gave in. The beating could go on a good thirty minutes to an hour. Mildred would get tears in her eyes from the pain. She'd quietly ask Jesse to stop, it hurt. But she never really got mad at him over it."

He wanted her self-esteem so low that he could continue to humiliate and degrade her and she wouldn't leave him. When it came to Cummings, Mildred fit the bill. Where he was concerned, she had no dignity or will of her own.

Cummings enjoyed taking pills even more than dispensing them to his family. Percodan was his drug of choice, and he was terribly addicted to it. To ensure that he never ran out, he used a list of phony maladies and a variety of doctors, none of whom knew he was seeing the others. A bullet lodged in his hip from a violent encounter in the past provided his quickest and most effective guise with which to get the drug refilled.

Cummings took the painkiller by the handfuls, sometimes as many as ten to twelve at one time, starting from the moment he got up until he went to bed. It was amazing he could even function on that high a dosage. The one function it allowed him to accomplish best, though, was to allow him to unbridle his rage and not feel physical pain because of it. His pain tolerance was so high it enabled him to assault the people around him all day long without getting tired or feeling pain.

Anita shuddered when sharing the memory. "If he come in and beat us up, we'd be hurtin' too bad to get out of bed. He was so stoned on the pain pills he didn't feel nothing, even if his hands or fists were all cut up and beat up from hitting on us."

Even with a month's supply of one hundred Percodan written for him by several doctors, in the depths of Cummings's addiction, he would quickly run out. When this happened and he could not find a doctor to write him a prescription, he would call on Mildred Tucker. She would go to her doctor and have him write her a prescription for the drug. It was another practice he had to cause harm to another. He had Tucker getting prescriptions on a regular basis for Halcion, a powerful sleeping pill, and Soma, which is a strong muscle relaxer. Cummings used the combination of the two drugs to slip in unsuspecting women's drinks to knock them out. When the drugged victim was unconscious, he would have sexual intercourse with his prey. Later on, the game would become much deadlier than the sexual assaults he was committing.

Twelve

Christmas at the Cummings household was not surprisingly strange. Jesse always picked out the tree. He had the women decorate it as he watched, instructing them what they could or could not put on the tree. "We couldn't put on glass bulbs, just the ones with string, and we were allowed only one string of lights. We wanted to decorate around the window or outside of the house, and he refused to let us," Sherry recalled.

It was Cummings who went and picked out the presents. "Mainly, he just got presents for the kids," Anita remembered. "We'd have maybe one present. He didn't get a present from us because he didn't want one, and that was fine with us, 'cause we didn't want to get him one, either.

"Usually he'd have one of us wrap the presents, but he'd be in there telling us what to do."

Sherry joined in the remembrance. "The presents stayed in our bedroom till Christmas Eve. After the kids went to bed, we could put the presents under the tree. Sometimes he would wait until Christmas morning and wake us up really early. We'd quickly put the presents under the tree, then go wake the kids up. A lot of times it was like one or two in the morning when we woke the kids 'cause according to Jesse it was legally Christmas morning. When the kids got out there, either Anita or I or both would start to hand out the presents. That early in the morning the kids were too sleepy to care. Jesse'd say, 'Well, here I'll help you.' And he'd open the presents and give it back to the kids."

Cummings opened nearly every present that was under the tree. He bought the children little plastic toys that never cost over a dollar at the most.

According to Sherry, "He was like, 'It's Christmas. Let's just get it the fuck over with.' "

Many Christmas mornings Cummings forced the women to go out into the cold of the winter and haul wood. He would tell Sherry and Anita that the holidays were the same as every other day.

He felt that way about other occasions, as well. Anita coldly recounted, "On our anniversary, at first I'd want to celebrate it and he'd say, 'Our anniversary ain't no different than any other day.' Said the same thing about birthdays, too.

"The kids knew better than to ask for a party. It was where we couldn't have parties, the way Jesse behaved and all."

The year 1990 started and ended pretty much the same way in the Cummings house. Jesse Cummings controlled everything, daily beatings and torture went on, and the women were forced to endure prostituting their bodies.

There was one particular incident that would stand out that year. It would also bring into Jesse's, Sherry's, and Anita's lives a ruggedly handsome young trooper by the name of David Cathey [no relation to Pat and Lisa Cathy], who would one day have an impact on each for the rest of their lives.

Cathey, barely thirty years old, was striking in appearance. The trooper's thick dark hair was lightly dusted with the gray his ample mustache managed to escape. His most striking feature was his incredible blue eyes, eyes a woman could easily get lost in.

He had been a trooper for the State of Oklahoma for six years and was one of several troopers responding to a disturbance at a rest stop. When he and other troopers arrived on the scene, the disturbance had dissipated, but he would still vividly recall the incident years later.

On this particular chilly January night, Cummings had taken Anita to prostitute at a rest area. It was stationed along a highway leading from Texas to Oklahoma City along mile marker number three.

A black pimp Cummings had run-ins with before, showed up, infringing on Cummings's territory. Heated words were exchanged. Cummings instructed Anita to get back in the car; they were going to mile marker number thirty-five.

Anita did as she was told. Agitated about being run off from what he felt was legitimately open territory, Cummings started the drive to mile marker thirty-five.

Unfortunately, the pimp and his girl followed him to the area. Cummings wasn't going to be generous enough to leave the area this time. He and the other man got in a shouting match that grew louder and more obscene.

Cummings went back to the car to get his gun, telling Anita to get out. She obeyed. Instead of getting out of the way, she jumped on the hood of the car making herself a perfect target for the whizzing bullets flying by. Cummings screamed at her to get behind the car before she got shot.

Anita explained her actions in the following way. "Here, I'm trying to get the guy to shoot me. 'Cause I'm figuring, if he shoots me and he don't kill me, then Jesse ain't gonna bring me back out here to work. The prostitution would finally be over. Frankly, I was hoping he'd kill Jesse. But the ignorant guy just kept shooting at Jesse and missing. And he never did pay a damn bit of attention to me."

During the exchanged gunfire, a bullet from Cummings's gun supposedly hit the other pimp's woman. Cummings ran around the side of the car, grabbed Anita, and roughly threw her in the backseat. Just as he was doing this, the other pimp returned fire once more, shattering Cummings's front passenger window. Cummings peeled out, profusely cursing his wife. "You stupid fuckin' bitch, was you trying to get yourself shot?"

Anita took a second to think on the matter. She bit her tongue and thought, Well, yeah! That's exactly what I was doing.

Cummings knew the disturbance had undoubtedly been reported on the truckers' CBs. He wanted to put as much distance as possible between himself and the rest stop. As soon as he had accomplished that, he pulled off the main highway and onto a dirt road. He stopped the car, went around to the backseat, and jerked Anita out onto the dirt.

Cummings proceeded to beat the daylights out of her. Fortunately for Anita, the beating, although savage, was short. Cummings was concerned that the truckers witnessing the gun battle had called the cops and they would trail him any moment. He threw Anita into the backseat and peeled out, heading back to the main highway.

Always prepared, Cummings had another car identical to the car he was driving, except in color. He pulled into his driveway, exited the vehicle, went inside, and woke Sherry. He ordered her to find lamps with extension cords, which Sherry obediently rounded up. He then ordered the confused woman to go in the house and stay there.

Anita and Cummings went to work like pros, fixing the damaged car. The window was replaced, the car painted, and the license plates switched. Holes in the door of the car were quickly repaired. The two worked all night to get the rest of the damaged car fixed.

Cummings's angst was caused by a report he heard on his scanner. He listened to the account of a black woman who had been shot. He knew it was his bullet that did it. He'd be damned if he would go to jail over that pimp and his whore. Cummings was never arrested for the incident, and the matter quietly went away.

Although she and Jesse had different fathers, Judy Moody loved and treated Jesse Cummings, Sr., like he was her natural father, and he felt the same way toward her. So much so, that people who met the three when they were together mistakenly assumed that Judy was his natural child. More importantly to Judy, though, was that Melissa loved her stepgrandfather immensely, and he loved the little girl, too.

Cummings's hatefulness and meanness were tolerable because they were offset by the sweet nature of his father toward people. Children always brought out the best in the old man, and he had mellowed as he was closing in on sixty-five. The only people Jesse, Sr., couldn't seem to get along with were his wife and his son. Judy never knew of him to get in fights with anyone else.

As was the case from almost the day Joyce Denman and Jesse, Sr., were married, they were in a constant state of separation. However, shortly after Jesse, Sr., had been diagnosed, they would separate for the last time. The altercation began, as usual, in a shouting match. This time, however, it escalated to the point that Joyce was furious and stormed out on her husband. She was so mad she had decided she wanted him killed and sought out a man she knew who would hurt or even kill people for money. All reason abandoned, Joyce located him. By the time she did, her anger had abated enough that she did not want him killed, just hurt. Joyce paid the man, told him that her husband would be in a certain bar that night, and instructed him, "Cut him up bad, real bad. I want you to teach him a lesson he ain't never gonna forget!"

Ironically, Jesse, Sr., was spared the savage attack because word had quickly gotten to his well-connected underworld son that Joyce had hired a man to follow Jesse, Sr., to a bar where he would be attacked. The father and son's relationship was one where they would get in a knockdown drag-out, then go out and get drunk together. The abnormal alliance between Jesse and his dad mirrored the rest of Jesse's acquaintanceships. In fact, he had never had a normal relationship with anyone his entire life. With no rhyme or reason to his life, he became enraged after being tipped-off about the forthcoming attack. Jesse Cummings grabbed up a baseball bat and knife, pulled one of the women aside, and handed her the bat and told her to go find Joyce. His instructions to her upon finding Joyce were simply, "Beat the holy shit outta that bitch!" Joyce's injuries were so severe that after the attack, she was taken to the nearest emergency room. Joyce, her body bruised and broken from the savagery of the attack, sat in stone silence, and the doctor on duty was told that she had been pulled in an alley and mugged. Joyce knew if she wanted to live, she would not contradict the story. The one and only time she discussed the brutal attack was to lie when she stuck with the story while being questioned by the detective assigned to the case. Joyce disappeared a couple of days after the attack with Shelly Marie and went into hiding.

At this point in Cummings's life, the supposed outrage was most likely just a reason for him to go into a violent rage. From the time that he reached adulthood, not one single day went by that he didn't hit someone. The only thing that varied in his everyday violence was the magnitude of the brutality he inflicted on his victim of the moment. Cummings breathed violence to survive like normal people breathe air to stay alive.

As Jesse Cummings, Sr., began to feel worse, he swallowed his pride and asked his son for permission to move in with him. Surprisingly, Jesse welcomed him into his house. With very little room to spare, Jesse, Sr., slept on a fold-out bed in the front room.

In the early part of 1991 Judy Moody met a native of Tushka, Eugene Mayo. Although Mayo was a decade younger than Judy, which made him even younger than one of her sons, an attraction existed between the two, and before the month was over, Judy and Eugene Mayo were married.

As if Melissa wasn't under enough strain hoping that Mayo would make her mother happy, she was a frequent target of her classmates' cruelty, and had been all year. One day during a lice check, some were found in Melissa's hair. Lisa Cathy explained why, "She would get lice when Melody had her kids around her, then when the school found 'em, the other kids teased her and called her names about it."

Melissa, having just turned eleven, was growing weary of being made to feel like less of a person because of things she could not help, and was counting the days until she and Lisa were out of the cruel place for the summer. Children are usually too immature to know the pain they can cause. They make fun of anything they can find to make fun about. With Melissa's slurred speech she was an easy target.

Despite her treatment at school, Melissa's disposition remained as constant as it always had. Regardless of what was going wrong in her life, she had her best friend. Lisa Cathy thought carefully before talking about the reason why she and Melissa had formed such a comradeship. "I think it was she was just different, like me. We both liked to write and draw, and I didn't know anyone else who cared for it. We both dressed different than the other kids, wearing black a lot. I just felt we were connected. For whatever stupid reason she got picked on a whole bunch more than me. It wadn't right."

A little smile began playing across Lisa Cathy's face as she remembered things the two friends did together. "When me and her would spend the night at my house, we'd sneak out and sleep in the car 'cause it was neat and fun. We did that a lot, especially in the summer. Just to do it. Melissa was just a regular kid, you know. We talked all the time about what we wanted to be when we grew up. Melissa loved to sing and act and wanted to grow up to be a star. We'd go walking and sometimes we'd go ride our bikes in the country." Lisa rolled her eyes and cracked a grin. "But school sure cut into a lot of our fun."

Now that his father was ill, Jesse Cummings seemed to calm down where his dad was concerned. They got along most of the time. Anita and Sherry both loved Jesse's father and thoroughly enjoyed his company. He always took time to sit and chat with them.

The fact that Jesse, Sr., was there had no bearing on his son's continuous battering of them. Jesse, Jr., beat the women so often now, he had it down to a science. He knew exactly the maximum pain he could inflict with the minimum amount of internal damage. Anita remembered his gift. "He would hit me on the breast-bone with his fist so hard, it would feel like my heart literally stopped. I would pass out or come close to it from the jolt," she recalled.

Sherry had her own memories. "Jesse could take one finger, just one finger, and leave bruises that covered several inches of skin. I tried to fight him back one time. Actually, all I did was bring my arm up to keep him from hitting me in the face. I was down on the floor in a corner cowering. When I raised my arm, my hand was closed into a fist. He beat me worse than he ever had screaming at me each time he struck me, 'You wanta hit me? If you think you can hit me, come on and do it!' "

Cummings had a favorite expression he liked to use on his wives when he was trying to intimidate them. He would snootily remark, "If you feel froggy, jump." Meaning if they thought they were big enough to jump him, they should go ahead and try.

Cummings slowly began to incorporate violence with sex. It was around eleven o'clock at night when Sherry fell victim to the trend. The household was quiet; Anita had left to pull a double shift at her job. The children had long since been asleep. Cummings decided a little sex and bondage with his remaining wife would be entertaining.

He handcuffed Sherry to the bed and proceeded to have sex with the shackled woman. That night, however, he put a maniacal twist on the sexual ritual. Sherry was positioned on her back with Cummings over her, as the two had sex. He started violently punching her in the ribs with his clutched fists.

Panicked, Sherry fought back. The more she screamed, kicked, and begged, the more excited Cummings became. He started encouraging her to fight harder. Throughout the attack he called Sherry "Dorothy Louise," just like Marie had done to him with the name "James." He knew Sherry vehemently hated his girlfriend, especially after she found out that Dorothy Louise was responsible for giving him gonorrhea years ago.

Sherry finally realized the fighting was arousing her husband. Immediately she ceased all resistance and lay motionless. A passive Sherry was not nearly as much fun as a fighting one.

He quickly finished, unshackled her, and got up and walked out of the room as though nothing unusual had transpired.

Cummings became enraged when his women did not move during sex. A favorite saying he would venomously hiss at the passive partner was, "Don't just lie there like a dead fuck!" His point was always punctuated by a well-placed jab to the offending party's rib cage.

Violence seemed to be the only aphrodisiac that temporarily satisfied Cummings's never-ending appetite for sex, and the propensity was growing fast as the beauty and color of the spring rushed in, sweeping away the bleakness of a long, hard Oklahoma winter. Cummings thought up more and more demeaning, hurtful things to do to his wives as time passed. He went through one phase where he would pinch them on the breasts until they would scream from the pain. Other times he would pinch them as hard as he could on the clitoris. The pain was unbearable, and that's exactly why he liked to do it. He also loved to pull hair. Anyone's—the children's, wives, girlfriends— it didn't matter. He would yank handfuls of head hair out at a time, for the pure meanness of it, and he always loved the high-pitched screams it would evoke. Without warning or provocation he would sometimes grab their pubic hair and actually yank patches out, too.

Pat Cathy vividly remembered a visit at Judy's when Jesse and Anita were there. "I couldn't believe it. I was sitting on the couch, and Jesse walks up behind one of his wives and grabs her around the throat. She went out like a light. I just looked at him. I didn't know what to do. He never said a word. I don't know if he did that to scare Judy or what his reason was."

Sherry's fourteen-year-old sister, Sarah Yaws, had recently moved from Missouri back to Oklahoma with her mother. At the time Lahoma Yaws found out where Sherry was living by total accident.

Cummings had a firm rule about mail. Any letter written had to be read by him before it was mailed. He distributed the stamps. He knew when mail was being sent out. For long periods of time, neither Sherry nor Anita could write her mother. And neither was allowed to call. As with everything else in Cummings's life, he had a good explanation for all of his rules. This one strengthened his control and insured his wives isolation from support.

Sarah and Lahoma had been in town for only a couple of weeks when Cummings made the grand gesture of telling Sherry to call her mother and see if she would let Sarah come visit her sister. He told Sherry she could help tend to the kids. Cummings wanted Sarah to spend the night there. Sherry would not be suspicious if he justified her sister spending the night to catch up on things, so he said what he knew she would buy. Jesse explained that Sarah spending the night would give them longer the next morning to play around. It was not the first time she had spent the night at the Cummings house. She had dropped by once before when they had just moved into their house. But it would be the last visit.

The day had gone smoothly enough. Cummings had made himself scarce the better part of the day, so the women didn't have to put up with him. The trouble began shortly after nightfall. Tired from the long day tending to the children, Sarah prepared for bed in a tiny spare bedroom.

Cummings was sitting in the front room and appeared to be preoccupied with a show playing on television.

The worn-out girl was still fully clothed when she lay down on the bed. It didn't take the exhausted teenager long before she fell into a deep sleep. Cummings came into the room where Sarah was. He shook the girl awake and began harassing her, trying to talk Sarah into having sex with him. In no uncertain terms the teenager told him it wasn't happening and to get out of the room.

Cummings slunk back into the front room to sulk in front of the television. The rejection played over and over in his mind. Who in hell'd that bitch think she was. No one said no to Jesse Cummings. No one!

Sarah, thinking the matter settled and under control, drifted back to sleep. In the middle of the night, a startled and frightened Sarah woke when Cummings plopped down next to her, perched near the edge of the bed. Sarah remembered the ensuing nightmare, "I started really getting scared 'cause I'd never really trusted him anyway."

In the darkness of the room, Sarah tried to sit up. She could not move. A heavy pressure was against her stomach. Cummings had gotten on top of her as she slept, straddling the teenager and effectively pinning her down.

He roughly shoved Sarah's skirt up around her hips. A tear slipped from her eye and ran down her terrified fourteen-year-old face. Panic caused her to suck in great slurps of air. Her piercing scream filled the night air, followed by another, until one hand closed over her mouth cutting the shrieks off. She began to struggle, futilely trying to pull in air as Cummings held his hand firmly over her face to muffle any further cries. Sarah's lungs began to burn. "I knew I's fixing to pass out. I just kept fighting Jesse to keep him from doing what I knowed he was gonna." Sarah, sure she was going to faint from the pressure blocking her airway, lost consciousness within seconds.

Anita, who was asleep in bed, woke to the gut-wrenching scream. She jumped up and went to investigate the noise. When she saw Cummings straddling Sarah, her first thought was, *What the hell's going on?* Years later, she recalled the scene still so fresh in her mind. "Jesse was wrestling with Sarah on the bed and she was screaming, kicking, and hollering. Jesse turned and just stared hard at me. My attention was on the bed, so I don't know if Sherry was in the room or not at that moment."

Conditioned to feel nothing, Anita announced, "I'm going back to bed. I didn't see this."

Anita explained her bizarre response, "I knew I couldn't stop him. I started to leave the room and he says, 'No. You're gonna watch this.' " It was then that Anita noticed Sherry for the first time. She was standing frozen near the end of the bed. "Sherry had this look of disbelief on her face. It was an 'I'd really like to kill this bastard' look at the same time."

The horrified Sarah believed that both women were holding her legs down, Anita holding one leg and her own sister holding the other. Sherry and Anita emphatically deny having anything to do with Sarah's rape. Anita explained why she believes Sarah was confused, "The way Jesse was lying on her, it could've felt like we was holding her legs, 'cause he had his feet wrapped around her ankles, pinning her down. I never held her leg and I doubt Sherry did, but I can see why she thought that. Plus, she was obviously scared to death. After that night, Sherry and I never spoke of it again.

"The harder that girl fought, you could tell the more he liked it. She tried so hard to escape from him, to wiggle out from under him, but he had his arms on her chest. And Jesse, at that time, had a muscular build and was very strong. At one point she quit fighting him and laid real still. I guess that's when she musta passed out.

"I remember hearing her cry out for her mama as Jesse raped her. And I remember thinking, your mama's not here and even if she was, I doubt she coulda done anything."

When the attack was finally over, Anita slipped away tiptoeing back to her bedroom. She crawled underneath the covers, then felt the other side of the mattress give as Jesse and Sherry lay down. The man who was never satiated sexually shocked the women when he commented in the darkness, "Whew, man, I couldn't get it up again right now, if I wanted to."

Poor, horrified Sarah had no choice but to spend the night under her rapist's roof. She never went back to sleep, and her body didn't cease shaking for hours. Since Sarah's family had just moved to Oklahoma from Arkansas, Sarah knew no one. She barely knew the way back to her new home. She had no choice but to wait for the interminable darkness to fade so the light of day could come and whisk her away from her despicable brother-in-law.

Anita consciously avoided the teenager before her departure.

"I stayed off by myself. I couldn't believe he'd done it, and I didn't know how to deal with it. Later that day Jesse and me got in a huge argument over the incident. Jesse was saying, 'Well, you know she's done it before.' " In Jesse's warped mind that somehow made Sarah open game.

Cummings threatened his sister-in-law before she left the next day. If she told anyone about the rape or tried to go to the police, he promised he would kill her and her mom, vowing to burn their house down with them trapped inside. The petrified teenager believed every threat he made to her that day. Sarah was delivered home that afternoon when Cummings got around to it.

Sherry was admonished by her husband that it was her responsibility to make her sister "a believer." Continuing with the same threat he had used earlier on Sarah, he warned Sherry, "If she turns me in, I'll sneak in after everybody goes to bed, kill all of 'em. I'll start such a bad fire, they'll die as the house burns to the ground. And everyone'll think they died from the fire."

Sherry never discounted Cummings's threats, and he made sure she didn't discount this one, either. "He went so far as to find out my mama and them's routine to see when they was awake. He told me he could just as easy blow up the house. Jesse'd go on about plastic and dynamite after that statement to let me know he knew exactly what he was doing."

Anita recalled that shortly after Sarah's rape, Darren Cooper and Cummings stole some dynamite. "Eight sticks, I think. I don't know whatever happened to 'em, but they disappeared."

Sherry vowed to herself that although she had been unable to protect her sister that night, she would do so from the next day forward as best she could. On the occasions when Cummings instructed Sherry to see if Sarah could spend the night, she would walk over to her sister's house. There they would concoct a lie as to why Sarah could not come over. Around Cummings a simple "no, thank you" would never suffice.

After the incident, Sarah avoided Cummings like the plague.

She never spoke to him again. And she didn't dare go to the police to report him. The only thing left for her to do was to try to forget it ever happened. So Sarah pushed it all down into a secret place deep inside of her. Sarah soon forgave her sister for not rescuing her that night. The teenager would later testify, "Jesse was holding over her [Sherry's] head, if they ever separated, he was taking their daughter and leaving. Sherry would do anything for that little girl. Anything."

By May it was obvious that Judy and Eugene Mayo's marriage was not working. Judy fought admitting it, she needed Eugene's companionship so desperately. The younger man, however, did not need their relationship like she did, so he had no real incentive to work on their problems. At the end of the month, Eugene packed his things and left. Judy cried for days.

Knowing Judy was always looking for ways to supplement her government checks, Cummings took advantage of her disadvantages. He was a master at using other people's troubles to his advantage. The fact that he would do it to his own sister made the act even more repugnant. The minute Mayo packed his things, Cummings had Judy running all over the place for him doing whatever he ordered her to do. It seemed as though Cummings was now making Judy do things for him for reasons that looked a whole lot more like control than a need to help his sister out of her financial straits.

Melissa Moody and Lisa Cathy were now out of school, and they spent every waking moment together. Distraught over the very thing she had feared Eugene would do, and unable to do anything to ease her mother's pain, Melissa preferred to escape, rising early every day and heading to the Cathys' house. Like most little girls at the time, Melissa and Lisa delighted in weaving colorful friendship bracelets to exchange. Now that she had the time, Melissa would spend countless hours in Lisa's living room sitting with her on the floor and carefully constructing more bracelets. There were four of them, in particular, she cherished and wore at all times. One of the bracelets held special meaning for the two young girls. It was one that Lisa had made for her that summer.

Melissa had not been with Lisa when her friend sequestered herself in her room and steadily worked on it, carefully twisting and turning the twine together. She worked diligently on the bracelet, because this one would be special and had to be just right. When Lisa surprised her friend by proudly handing it over the next morning, a huge smile crossed Melissa's face and she instantly loved it. Lisa had known Melissa would love it because she knew what her friend's three favorite colors were. Melissa eagerly slipped the other three bracelets from her arm and before putting them back, she slipped the new one on. She did love it, and she loved her friend who made it. Melissa slipped it on first so it would be the one worn closest to her heart. The bracelet was white with purple and gold twine interweaved.

But summer brought some unpleasant activities for the girls, Melissa in particular. With school out she had to spend more time on Jesse's farm because Judy always seemed to be doing things for him.

Melissa never showed affection toward Cummings in Lisa Cathy's presence, according to Lisa. But when Cummings walked by, Melissa would smile politely and greet her uncle. She always tried to get Lisa to come with her, and Lisa almost always did. She would have put up with a hundred Jesses to be with her best friend, anywhere, anytime.

Cummings was described by Lisa as "scary" in what he was known to do for a living, and in how he looked. "His reputation was pretty bad 'cause he dealt in drugs and made and sold whiskey. He looked strong, like you didn't wanta mess with him. He wore these plain ole brown glasses and walked around grim, like he had a chip on his shoulder, and had lots of whiskers and stuff on his face. There was a bad-looking scar on the back of his head. And he was scummy-looking with that shaved head that he had back then. I thought he looked like a psychopath."

Outspoken and sometimes blunt like her friend, Melissa

didn't mince words, either, when she spoke with Lisa in private about her uncle. She confided that she hated Jesse because he was so vindictive and mean. Lisa spoke about the sweet personality and warm smile of her friend, "She had the brightest smile of anyone." Suddenly sober in the next memory, Lisa described a change in her friend. "As it got closer to summer, Melissa would go into these real depressed moods. We never really talked about it. When she got like that I just tried to cheer her up. I know a lot of the depression was 'cause she was over at Jesse's so much 'cause of Judy's money situation. Judy always had money problems 'stead of helping her out he'd just use her."

Several months before Judy's eventual disappearance, she and Melody Thompson got into a fight. Pat Cathy remembered, "Melody was cussing Judy and her kids, and Judy told her, 'You better shut up or I'm gonna smack you. That's not right and you're gonna quit doing that in my house.' Well, she did it again, and Judy smacked her good. Melody left.

"Judy had received her divorce papers in the mail that day and was already crying and upset before Melody came over and started something up with her."

Always a loyal daughter, Melissa would become angry at anyone who didn't show her mother respect. Lisa Cathy put into words how Melissa felt, "Anybody that had no respect for Judy, well, Melissa had no respect for them. She stood up for her mother, always. And I think that's why she started hating Jesse so much."

In July, Jesse Cummings started driving his father back and forth to Oklahoma City for treatment of his disease. This type of generosity was totally out of character for Cummings. But as was always the case, he wasn't as interested in his dad's health as he was in constructing an alibi for the mayhem he was silently planning.

On August 2, Anita turned twenty-two. Cummings told her he was going to take her to a local tavern to have a beer or two as a birthday celebration. The only other time Anita had been to a bar was on her twenty-first birthday.

During the day Cummings received a call to go to Texas to haul hay. His dad had been after him all day long about taking both Anita and Jesse out to celebrate the event with a few beers.

Anita worked until ten-thirty that night. Cummings instructed his father to pick Anita up when she got off work. Around eleven o'clock, Jesse, Sr., picked Anita up and told her about Jesse's unscheduled trip to Texas. The old guy assured her that he had gotten permission before his son left to take the birthday girl to a bar as planned.

With no time to go home and change, Anita wore her work uniform to celebrate in. The two went to a local tavern and danced a couple of dances. Anita recalled the evening vividly. "His dad drank his beer, and I drank maybe a total of half my bottle. I had gotten my sixth bought for me, and I was passing 'em off 'cause I knew better than to get drunk. I knew what Jesse would do to me if I did. At the time I had lost so much weight from stress, I barely weighed a hundred pounds. And I hadn't drank in over a year, so a half of a beer almost got me plastered."

Jesse, Sr., and Anita left the bar and headed home. When they got into town, the police stopped them. "They told Dad he was drunk. The cop came around to my side of the car and had me get out. He talked to me for a few minutes then picked me up, and said, 'I bet you don't weigh a hundred pounds.'" Anita smiled at the accurate guess and nodded. He asked Anita how much she had to drink and was informed only one beer. They arrested Jesse, Sr., and let Anita go, but they impounded the car.

Anita was forced to start walking home. "It was too far to walk at night. I'd done seen too much evil from Jesse. I knew what people were capable of. I hadn't walked far when one of Jesse's friends spotted me and offered me a ride home.

"I no more got home and was telling Sherry what happened when Jesse pulled up in the driveway. I went out and told him about it. He was majorly pissed-off and proceeded to beat the living daylights out of me."

According to Cummings, it didn't matter that he had given his father permission to take Anita out. In his way of thinking, she should have told his father that she just didn't feel right going to a bar without her husband.

"I tried to reason with Jesse saying, 'Well, you said I could go, Jesse.' I got backhanded hard across the face. I was standing in the front yard, unfortunately right next to the clothesline. It caught me right across the throat. As I bounced off the line, Jesse grabbed my arm and was jerking and pushing me around. He kept ranting that I went whoring around, and that I was probably messing around with his father.

"Then, Jesse kicked me across the yard. I had bruises everywhere, especially on my arms, chest, and legs. I had ones here on my arm that looked like fingerprints. Plainly you could see four finger imprints and a thumbprint underneath the arm.

"After Jesse got done beating the shit out of me, he took me inside and took pictures of the worst bruised arm. Early the next morning, Jesse got me out of bed. I was so sore I could barely move.

"Dad took up for me a lot but he wouldn't have interfered with this beating, 'cause if he had Jesse would've turned on him and beat the hell out of him, too."

Before Cummings left to pick up his father, he instructed Anita to wear blue jeans, socks, and tennis shoes. Her shirt had to have three-quarter-length sleeves.

"It was the middle of a burning hot August and Jesse didn't want me to show any skin except from my elbows and the neck up. He made me tell the police that the man that arrested Dad had done this to me. Jesse planned on using it for leverage to get his dad out of trouble. Sorta like, you drop my dad's charges, and my wife won't pursue assault charges."

Jesse Cummings, Sr., was released from jail. Anita was told to come back the next day to file a formal complaint against the officer. When she went back, they wanted her to take a lie detector test. Anita went home and told Cummings about the request. "Jesse was like, 'You go down there and tell 'em you'll take their damn lie detector test.' I went back and told 'em I'd take it. I was surprised when they said it wouldn't be necessary. All charges against Dad were dropped.

"They made me go face-to-face with that officer, and I had to stand there and look the man in the eye. Oh man, you talk about something to go through. I had to stare him in the eye and lie. The officer just stared at me in total disbelief. I knew it would be easier to stand there and lie, then face what would happen to me at home if I didn't." For Anita, the choice was a simple one.

The police officer Anita had been forced to falsely accuse had one prior complaint on his record. It stemmed from him getting a little too rough with a prisoner. The prior incident topped off Anita's accusation and landed the innocent officer in a different police department.

Judy spoke often and lovingly of her stepfather. The two were so close most people thought Marie Cummings was the stepparent instead of Jesse, Sr. Pat Cathy remembered Marie's name being brought up only once. Judy had shown her a watch that used to belong to her mother. It was given to Judy shortly before Marie died. The other siblings were mad because Marie had chosen to give it to her. Judy held up the arm with the watch around it and truculently announced to Pat, "They want this watch. But I'm keeping it till the day I die!"

The beginning of September found Judy trying to recover from the depression her divorce from Eugene Mayo had brought on by dating a man that lived a few miles away from her.

By this time Judy's love for Jesse was fading fast, and she started seeing another local man by the name of DeWayne Snow. Judy was going to drop Pat Cathy off at work. When she arrived, Cummings and Anita were there and Judy was crying. This really surprised her, because Judy had been perking up from Snow's companionship. But then, it seemed to Pat every time she saw Judy crying lately, Cummings was somewhere around close.

"Judy had a little strongbox, a gray box, and it was sitting on the counter. On the way to work I asked her what was wrong. She finally told me Jesse was really gonna take her only method of transportation."

Pat Cathy believed the title to Judy's vehicle was in the strongbox. "I couldn't for the life of me understand a brother who'd do such a thing to one of his relatives. And I told Judy so. She was scared of Jesse, and the wives made out like they were scared of him, too."

Lisa Cathy had grown into a pretty and petite teenager with light blond hair. Her soft-spoken voice told about the night before her best friend's death. "Melissa begged Judy to let her stay that night at my house. There was a lot of reasons she didn't want to go over there. One of 'em was the living conditions were really bad, and the women were mean to her. But after August she made ever' excuse in the world not to go because Jesse was acting so weird. Come to think of it, I think she managed to keep from going in August. If she'd gone I'd known, 'cause we was together all the time that summer. And I know she didn't go back out there before the Fourth 'cause we was trying to crowd in as much time as we could doing fun things 'cause school was fixing to start."

The last time Pat and Lisa Cathy saw their two friends was on Wednesday, September 4, 1991, the night Melissa and Judy went over to the Cummingses'. Melissa begged her mom to let her spend the night with Lisa instead. Pat chimed in, hoping she might be able to influence Judy. But, Judy was adamant, "Not tonight!" A vocal Melissa stood toe-to-toe with her mother insisting she wasn't going to go. "I'm not going out there! I told you, Mama, I don't like it!"

Pat Cathy took Judy aside and beseeched her, "Don't go out to Jesse's. If you gotta have a place to stay, come to my house." Pat Cathy tried to ponder Judy's motives. "She never did say why she had to go, just [that] she had to get some things settled. Then, me and Lisa tried to talk her into at least letting Melissa stay with us. But she was adamant she's taking Melissa."

After the two had become trusted friends, Judy had confessed to Pat how badly she had messed up in California with her kids. She told Pat she had suspected her husband was sexually assaulting their children. When she failed to speak up and protect them, Child Protective Services took them away. "Judy said she'd stayed quiet once, and it almost cost her everything in life she cared about. She told me she'd made up her mind that she'd hang on to the only child she had left. Fact of the matter her exact words were, 'If anyone ever lays a hand on Melissa, I swear to God, there'll be hell to pay!' "

Before school was to start, Melissa was becoming withdrawn and even more quiet. She seemed troubled. Both Pat and Lisa Cathy remembered that Melissa had stomach problems, which would only flare up when she had to go to her uncle's house. Sometimes Melissa would double over with pain at the mention of Cummings's name. Pat Cathy could not prove it, but she strongly suspected Cummings was molesting Melissa. "I just had the feeling Jesse was messing with her, 'cause she hated going over there so much. I think Judy found out Jesse was molesting her. She'd lost her other kids by not standing up for them. She'd told me she'd never make that mistake a second time. Melissa was all she had left, and they both loved each other a lot."

As the morning was turning into the afternoon, Pat and Lisa, not willing to give up without a fight, followed Judy to her house to once more try to talk her out of taking Melissa with her. Judy had put on makeup, applying a bright blue eye shadow that mirrored the color of her eyes. She appeared to be priming herself to make the overnight stay, something she had never done from the time she moved to Tushka. Lisa Cathy recalled, "I remember Judy saying her and Jesse, Sr., were going out to a bar that night. Mom thinks she was just trying to keep her mind busy till her and Jesse took care of what it was they was suppose to."

A smile crossed Lisa's lips as she remembered how Judy looked, "She had on a black shirt with this black lace 'cross it and a pair of these peach pants on. I'd never seen her all fixed up before."

Whatever was troubling Judy would temporarily be put on hold. Tonight she was determined to have a good time. She would worry about settling things with Jesse the next day.

When Lisa hugged Melissa goodbye, both lingered a little longer than usual. She couldn't put her finger on what, but something was wrong, very wrong. Melissa's face showed concern, not disappointment or sullenness. A distant look captured her face as she sat quietly waiting for her mother to finish getting ready and dreading the thought of spending the night inside Jesse's house. Lisa was disheartened that she was unable to persuade Judy to leave Melissa with them.

Lisa recalled, "I remember the first time I ever went over there. Judy always got a cup of coffee and she'd sit down at the table. That's where everyone would gather and Judy'd talk with Jesse and his wives. Me and Melissa was told to go outside and play. We were never allowed inside when the adults were talking at the table. I felt something was being discussed in there, but I knew it wasn't any of my business, so I never asked." Lisa continued her tale with a distant look on her face, "I wish for once I had disobeyed Judy and eavesdropped on their conversation around the kitchen table. Maybe I'd better understand this whole thing." It was small comfort to the teenager that the madness compelling Jesse Cummings had no rhyme or reason to it.

Judy was more aware than anybody of all the illegal activities her brother was into. Judy had never really trusted Jesse when it came to money, but she had always trusted him where Melissa was concerned. The knowledge of her brother's criminal endeavors, along with her mistaken trust of Cummings with Melissa, would have horrible consequences. Judy's costly decision to take her daughter with her instead of letting her remain behind with Pat and Lisa, would be paid in Melissa's blood.

Thirteen

Thursday night Judy and Melissa headed toward Jesse Cummings's farm. Jesse, Sr., and Judy decided, since she was spending the night at her brother's, the two would go out drinking at several bars and just have a good time. Jesse, Sr., depressed over his battle with cancer, felt this would be a good pick-me-up.

The month prior, Cummings had talked to his sister about moving closer to him. It was Cummings's practice to keep those he controlled close to him. It made management so much easier. Judy hadn't said a word about moving to Pat Cathy. It was unlike her not to share the information with her good friend.

Whether Cummings used his persuasive abilities on Judy, or she was simply placating her brother, she agreed to look at houses the next day.

That evening Cummings secreted Sherry into the bedroom. Pensively studying his wife, Cummings described the house-hunting expedition he wanted Sherry to go on with Judy. Sherry readily agreed to take her sister-in-law out.

Cummings looked sternly at Sherry and said, "When you take Judy to look for a house, find an empty one out in the country, away from everybody."

Confused, Sherry agreed, then questioned her husband as to why he wanted specifically for them to go to the country.

With no more emotion than someone giving directions, Cummings explained, "Because when you get out there, I want you to take her in that empty house and shoot her in the head."

Most ordinary people would have been staggered by the statement. But in the totally dysfunctional Cummings household, Jesse was always doing crazy stuff like this. The demand didn't shock Sherry, but it did catch her off guard.

She responded, "I can't do that. I grew up around Judy and I love her."

Cummings countered, "If you love *me,* you'll do it. Will you do it?"

Sherry stressed again she couldn't do that to someone she had known so long. At this point Sherry didn't know if Cummings was just playing mind games with her, perhaps testing her loyalty, or if he was actually serious.

Cummings repeated again, "If you love me, you'll do it."

Sherry looked her husband straight in the eye and shocked him when she replied, "Jesse, I haven't loved you for a long time now."

Cummings looked surprised and rebutted, "Then why do you stay?"

Astounded, Sherry shot back, "You *know* why I stay. You won't let me leave and take Jessica." Cummings walked out of the room and never again mentioned the matter to Sherry.

Sherry knew it was just like Cummings to come out of left field with something like this. And she knew if he really wanted you to do something, he would never back off. If anyone defied his orders, a severe beating was inevitable. There was no beating, so Sherry thought he was messing with her.

Judy and Jesse, Sr., partied until around two o'clock in the morning. When they walked in the house, both were a little inebriated and exhausted. They went to bed as soon as they got in. With the revelers safely tucked in, the Cummings house fell silent.

Shards of sunlight peeked through the shabbily pieced-together carpet covering a broken window, and ushered in the fateful Thursday morning.

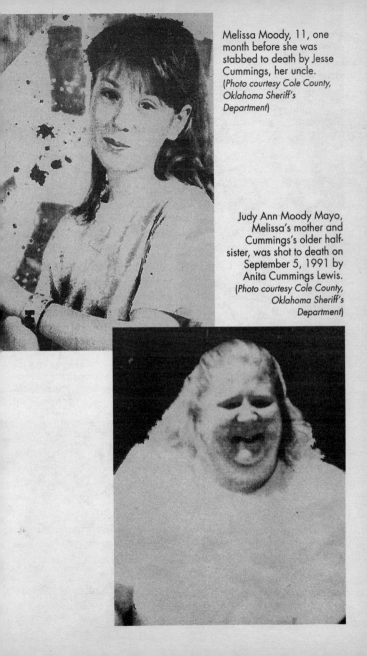

Melissa Moody, 11, one month before she was stabbed to death by Jesse Cummings, her uncle. (*Photo courtesy Cole County, Oklahoma Sheriff's Department*)

Judy Ann Moody Mayo, Melissa's mother and Cummings's older half-sister, was shot to death on September 5, 1991 by Anita Cummings Lewis. (*Photo courtesy Cole County, Oklahoma Sheriff's Department*)

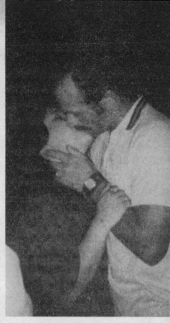

On June 14, 1989, Anita Lewis became Jesse Cummings's fourth wife. At the time, he was still married to two other women. (*Photo courtesy the Lewis family*)

Anita Lewis graduated with honors from Cushman High School in Batesville, Arkansas, the only female in her class to achieve that status. (*Photo courtesy the Lewis family*)

Sherry (left) holding daughter Jessica and Anita holding son Scottie. (*Photo courtesy Anita Cummings Lewis*)

Cummings forced his wives to prostitute themselves. Seated in a cluttered bedroom, third wife Sherry Yaws Cummings has on the outfit Cummings chose for her to wear to pick up men at a truck stop. *(Photo courtesy Sherry Cummings)*

Jesse James Cummings in the bedroom he shared with wives Sherry and Anita. *(Photo courtesy Anita Cummings Lewis)*

Cummings with his daughter Jessica and Anita's son Scottie. *(Photo courtesy Anita Cummings Lewis)*

Cummings dressed in a security uniform with his younger sister Debra. The .38 in his holster is believed to be the missing murder weapon. *(Photo courtesy Anita Cummings Lewis)*

The cellar behind the Cummings's house in Phillips, Oklahoma where Cummings punished the children and planned to keep a woman as a sex slave.

Cummings tormented the children by telling them maggots would crawl up and get them in the outhouse.

After deciding to adopt Anita's son, Cummings had to move his family into a house with indoor plumbing to satisfy Child Welfare's requirements.
(Photo courtesy Wonda Utterback)

Judy Mayo's body was found in a pond near Atoka Lake. Cummings had stripped the body of upper clothing to make it look like she had been raped and murdered.
(*Photo courtesy Cole County, Oklahoma District Attorney*)

Mayo's bra and underwear were discovered in the river next to the pond.
(*Photo courtesy Cole County, Oklahoma District Attorney*)

A package of cigarettes pierced by a bullet that had fallen out of Mayo's blouse when Cummings stripped her body.
(*Photo courtesy Cole County, Oklahoma District Attorney*)

Cummings used Mayo's truck to transport her body to the pond. The truck was later found abandoned by the side of the road.
(*Photo courtesy Cole County, Oklahoma Distract Attorney*)

Multiple sets of handcuffs found in Cummings's bedroom.
(*Photo courtesy Cole County, Oklahoma District Attorney*)

Cummings planted some of Melissa Moody's clothing with Mayo's to make authorities believe Melissa had been killed with her mother.

Her four friendship bracelets were still around Melissa Moody's left
wrist when her remains were found.
(*Photo courtesy Cole County, Oklahoma District Attorney*)

The skeletal remains of Melissa Moody. Her skull, with a few strands
of hair, is to the left.
(*Photo courtesy Cole County, Oklahoma District Attorney*)

Convinced that Cummings was planning to kill her, Anita Lewis confessed to police she shot Judy Mayo on Cummings's orders. (*Photo courtesy Cole County, Oklahoma Sheriff's Department*)

Sherry Yaws was arrested for capital murder after Lewis's confession. (*Photo courtesy Cole County, Oklahoma Sheriff's Department*)

Jesse Cummings was found guilty in the murders of both Judy Mayo and Melissa Moody and received the death penalty. (*Photo courtesy Cole County, Oklahoma Sheriff's Department*)

Sherry Yaws (left) and Anita Lewis before leaving court for prison.

OSBI Agent David Cathey with
Prosecutors John McPhail and
James Thornley, District
Attorney.

Judge Douglas Gabbard II
presided over Cummings's trial.
(*Photo courtesy
Judge Douglas Gabbard II*)

From left to right, OSBI Agents Chuck Jeffries, David Cathey, and Dale Birchfield receiving commendations for their work on the case. (*Photo courtesy OSBI*)

From left to right, OSBI Agents Reanae Childers, Chris Dill, and Charlie Mackey with their commendations. (*Photo courtesy OSBI*)

Lewis (left) and Yaws in their cell awaiting transfer to state prison, where Lewis will serve a life sentence.

Melissa Moody's homemade gravestone was donated by the volunteer firemen who had diligently searched for her body.

Jesse Cummings was driving his father to the hospital in Oklahoma City for the cancer treatment he had to have. The drive was a long, tiring one, so Jesse planned to leave around seven o'clock that morning.

Members of the family began to slowly come alive one by one. Sherry was the first one up. She headed to the kitchen to prepare breakfast.

As Jesse, Sr., quietly dressed for his trip, Judy lay soundly sleeping nearby, hung over from the night of partying. Melissa slept beside her mother.

Cummings lay beside Anita, patiently waiting for her to wake up. When Anita opened her eyes, she turned over and saw Cummings lying next to her just staring at her.

Anita recalled, "Jesse told me he wanted me to do something for him while he was in Oklahoma City with his dad. He said, 'I want you to kill Judy and use the .38 because it's untraceable.' I told him I wouldn't do it."

Cummings then did what always worked, he threatened to kill Scottie. "He told me if I hadn't killed Judy by the time he got back, he'd kill Scottie and make me watch. It was gonna be my choice who got to die."

Anita had learned in her terrifying years with Cummings to ask no questions. She also knew he was a man of his word when it came to something like this. Stunned and speechless, Anita sat up and stared at Cummings as he walked out the door.

He turned on his heels with one parting instruction, "Remember, you decide." No one would have known from his demeanor that he had just ordered the execution of his half sister.

Later that morning Sherry took Judy to look for houses as she had agreed to. Anita watched them leave. She felt sickened and dazed. Most of the morning she lay on the bed, just staring out the window, as she tried to deal with the burden foisted on her.

She couldn't erase Cummings's threat from her mind. "I knew he'd do what he said to Scottie, 'cause he'd already come close to killing Scottie more than once."

A little after noon Anita heard Judy and Sherry come into the house. Her stomach knotted up, plagued with the thought of Cummings's orders. All morning she'd been trying to think of a way out of this. The pressure in her temples increased as her heart pounded harder. Her mind became a whirlwind of activity.

Anita knew Cummings; knew the depth of his cruelty, the depth of his evilness. And she also knew there would be no way out of this.

With an all-too-familiar sigh of resignation, Anita raised up off the bed and walked over to the window. She gazed out to watch her little boy playing with Jessica and Melissa. Tears slid down her cheeks. She knew the only answer to this nightmare would end in a life being taken by her hand.

Anita walked through the house, moving as if she were programmed. She spotted Judy relaxing on the sofa, engrossed in a television program. Anita glanced out the back door and saw Sherry on the porch watching the children play.

She blankly stared at the .38 in her hand. The zone she practiced reaching when being tortured by Cummings had kicked in. Her soul was completely barren of emotion.

Fatigue and stress were etched into Anita's face. Weary beyond words, she focused a final time on her son outside playing. She needed one more reminder of why she had no choice.

Anita's attention focused back on the body on the couch. She began to move in slow motion. The cadence of her heart was overwhelming as the gun was aimed in Judy's direction. With eyes tightly closed, Anita pulled the trigger. The sound of the gun echoed, pounding like a hammer in her ears.

Anita pulled the trigger again. Then again and again and again, until she heard the click of the hammer striking against the empty cylinder. There were no screams. No cries. Just deafening silence.

The acrid smell of gunpowder permeated the room. It hung in the air like heavy fog. Slowly Anita opened her eyes. She saw that one bullet had splintered the wood frame of the couch.

Her eyes traveled upward to Judy. The body was leaning back against the couch. It looked as though she had merely fallen asleep. Anita noticed blood spattered on the bottom of the couch, floor, and walls. The maroon couch was blood-soaked but its color hid the secret. Anita lowered her arms, with the gun still clutched between trembling hands.

Outside Sherry jumped when she heard the shots fired. She knew without question Judy had been shot. Her refusal hadn't made any difference after all.

The kids were playing in the pasture in back. If they heard the gunshot, they never indicated it. Even if they had heard the pistol being fired, it was not an unusual occurrence. Gunshots coming from the Cummings house were an all-too-familiar sound for them.

They had learned long ago to shut out external noises, the screams, the sound of their mothers' bodies being slammed up against the wall, and furniture and dishes breaking as Cummings terrorized his family.

Inside the house the still-dazed Anita laid the gun on top of the television cabinet. She walked toward the porch, her eyes tired and searching. Anita's only thought, her only focus, was to get to Scottie and hold him—just hold him. Then everything would be all right.

Sherry spotted Anita heading toward the pasture. She hollered at her, and the call stopped Anita in her tracks.

As the two women looked at each other, a slow panic began to build within both. They briefly discussed getting the kids inside. Anita called to Jessica, Scottie, and Melissa to come in. The obedient trio ran to the porch.

Without explanation the children were told they were going to have to play inside the house for a while. It never occurred to the kids to ask why. Cummings's beatings had trained them never to ask questions.

Sherry gathered Jessica in her arms and placed her hands over her daughter's eyes. She walked through the kitchen, past the bloody corpse in the front room, and secured Jessica in the master bedroom. She shut the door as she left.

By the time Sherry made it back to the porch, Anita was carrying Scottie in her arms, his eyes also concealed while she made the same journey. Melissa was the last to be taken inside. Her eyes were also shielded from seeing her murdered mother's body. The bedroom door was fastened with a nail from the outside, locking the children in.

With a shared understanding Anita and Sherry went to work. A white hospital mattress pad, one of many in the house from Jesse Sr.'s hospitalizations, was wrapped around the body. Using the pad for leverage, the women pulled their heavy burden through the house and out the back door.

Adrenaline was pumping so fast, neither woman paid mind to the heaviness of the corpse. They both described the way they were feeling: "It was like we'd stepped outside our bodies, and watched this drama being played out in slow motion, in front of our eyes."

The back door was propped open. Acting in concert, both women anticipated each other's moves. They pulled the dead body onto the front porch. The women heard a car coming. They stopped pulling their bundle and quickly crouched down. When the car was gone, they finished pulling the bundle off the porch. The body thumped as it hit each step on the way down.

Cummings had drummed into their heads, if anything ever happened and they shot someone, they were to put the body in the cellar and leave it there until he got home. That's precisely what they did.

The dark, dank cellar filled with stagnant water and slithering snakes became Judy's resting place until her half brother's arrival home. The corpse's back and side were propped against the side of the cellar wall, its bottom rested on the second step. The legs were leaned to the side, and the feet dangled in the rancid water. The cellar door was then placed across the opening.

Back in the house the women worked in silence. They cleaned up the blood while the children played in the locked room. Sherry took the cushions off the couch and carried them around back. A water hose was used to soak each cushion thoroughly. The wet cushions were then leaned against the cellar door to dry.

Anita mopped the blood off the floor, wiped down the walls, and cleaned the corner of the couch where blood had sprayed. Wandering in a stupor onto the back porch, Anita looked down and noticed a small drop of blood.

She dropped to her knees and began furiously scrubbing the small blood drop with the sponge still in her hand. As she cleaned, Anita broke down for the first time. Weeping at the memory, Anita explained, "I kept rubbing that spot while I cried. I rubbed and rubbed but it wouldn't come off." Her voice faded as she replied once more, "It just wouldn't come off."

Sherry pulled the crying woman away from the now nonexistent spot and pushed her inside. Anita had to get herself together to go to work. She knew she had to act as if nothing out of the ordinary had transpired that day. Jesse would beat her if she deviated from her everyday routine.

A cook at the Dairy Queen in Atoka, Anita was to report to work at five o'clock that afternoon. The time was drawing near. Sherry went back outside and hooked up the garden hose so Anita could shower in the backyard. Quickly Anita hosed off and hurried back inside.

She rushed into the bedroom to put her work uniform on. While dressing, she observed Melissa playing with Jessica and Scottie. Anita left the room, replacing the makeshift lock. Sherry was sitting cross-legged in a stupor on the floor. Her eyes were looking in the direction of the television but not seeing.

Anita noticed during her absence a small dresser had been placed where the couch had been. The rocking chair had been brought in to make the room look fuller.

Anita went over to Sherry and begged, "I've gotta have a

cigarette, but please don't tell Jesse I smoked one." Sherry nodded her head and handed one to the shaking woman.

Judy's red truck was parked directly behind the truck Anita was to drive to work. In a quiet hysteria Anita mistakenly put the gear in reverse. Her body was jolted forward when her truck slammed into the front of the red truck.

Shaking and in tears, Anita jumped out and checked the damage. It was minimal. She got back into the truck and hastily drove toward Atoka.

Anita hadn't traveled far when she realized something was wrong with the truck. Pulling over at a self-serve gas station, she got out and made a quick inspection. To her dismay, a tire was low and losing air fast.

Aggravated and frustrated, Anita started to panic. Her mind started swirling as she tried to think. The tires on the truck were too big for the now ninety-pound woman to even think about trying to change.

She started walking to a nearby friend of Cummings's. Once there, Anita phoned her boss at Dairy Queen to notify her why she would be late. A hard worker, Anita always got to work on time and volunteered to stay late. She seldom used a sick day. Her devotion was simple—at work she didn't get hurt, and she didn't have to be around Jesse.

As soon as the tire was changed, Anita jumped back in the truck and sped toward Atoka. Forty-five minutes late, she scrambled into the Dairy Queen, grabbed her apron, and put it on as she walked.

Anita was visibly upset. A coworker, misreading the circumstances surrounding Anita's distress, told her to calm down. She assured Anita she wasn't in trouble because she had called in. Like a robot, Anita grabbed a hair net, tucked her hair underneath it, and started cooking.

"I didn't have to think at that point. It was like mechanical. Fry hamburgers, dress the buns, do the fries. It was automatic." The busier she stayed, the less time she had to think about the horrible tragedy that had transpired earlier.

Back at the Cummings house Sherry mourned the loss of her sister-in-law. Her emotions ran the gamut from terrified to giving in to the sobs fighting to get out. Cummings had crossed the line this time, and it had cost a human being her life.

At the moment she had no reason to be concerned for Melissa's safety. Years of dealing with Cummings's warped mind kept alarm about Melissa to a minimum. She figured he would seize the opportunity to adopt Melissa and use her as the sex slave he had been looking and planning for.

Sherry cooked supper, then went in and brought the kids out of the bedroom to eat. They played with their food, eventually ate, then jumped up from the table to play some more. They never questioned Judy's absence.

After the meal Sherry told Scottie and Jessica to go outside and play while there was some sunlight left. She escorted Melissa back to the bedroom. Bewildered about what she had done wrong, Melissa, nevertheless, accepted her perceived punishment without quarrel.

Ensconced in the locked room, Melissa busied herself playing with the women's makeup and clothes, trying to pass the time until she had done sufficient penance, and trying to bury the horrible dread mounting inside her that she was not locked up for penance sake. Something else was going on, something the girl would not allow herself to think about right now.

After cleaning the kitchen, nervous energy sent Sherry pacing throughout the house. Occasionally she peeked in the bedroom to check on Melissa, who had been locked up since three o'clock that afternoon. It was now getting dark. Each successive time Sherry would check on Melissa, the girl's face registered more concern.

When the daylight waned, Scottie and Jessica were called into the house. They parked themselves in front of the television. Neither inquired about Melissa.

Sherry heard her neighbor Betty hollering, "Sherry, Anita, you got a call."

"We didn't have a phone at the time. If we got a call, and it was dark, Betty wouldn't come over and knock. She'd just yell," Sherry revealed.

Sherry did not know the exact time when the call came through, but she knew it was before nine o'clock because the children were still up. Even with Cummings gone, his rule that the children be in bed by nine was never broken.

Sherry walked the short distance over to her neighbor's house. Crossing the threshold, she headed toward the phone. Its black receiver lay on its side. She picked up the phone and heard Jesse's voice, "Is everything done?"

"Yes," Sherry answered. Cummings said he wanted one of them to handcuff Melissa to the bed. Sherry listened as he spoke. His last response was short and curt, "I'll be home in a little while."

Still maintaining silence, Sherry listened as her husband told her goodbye. The receiver was returned to its perch. Sherry thanked Betty and headed back home.

Betty was the only neighbor in a position to hear the cries and screams coming from the Cummings household, but she never reported them. Betty had two wild, rebellious girls who loved to party and play loud music at the house. The deal struck with the Cummingses was simple, "You don't call the police on my girls' loud parties, and I won't call 'em about the noise coming from your house."

When nine o'clock arrived, Scottie and Jessica were put to bed. Sherry went in and checked on Melissa. The girl needed to go outside to the bathroom. Sherry accompanied her. When Melissa was placed back in the bedroom, Sherry sat down in front of the television set.

Around ten-thirty that night Anita got in from work. Cummings had not made it back yet. She headed for the bedroom to take her uniform off and change into shorts. Glancing toward the bed, she saw that Melissa was asleep and handcuffed. The child was lying on her back with her arms extended above her head.

Hardened to such sights, Anita quietly stepped out and wandered back to the front room. She sat down by Sherry. In stark silence both stared at the television screen, as if hypnotized by it.

Although Melissa had seen her cousins cuffed before, it was still a frightening experience. The whole day had been strange, and she began to worry about where her mother was. She knew something was very wrong. What it was, wasn't quite clear.

Despite the uncomfortable position the handcuffs placed her in, Melissa, tired and bored from being kept captive in the room most of the day, fell sound asleep.

As the women sat and stared at the screen, they both listened for Jesse's car to pull in the driveway. It was almost two o'clock Friday morning when they finally heard the car. Melissa had been held captive for almost ten hours.

Anita and Sherry walked outside and approached Cummings. Before he could speak, Anita nervously blurted out the secret that she had smoked a cigarette of Sherry's earlier that day. Sherry was flabbergasted. Anita had pleaded with Sherry not to tell on her and she had just squealed on herself.

Anita defended her actions. "I was afraid she'd tell him. And if I told him first, he wouldn't beat me so hard."

But Cummings wasn't worried about beating anyone at the moment. He had only one question, and it was directed at Anita, "Is it done?"

Anita hung her head and softly nodded. Cummings ordered her into the house. As Anita walked off, she heard the sharp sound of an open hand coming in direct contact with soft flesh as Cummings forcefully backhanded Sherry, knocking her backward into the car.

Sherry brought her hand to her stinging face as tears gathered in her eyes. She knew the slap was a result of his anger over her disobedience. Neither said a word as they walked inside the house.

The first thing Cummings did was gather up all the car keys. He didn't want anybody going anywhere. That done, he directed his wives to accompany him to the cellar.

Outside the only illumination was courtesy of a streetlight. The door to the temporary morgue was removed. Judy's massive body filled the doorway of the cellar. The two women stood and watched as Cummings strained tugging on the mattress pad surrounding it.

When the body was dislodged from the opening, it was placed on the ground in front of the cellar. As the women stood guard, Cummings disappeared and emerged with a rope in hand. He bent down next to the corpse and tightly wrapped the rope around its ankles and shoulders.

Cummings ordered his wives to help pull the remains to his sister's red Chevrolet flatbed pickup, parked only a few feet away. With only the streetlight to guide his moves, he laid the corpse on the ground beside the passenger door.

Together the three hoisted the tightly wrapped bundle onto the passenger seat. The women held their cargo up by bracing its girth with their shoulders. Cummings walked to the driver's side and got in. He instructed Sherry and Anita to push on the body as he pulled on the rope.

Once the body was secured inside the truck, the passenger door was shut. Cummings directed Anita back into the house, instructing her to stay inside and answer the door for no one.

Sherry was ordered to get in the blue Toyota Celica and follow closely behind him.

Both women's recollection of the event reminded them of a drama playing out on a television screen, with the sound turned all the way down. They could see Cummings's mouth move but couldn't hear what he was saying.

Cummings traveled along Highway 43, turning east down a small dirt road leading to a boat landing at Atoka Lake. He then turned onto a dirt path made by campers and fishermen. The lights were shut off as the truck rolled to a stop.

Climbing out of the flatbed truck, Cummings motioned Sherry with a flashlight to pull down closer to the water and park. Sherry drove the car into position, killed the engine, then shut off the lights. She sat in darkness surrounded by silence.

The truck was slowly eased toward a small pond close to the lake. The passenger door was opened. Cummings tugged on the rope wrapped tightly around his sister's body. One hefty pull sent the load tumbling heavily to the ground. He dragged it to the edge of the pond and removed the rope binding it.

Without feeling, without remorse, Cummings removed his sister's blouse, bra, and panties, then rolled the half-naked body into the pond.

Sherry heard the pickup start. The lights remained off as the truck approached the Toyota. The flashlight was held out the window and flicked a couple of times, signaling her to follow.

Traveling west onto the old dirt road, the truck headed to Highway 43, then turned in an easterly and northerly direction toward Highway 69. Approximately half the distance to Highway 69, Cummings pulled Judy's truck off the road and onto the gravel shoulder.

Sherry pulled up behind the truck but left the car running. Exiting from the pickup, Cummings went to the front of the vehicle and raised its hood. He walked back to the car and had Sherry scoot over to the passenger side. The two people sat in stone silence as they headed back to Coalgate.

Anita heard the car as soon as it pulled in. Frozen in shock since Cummings and Sherry's departure, Anita had not moved from the time they left until they got back. Not even to check on Melissa.

The front door swung open as Cummings walked in, followed closely by Sherry. A directive was issued to the women to go into the bedroom and uncuff and undress the shackled child. The shared look between Sherry and Anita acknowledged what was about to occur.

Knowing they couldn't stop him, never even entertaining the idea, the women shut down their feelings and did exactly what they were told. Anita flipped the light switch on and gently woke the sleeping girl. Sherry handed Anita the key to the handcuffs.

Melissa's arms had remained extended over her head for

hours. Administering the only act of consideration that night, Anita cautiously pulled Melissa's stiff arms down. She rubbed the child's arms between her hands to bring back circulation.

Systematically the women began to tug, unbutton, and pull the red-and-white-striped shorts and the shirt sporting an alligator in the upper-right-hand corner from the child's rigid body. Cummings stood in the doorway and watched.

Melissa seethed with hatred for every person in the room. The girl known for her fiery spirit and outspoken manner was too terrified to speak.

Once the task was completed, Cummings crossed into the room and shut the door. He pulled his shirt over his head, then tugged his blue jeans off. They were rolled up and placed underneath the mattress where he always put them to protect them from prying hands until he retrieved them.

Melissa awkwardly attempted to shelter her nudity by strategically crossing her arms. Defiance crossed her face as she stared caustically at the uncle she despised. The question looming in Melissa's liquid chestnut eyes was answered when Cummings curtly stated, "You know what I want." A tremulous sigh escaped the child's lips as she sat on the bed.

Anita and Sherry turned to leave but stopped when he barked, "Nope! Y'all are staying here and watching." Blotting out the reality as she had done so many times, Sherry looked away as the rape commenced.

Anita focused her gaze directly above the bodies on the bed, hoping to avoid her husband's wrath if he looked over to make sure she was watching the perverse show.

The women, who had endured an existence of nonrecognition and pain, treated the young rape victim with the same indifference that had always been shoved their way.

After Cummings had climaxed, he instructed Melissa to "clean him off." Trying to control her quivering voice, Melissa softly replied she didn't understand what he wanted. Agitated at her obvious inexperience, Cummings told her to put his penis in her mouth. Melissa shut her eyes for what must have seemed an eternity, only opening them when he withdrew.

The creak of the bed as Cummings got up signaled to the women that the sexual assault was over. He directed Anita to get a pair of blue coveralls stacked on top of one of several piles of junk in the cluttered room.

Anita nervously searched for the coveralls, while Melissa grabbed up her clothes, quickly pulling them on to banish the sensation of her uncle's eyes on her body.

Once located, the coveralls were placed near the end of the bed. Anita turned on her heels and practically broke into a run to leave the room.

Anita had watched her husband rape his fourteen-year-old sister-in-law, Sarah, just as he had his eleven-year-old niece tonight. The memory of Sarah's and Melissa's rapes flooded her mind, blurring the two images.

Anesthetized from years of Cummings's torture and abuse, Anita found herself standing numb in the front living room. Barren of normal feelings, she didn't try to escape or try to stop any further injury to Melissa. She just stood there.

The bedroom door opened moments later. Cummings, wearing the blue coveralls, walked out. Melissa was sandwiched between his body and Sherry's.

The man made a revolting remark to no one in particular. "I've been wantin' to do that for a long damn time!"

He stopped long enough to glance over his right shoulder to inform Melissa, "We're taking you to your mama." Fully understanding the implication of the brusque remark, Anita's stomach churned with revulsion.

"When I first left the room, I figured Jesse was gonna keep Melissa to mess with. After he told her he was taking her to her mama, I knew he wasn't gonna bring that baby back."

Anita was right.

The entire week preceding the attack on Melissa, Cummings had stayed in a highly agitated state. When he was like this, neither woman knew what he might do. Knowing their husband was capable of all sorts of depravity, the terrified women took Mini-Thins by the handful to stay awake and alert in the event he went over the edge. Critically fatigued, both wives continued to fight sleep.

The actuality of Cummings's murderous intent hit Sherry, shortly after Anita's mind had absorbed it. Seconds later he informed Sherry she would be coming with them. He scrutinized his wife's face for a reaction. Years of hiding emotions served Sherry well. The emptiness in her eyes concealed the desperate fear enveloping her. Aware that he thrived on people's fear of him, delighted in it, Sherry fought to deny Cummings that one small pleasure.

Melissa and Sherry followed Cummings to the car. He placed Melissa in the backseat and closed the door on the petrified girl. Sherry opened the passenger door and got in as Cummings headed around to the driver's side.

When he pulled out of the driveway, Sherry stifled her sobs trying desperately to keep her panic in check. The instant Sherry felt a tear trickle down her cheek, she quickly brushed it aside with the back of her hand so he wouldn't see.

The valiant but despondent Melissa hopelessly battled to keep from surrendering to tears. As the car moved farther down the highway, the little girl succumbed to the panic gripping her. Quiet sobs emanated from the back of the Celica.

For over an hour Cummings drove. During the long ride Melissa's tears faded into blunted silence, almost as if she had drawn a curtain across her emotions. A sign informed travelers that they had just crossed from Cole County into Choctaw County. Cummings navigated the car toward Crystal Road and the Twin Set Bridges, which crossed over Clear Boggy River, north of Boswell, Oklahoma.

It was close to four in the morning. Sherry closed her eyes but quickly opened them when she felt herself start to nod off. Despite being wired on Mini-Thins, the exhausted woman still had to fight the sleep her body dearly needed.

The car slowly rolled to a stop on the dusty shoulder of the

Twin Set Bridges. Cummings parked. But for crickets chirping in the woods, the silence was deafening. The early-morning air was fraught with tension as Melissa and Sherry waited for Cummings's next move.

A pair of surgical gloves from the car's floorboard was retrieved. Cummings slipped them on. He opened the car door, stepped out, and went around to get Melissa. He directed Sherry to unlock the back door. He tugged it open and reached in, forcefully pulling out the quivering child.

Sherry took one last look at her niece. Silken wisps of hair framed the panic-stricken eyes as her fragile body trembled with fear. Melissa looked into her aunt's eyes, searching them with her own—silently pleading for help. Sherry, unable to bear the vision, turned back around and stared straight ahead into the darkness.

Cummings's face remained stone cold. A paralyzed Sherry watched as he climbed over the rail of the bridge, taking Melissa with him. Soon the two disappeared from sight.

Sherry has attempted to explain her inaction. "People expected me to stop Jesse. I know no one understands it, but I knew if I tried to stop him, I wouldn't leave this place. There was no escape."

Melissa's shaking hand was tightly gripped by her uncle's as she was led down a dirt path from the bridge. An unfamiliar flutter in the pit of the child's stomach must have crescendoed as she followed Cummings into the woods. A silent, empty place was chosen and the two stopped.

Cummings issued an obdurate directive to his terrified niece to disrobe. Melissa whimpered faintly as she discarded her shirt, then her shorts; the question "Why?" had to be crying out from her silent lips.

Cummings drew the naked child close to him, her back against his chest, then uttered the last words the adolescent would ever hear, "I wanta fool around 'fore I take you to your mama."

Assaulting Melissa once more, Cummings stripped away the

last shred of dignity the girl possessed. When finished, he reached with his right hand and pulled a hunting knife from the scabbard of the belt fastened around the coveralls.

His left arm hugged Melissa's neck, gripping her tighter as he stretched to cover the child's mouth with his hand to stifle the screams to come.

The first time the knife invaded Melissa's body, she momentarily tensed. With each additional wound, the girl's life slipped further from her grasp. The knife was withdrawn and Melissa slumped against her uncle, dying from the mortal injuries.

With icy indifference, the monster of Melissa's worst nightmare malevolently placed the knife on the left side of the young girl's neck and deftly slit her throat. Cummings backed up and watched the limp body crumple to the ground.

Melissa's beautiful, dark chestnut eyes stared blankly into nothingness as the cold breath of death snatched the eleven-year-old's life away.

Cummings looked around, almost casual about what had just transpired. He stooped and gathered up Melissa's clothes, then walked off, leaving his niece lying like discarded garbage on the dusty path.

Sherry waited in the darkness with the window rolled half-way down. The woman braced herself and listened for a scream to escape the woods. Only quiet prevailed. Sherry's muddled mind was unable to determine if minutes or hours had passed from the time the two figures had disappeared from sight.

The side mirror on the passenger-side door unexpectedly reflected Cummings's silhouette as he walked toward the trunk of the car. The movement startled Sherry.

Cummings moved from the trunk to the driver's side and opened the door. He reached inside, placing his hand on the steering wheel for leverage, as he slid behind it.

When the overhead light briefly came on, Sherry focused on the ominous shadows cast by the moonlight on Cummings's gloved right hand. Her gaze transferred from his hand to her own. In a matter of seconds she realized the shadows on the glove were not the result of the moon but splattered blood.

The horrible truth slammed home. Melissa really was dead, and Sherry had done nothing at all to stop it from happening.

The snap of the surgical gloves broke the silence and intruded on Sherry's train of thought. Cummings stripped the right glove off first, then yanked off the other. The odor that accompanied him was foreign to Sherry. Recalling the smell today, she shuddered. "Human blood's different from anything you'll ever smell. It was that moment I knew without a doubt he'd killed her."

Cummings stuffed the gloves in the pocket of his coveralls, then wiped the bloody steering wheel with the right sleeve of his coveralls. He started the car and pulled off the shoulder and onto the main highway.

Approximately fifteen minutes into the drive, Cummings turned off onto a dirt road. The strained silence between the two remained unbroken. His face remained expressionless. Fatigue and stress veiled Sherry's emotions as she hugged the passenger-side door, fearing she was next.

"I kept telling myself, 'don't go to sleep . . . don't close your eyes. Jesse shifted in his seat, and I thought he was gonna kill me right there in the car. I started to pray, and that was a mistake. I was so tired, the minute I closed my eyes, I dozed off," Sherry admitted.

Sleep brought Sherry no respite, as the nightmare of what had happened drifted in and out of her subconscious. "In my dream I thought, when I wake up this'll all be a dream, and I'll be at home in bed. The couch is gonna be fine, Anita's gonna be fine, Judy's gonna be there, and Melissa'll be with her."

Cummings pulled into an area near a lake along the dirt road. A large chug hole jostled Sherry awake as the tire dropped into it. Stark realization overwhelmed her, and she knew none of this was a dream. Things were not going to be fine. Things would never be fine again.

The car rolled to a stop. Without a word Cummings got out

and walked toward the water. He stopped near the edge of the lake and kicked off his tennis shoes. The placid night echoed the sound of each shoe splashing in the water as it landed.

Senses intensified by fear, Sherry could hear the snaps of the coveralls as they came undone, followed by the zipper. Shedding his clothes like a snake does its skin, Cummings pulled the bloodied coveralls down, turning them inside out in the process. The belt, with the sheath holding the murder weapon, was placed on the ground close to the killer's feet.

To remove any traces of evidence, Cummings splashed water on his chest. Sherry listened as the cold-blooded murderer squealed, then complained, "Goddamn, this water is cold! I should'a fuckin' waited till I got home. Shit!" A quick swish washed the remaining blood off his submerged hands.

He waded out of the water and used the coveralls to pat himself dry. Rolling the clothing up, he headed back to the car. The clothes were stuck behind the seat of the car as he climbed in. The only clothing remaining on Cummings was a pair of green swim trunks, which had been concealed beneath the coveralls.

The car pulled onto the main road and traveled in the direction of Cole County. Scared of falling asleep again, Sherry took measures to stay awake this time. She fixed her gaze on the white line painted on the highway.

Her intense concentration was severed when the white line abruptly disappeared from sight. "I wasn't thinking at this point, just watching that line. All of a sudden that white line was way over here, so I looked up and seen we was next to a bridge by the radio station in Atoka. I knew we wadn't far from home."

The driver's-side window was rolled down and the bloody clothing tossed into the high grass. Cummings pulled back onto the highway. Sherry immediately turned her attention back to the white line. Her eyes never strayed from it until the car pulled onto the narrow road leading to their driveway in Phillips.

When the Toyota turned into the driveway, Anita was sitting on the bed, absently staring into the darkness. Cummings flipped the light switch on, grabbed his jeans, and jerked them on. He slipped on a T-shirt, tossed a look Anita's way, and said, "Let's go. We gotta get rid of the couch."

Anita followed him out on the porch. Each of them lifted one end of the couch and loaded it into the back of Judy's truck. The tailgate remained down. The cushions were tucked up underneath the frame of the couch. Cummings pulled out of the driveway and started toward Centrahoma.

As he turned onto the main highway, he made the only statement of the entire trip. He turned to Anita and told her Sherry had killed Melissa. A tremendous look of relief flooded Anita's weary face. She was terrified that Cummings was going to kill her. The first thought that popped into her mind now was: *He doesn't just have something on me, but both of us. He ain't gonna try to just bump me off.* The assuaged woman knew if two wives died, there would be a lot more questions than if just one did.

Anita sat hugging the passenger-side door exactly as Sherry had earlier. Cummings grumbled and told her to move over by him. When she refused, he reached over, grabbed the inside of her thigh, and pinched firmly until she acquiesced.

A bridge right outside of Centrahoma was the spot he'd picked to dispose of the couch. The furniture was tossed jointly over the bridge into the almost dry creek bed. The frame tumbled down onto the creek's rocky bottom, breaking into pieces. Enough water trickled downstream to inch the cushions along. Slowly they began to float away.

Neither spoke a word.

Sherry sat in the rocker the rest of the night. She didn't get up once. She wasn't rocking. She just sat staring vacantly at the muted television.

Anita tried to fall asleep, but never succeeded. She had to work the 10 A.M. to 4 P.M. shift at Atoka Dairy Queen. At nine o'clock that morning, Anita, exhausted from no sleep, dressed in her work uniform.

Sherry got the kids up and fed them. The kids were loaded

in the car along with Sherry and Cummings. They followed Anita all the way to work. When Anita parked, Cummings got out and walked over to her. She would never forget what he said. "I'm taking Scottie with me to Oklahoma City. That's our alibi for today." She stared at him, and he warned her, "By the way, you get anything in yore head 'bout goin' to the police, you just better remember Scottie's with me. Ya understand me, girl?"

Anita understood. There was no doubt in the mother's mind he would kill her child if it became necessary.

Fourteen

By Saturday, September 7, 1991, Pat Cathy began to really worry about Judy and Melissa. Pat worked at the Dairy Queen alongside Anita. Concerned, she asked Anita if she'd seen or heard from Judy. Anita mumbled she hadn't. More to herself than anyone else, Pat commented, "That's not like Judy. We talk every day. It's not like her at all."

Pat even bravely confronted Jesse Cummings when he dropped by later that afternoon. "I said 'Something's wrong. Me and her have coffee every day' at her house. I'm getting real worried 'cause I haven't seen her.' " Cummings admitted to the worried woman that he hadn't seen his sister for a day or so, either. Worry consumed Pat Cathy even more. She continued to press Cummings for answers. Annoyed, he replied, "You're just worrying over nothing."

A pissed-off Cummings took Anita home and sat the women down to fabricate a story. "That nosy bitch is gonna cause us trouble. I guess I'm gonna have to report Judy and Melissa missing. Shit!"

The next day, tightly clutching photographs of Judy and Melissa, Cummings trotted off to the Atoka Sheriff's Department with Anita in tow. It was Sunday, September 8. A young woman, Janette Dodson, sitting behind the filing desk greeted them. Cummings approached the desk and indicated he wanted to make a missing-persons report on his sister and little niece.

He advised Dodson that friends had spotted his sister's truck parked near Atoka Lake on Highway 43. It was broken down. He emphasized the fact that the hood of the truck was raised and the doors left open. He spoke of his fears someone had picked up the mother and daughter.

A description of the clothes Judy and Melissa were wearing the last time they were seen was provided. Without prompting, he dutifully handed over pictures of Judy and Melissa.

Anita kept her back to Dodson the entire time Cummings talked. She never spoke a single word.

After the missing-persons reports were filed, Cummings went straight back home. He gathered the family around the kitchen table and advised them of the story they would tell when asked about Judy and Melissa. Anita and Sherry were to stick to the following story: "Anita was in her room asleep, because she had worked the night shift and had to go to work that next day. Sherry, you was in town."

Little Jessica was approached separately. Cummings pretended that they were playing a game. He reiterated to his daughter, "You heard a black truck, like the one owned by Judy's boyfriend. It roared out of the driveway, spitting gravel. You saw two heads through the back window. No one's seen 'em since. Got it?" Enthusiastically Jessica nodded her head and set about memorizing her lines by heart.

Jessica would have done anything or said anything to please her father. She proved to have an excellent memory telling the story without hesitation when authorities came around.

Jesse Cummings kept both his wives under an even tighter rein. If Anita stayed at the house, he would take Sherry and Scottie with him. If Sherry stayed home, he would make Anita and Jessica go with him. It was understood that if either woman tried to flee or call the police, her child was as good as dead.

Before dusk on September 9, Ada fire fighter Steven Lee and his wife, Elizabeth, decided to end Monday right. They arrived at Atoka Lake ready to relax and do a bit of fishing. As the couple walked toward the lake, they spotted a pond and decided to try their luck there.

Lee spied what appeared to be trash in the pond. As he got closer, he realized it was the partially submerged body of a female wrapped up in something.

He told his wife what he saw. Realizing they had just walked into a crime scene, the two stepped backward, moving cautiously and being careful not to disturb anything. They ran to the nearest neighbor and notified the Sheriff's Department.

By the time Atoka County sheriff Gary McCool and his deputy, Junior Head, responded, night was beginning to fall.

McCool, a big, barrel-chested man in his early forties, stood medium height. The dark skin he sported was courtesy of many hours in the sun. The sheriff, known for his dedication and hard work, was an amiable man in his second marriage. He had a son and daughter from his first one. When a case involved a homicide, policy dictated that the Oklahoma State Bureau of Investigations, more commonly known as OSBI, be notified immediately and brought on-site. Sheriff McCool placed a call to OSBI field agent Reanae Childers.

Reanae Hamm Childers's brunette hair framed a flawless complexion. Her deep brown eyes veiled the intelligence and intuition that allowed her to see into troubled souls and soothe them. In February 1990 Childers worked as a criminalist with the OSBI, using the skills she had learned earning her coveted bachelor's degree in chemistry. By necessity the young woman worked with many different and potentially dangerous chemicals. She wanted children, healthy children, someday. Concern about the effect the substances she worked with could have on her body prompted her to apply for an agent's position within the agency. Within a month after her application was submitted, she was accepted. She deftly exchanged career hats and was sworn in as an OSBI agent in the homicide division.

Agent Childers had put in a long and tiring Monday in Murray County, about seventy miles away. She was working security detail in the courtroom while notorious murder defendant Michael St. Clair stood trial. Because of threats received, the agents wanted to be cautious. Childers had invested weeks in the trial and was anxious to hear the verdict.

The strain and extended work hours had left the agent drained. On the lengthy drive home, she mentally went through a list of things that needed to be done at home. Her husband, Keith, a veteran police officer, matched his wife's personality well. The working couple had agreed when they first married that their partnership would be one of equality. In the spirit of that equality, they shared the household duties and cooking responsibilities.

Agent Childers served as an inspiration to many young women at the time as to how a good marriage runs well. She efficiently managed her responsibilities to the agency and her family, which right now consisted of Keith.

After a quiet dinner the couple retired to the living room to relax and watch a little television before going to bed. The peaceful quiet abruptly ended with the shrill ring of the telephone.

Agents with the OSBI are required to be on call twenty-four hours a day. The hours are essential because all homicides are handled by the agency. A knowing look passed between the couple as she reached to silence the noise.

Childers spoke softly into the phone to Sheriff McCool, then returned the receiver to the cradle. She quickly retrieved it and dialed the residence of Chris Dill, a criminalist for the OSBI. The two had paired with each other for security duty during the St. Clair trial. As the next agent on call, Childers would be the case agent in charge of this particular homicide. The conversation was short and to the point. Hanging up, the agent told her husband what he already knew—she had to leave.

As Childers drove toward Atoka Lake, Chris Dill, a young man in his late twenties, kissed his wife, Cheryl, and his baby girl, Chrissy, goodbye and headed out the door. Dill's chiseled good looks were surrounded by a shock of thick black hair. Tiny golden flecks braided through his coffee-colored eyes. As intelligent as he is good-looking, the criminalist had earned his bachelor's degree in chemistry at South Eastern Oklahoma State in Durant.

Dill and Childers had a long-standing friendship and were more like sister and brother than coworkers. The two understood each other well. Childers knew Dill's job inside out, and was aware that a criminalist could make or break a case. Her prior experience trained her to know an excellent criminalist when she saw one. Childers had no concerns when it came to young Chris Dill.

Dill pulled off of Highway 43 and encountered a dirt road, which he followed around to a smaller logging road. He pulled beside Childers's just-parked car. Dill's job, simply put, was to process the crime scene, collect the evidence, and take it back to the lab for analysis.

Stepping out of his car, Dill immediately spotted the body of a female floating in a pond near the northwest edge of the lake.

Sheriff McCool quickly filled Childers and Dill in on the missing-persons report that had been filed by Jesse James Cummings. From the physical description distributed in the report, it was a pretty safe bet the body was that of the missing sister, Judy Moody Mayo.

By now the sun had disappeared completely from the horizon. The darkness would require the difficult decision whether or not to wait for the morning's light. Both Childers and Dill were too experienced to even think about working a crime scene under the cover of night, where valuable information could easily be overlooked. Everyone agreed to return to the scene at daybreak. In the meantime an officer was assigned to protect the body and crime scene.

The most disturbing question for everyone working the crime scene was, If this was Judy, where was her eleven-year-old daughter, Melissa? The contemplation chilled them to the bone.

As Childers and Dill headed home, they both were radioed that a guilty verdict had been reached in the St. Clair case.

Michael St. Clair, a mass murderer, had been given a life

sentence without parole by the jury. Both Agent Childers and Chris Dill had spent two weeks at the trial, only to miss the verdict.

For Agent Childers, it would begin a chain reaction of missing key moments in the Cummings-Moody case, as well. Neither she nor Dill slept well that night.

As daylight broke on Tuesday, the agent and criminalist reunited at the crime scene. OSBI agent Dale Birchfield joined them on the scene to assist however he could. Sheriff McCool had returned with Deputy Junior Head to assist the agency with whatever was needed. Childers and Dill briefly talked to the two men, then set out to efficiently do their respective jobs.

Chris Dill began collecting potential evidence and looking for blood. As deputies on the scene aided Dill by doing the physical searching, Dill shot picture after picture of the crime scene. When he had used up his last roll, he poured a cast in the mud to trap the image of a tire track left close to the pond.

The wisdom and restraint shown by Reanae Childers and Chris Dill in waiting until daylight to process the scene, turned out to be an extremely prudent decision. "If we'd lost the tire track, we could've jeopardized the entire investigation," Dill explained. " 'Cause it turned out to be a key piece of evidence."

OSBI supervisor George McFarland arrived on the scene as the area was being methodically searched. McFarland, five-eleven, with hair just a shade darker than cinnamon, was of medium build. The supervisor, married and in his early forties, smoked incessantly. This case would cause him to up his normal daily consumption. As the supervisor, McFarland's job was to assist, give needed support, as well as technical advice. He managed to do so in a good-natured hands-off approach, stepping back to give the people under his charge considerable latitude to do their jobs. Today would be no different.

After tedious and laborious hours, one unpleasant task remained—removing the victim's body from the water. Bodies left in water tend to take quite a beating. The water turns the skin into something akin to wet newspaper. It's not unusual to have the skin literally peel away from the bones as attempts are made to retrieve it. The condition of Judy's body was disturbing, even for veterans. Judy's entire face was eaten away, as well as the fingers on each hand. Maggots had burrowed into her body.

After the processing had been completed, Childers remembers the heavy cloud that descended on the people who worked the scene. "We knew Melissa was either in grave danger, or worse, dead like her mother." An exhaustive effort to locate the child in the days and weeks to come would frustrate them all.

Everyone worked nonstop searching for a child they feared was already dead. Atoka firemen drained the pond to make sure it did not hide Melissa's body. Cadaver dogs were brought in for a search, which proved futile. Melissa was nowhere to be found. It was an arduous task, but everyone felt the urgency in trying to find the eleven-year-old girl, and everyone on the scene searched until they were too exhausted to go any farther.

When the close examination of the pond proved fruitless, the hardworking, dedicated firemen volunteered to go on a foot search for the missing girl. Agent Birchfield joined them. McCool and Deputy Head took out a boat and spent the better part of the day slowly prodding the pond and Atoka Lake for Melissa's body. The firemen fanned out to cover miles of acreage surrounding the pond. Although dead tired, they continued to search hour after hour, with little sleep or nourishment. The area, though extensively explored, yielded nothing. The search for Melissa would accelerate with each passing day.

Late in the afternoon, as soon as Childers finished processing the scene, she had the unpleasant task of notifying the immediate family. She asked Deputy Head to come along.

Deputy Junior Head of the Atoka Sheriff's Department was married and had children. The stocky, redheaded, fifty-something deputy's ruddy complexion matched his hair. Head's innately exceptional instincts merged with a lengthy career in law enforcement. He had been on-site most of the blaring, hot day. The deputy had lived in the area most of his life and knew the people of Atoka like the back of his hand. Deputy Head was considered a tremendous asset to the department. The agent knew that, and for that reason alone Childers asked him to accompany her to tell the family. His innate ability to reach people could prove helpful.

Deputy Head accompanied Agent Childers as the two left to break the bad news to the Cummings family. When told of the grisly find, Jesse Cummings hung his head in mock sorrow, then sighed as though his heart was broken. Sherry, Anita, and Melody, who had come out of the house to listen, started crying.

The street-savvy deputy was unimpressed with the drama playing out before him. From the day the missing-persons reports were filed, both Head and Sheriff McCool were convinced Cummings was behind the disappearances. McCool remembered with clarity when Cummings identified his sister's underwear. "I have a five-year-old, and I'm pretty sure I couldn't identify her underwear garments. Call it gut instinct. I felt from the first day that we found Judy's body that Jesse had done it."

On Wednesday Supervisor McFarland and Agents Birchfield, Childers, and Joe Holzendorf began a canvass. They started talking to neighbors, friends, and the family of the mother and daughter. A devastated Pat and Lisa Cathy were also interviewed. Reward posters appeared everywhere.

Childers visited the Cummings house again that Wednesday. She interviewed Anita first. Anita told the agent that she was asleep when Melissa and Judy left. She had been told that Judy and Melissa were seen "leaving with a man in a dark-colored pickup." Sherry was interviewed next. She told Childers the same story as Anita, except she added that the truck matched Gerald Sanford's, one of Judy's recent boyfriends.

The agent requested a recent photograph of Melissa from the family. She looked at the image she was handed, immediately struck by the lovely face that stared back. When the agent returned to her office that night, it was placed on her desk, where it would remain for the next three years.

A small tag-badge sporting Melissa's smiling face, which

was recovered from Judy's truck, was attached to the outside of Judy and Melissa Moody's file. Reminders of the sweet-faced eleven-year-old were soon scattered throughout Childers's office.

While the extensive canvassing was going on, criminalist Chris Dill, secluded at the OSBI lab, labored endlessly over the evidence from the crime scene, painstakingly searching for any clue to the killer.

Judy's bullet-riddled corpse was released from the medical examiner's office on Wednesday. Cummings paid the necessary visit to the local funeral parlor. A severely depressed Jesse, Sr., accompanied his son. On the drive Cummings told his dad, "We gotta get some money, and we gotta get some grave plots."

Startled at his son's use of the plural tense, Jesse, Sr., replied cautiously, "Well, let's just get the one for now, 'cause maybe whoever picked 'em up is still holding Melissa. Maybe she's still alive." The anguish of contemplating the loss of both his stepdaughter and grandchild could be heard in the old man's voice.

Judy's son Delbert was doing time in Lexington prison when his mother was murdered. Jesse, the "good brother," personally drove to the prison to speak with the warden. The warden okayed Delbert's temporary release to attend her funeral. He was to be delivered in shackles to his mother's grave-side service.

The funeral took place the next day. At the burial site, the cheap wooden casket's lid remained closed. The water had ravaged Judy's body so badly, it was unable to be viewed. There were no flowers or music. Longtime pastor to the Cummingses, Rev. Joe Lester preached a simple and short service. Pat and Lisa Cathy clung to each other, tears streaking their cheeks. Mr. Cathy stood beside his two girls.

True to its word, Lexington Prison delivered Delbert to Atoka for the funeral. Judy's son stood quietly with hands and feet shackled. Two deputies stood on each side of their prisoner closely guarding him, ready to whisk him back to Lexington the minute the service ended.

Another of Judy's sons, Henry, was present along with family and friends of Judy and Jesse. Since Jesse did not allow Anita and Sherry to have friends, they stood alone.

When the pastor said his final words and stepped aside, the atmosphere changed. Pat Cathy became disgusted with the crowd. "Everybody started laughing and carrying on like it was a ball game. I told my husband I had to get outta there. They didn't have no respect for her [Judy].

"Everyone eventually left to go over to Jesse's. I had heard Judy talk about her sister Debbie as caring and loving. I wanted to meet her, so I went to their house in Phillips. I asked someone to point Debbie out to me. I went over to her and said, 'Excuse me, Debbie, I'm Judy's friend, Pat. She was always talking about you.' "

Debra said thanks and reached to brush her hair from her face with her left hand. Pat couldn't believe what she saw. Judy's watch, the one that had belonged to her mother, the one she said she would never take off, rested around Debra's wrist. Pat and Debra's eyes met. Visibly uncomfortable, Debra quickly brought down her arm, excused herself, and walked off. Pat felt sick to her stomach and retreated to her home.

Coalgate sheriff Bill Ward attended the funeral. He watched Jesse Cummings and the women to gauge their reactions. "Jesse was just as solemn as could be. There weren't any tears from him, but the women showed emotion."

Sherry recalled the funeral, "It was hard on me and Anita. When it happened [the shooting], Anita wasn't Anita. It's hard to explain, she had tears and I could see the regret. I wadn't mad at her 'cause I knowed Jesse had said something to cause her to do it. I couldn't prove it, though. 'Cause she wouldn't talk to me, and I wouldn't talk to her." Cummings never even attempted to cry during the services. He kept his face an ice mask.

Shortly after his sister's body was found, Jesse, who never

asked anybody for anything, made the unusual display of asking Jerry Walker to borrow a horse to go looking for Melissa. Walker readily agreed and offered to go with him. The two men rode to Atoka Lake, searching the land for a sign of Melissa. When night fell, Cummings called the search off and the two men returned home. Pat Cathy has bitterly described another of Jesse's strange behaviors. "He started goin' around and collecting money to try and buy a headstone for Judy. That was just a bunch of bull. She never got a headstone, nothing to mark her place on this earth. So you tell me what he did with that money."

As the weeks went by, and Melissa was still not found, Cummings became bolder. He decided he better thoroughly clean the cellar to eliminate any possible evidence.

Just weeks after Judy's funeral, Cummings recruited Judy's son Henry to help him get rid of any potential evidence in the cellar. Of course, he didn't tell Henry that was the reason for the cleaning. First Cummings poured diesel fuel into the water to kill the snakes inhabiting the dank hole. Then he got a pump and pumped the water out. When the water got down to the rocks in the bottom of the cellar, he made Henry go down and kill any surviving snakes. When Henry had completed his assignment, he was ordered along with Anita and Sherry to go into the cellar and clean the rest of it out.

Sherry described the unpleasant task, "Jesse made us clean it out with ammonia and bleach. We had to scrub it, and I mean *scrub* it." A ring and bracelet were found resting on the concrete floor. Shortly before Judy's death, the cellar had been cleaned and swept out before recent rain filled it again. The jewelry had to be Judy's. The two pieces were turned over to Cummings, who acknowledged they belonged to his sister. They haven't been seen since.

Cummings would get a perverse kick out of laughing behind Henry's back, because the young man had unknowingly helped to destroy evidence of his mother's murder. Anita experienced revulsion: "Jesse really got off on that. He thought it was neat, here Henry had destroyed all this evidence and didn't even know he'd done it. I thought him laughing at Henry was cruel. But then Jesse was always cruel."

Sherry vividly remembered Cummings's warped attitude, too. "I thought it was disgusting that here he's having his own nephew, you know the woman was his mother, and he [Jesse] was having him clean up. Jesse thought the whole thing was funny, just hilarious."

Cummings was even brazen enough to actually visit Sheriff Ward at the Cole County Sheriff's Office and offer up leads. He told the sheriff what his theory was, as to what must have happened. According to Sheriff Ward, "His theory was this ole boyfriend messed with 'em."

Cummings relished laughing about his cleverness. In the weeks following Judy's funeral, he spouted off to both wives his scorn with the investigators working the case. He cornered Sherry in the bedroom and went on a diatribe of their total worthlessness, "These cops and OSBI don't know shit! They couldn't solve a fuckin' crime if it hit 'em right in the fuckin' face."

He would carry on to Anita, too. "Here's these two murders and they don't have a clue that there's a second one. Those idiots still think the second one's still alive." Cummings thought he was smart enough to beat them all. His last jab at the investigative body charged with finding Melissa was, "Cops are fuckin' idiots, or they wouldn't be cops!" He followed the insightful remark with a haughty laugh.

Within weeks of the murders, Cummings told Anita and Sherry if he ever got arrested he would get off because he had been in a mental hospital. Anita has qualified that disclosure. "I don't know that for a fact. I just took his word for it. And he had papers to prove he had amnesia. He said all he'd have to say was that he'd blacked out and didn't know anything that happened." Both gullible women believed him like the gospel.

While he was furnishing Ward with bogus leads, Cummings went hunting for a guy that had jumped bail. Sheriff Ward was astounded at his request, "First he wanted me to *deputize* him so he could bring this ole boy in for me. I told him I couldn't do that. Jesse says, 'Well, I might just bring him in anyway.' And, by gosh, he did bring him in—in *handcuffs!* I mean, he had me fooled 'cause he always seemed on the up and up."

As much as Cummings liked to rant and rave about the stupidity of law enforcement, he still loved playing cop.

Rubbing the stubble on his chin, Ward reflected back on this paradox. "The odd part about it was Joe Stalling—the sheriff when this happened—right off the bat says, 'Jesse Cummings probably done it.' I said, 'All right, what's his motive?' Joe said he didn't know unless Jesse wanted that little girl. I said I'd probably buy that 'cept he's got the perfect alibi. Joe come back that he don't know nothing about an alibi. He just got a gut feeling he did it. When the truth came out, he sure didn't hesitate to throw out the 'I told you so's' at me." The recollection made Sheriff Ward chuckle.

By the end of September, Cummings asked Darren Cooper to move in. Cummings told Anita and Sherry that it was better for all of them if they had someone in the house who could testify to their grief. Cooper witnessed a beating Anita received shortly after his move. The assault was so vicious, Anita's face was permanently scarred from the attack. The infraction that sparked the horrible beating was Anita's walking outside and leaving the children inside the house alone for a few minutes. Cummings pulled up in the driveway just in time to catch her standing out on the porch. He bailed from the car and started hitting her in the yard. Cooper just stood and watched the horrible beating. He didn't dare try to interfere with Cummings.

After the murders Sherry and Anita barely spoke. Anita was afraid to open her mouth, "If I talked about my past, I got in trouble. If I talked about things I wanted to do or anything besides the kids, I'd get in trouble."

Cummings continued to pit the two women against each other. No longer happy if the two just fussed at each other, he was only satisfied if they got into a fistfight.

Full of himself, he bragged to the women that he could talk them into anything. He reveled in the control.

One evening Cummings turned to Sherry and told her, "You know I got you right where I want you."

Sherry answered back, "Well, where's that?"

"Right on my front porch."

"The only thing on the front porch was the doormat. I thought to myself, Well I'm not really that low, yet."

Cummings continued, "I can get you to do anything I want."

A sparkle of defiance in Sherry reared its head and she responded without thinking, "You didn't get me to kill Judy."

"He got this look on his face and pointed his finger at me and warned, 'Your turn's coming up.' I didn't know if he was telling me I'd be put in the grave next, or if it was my turn to kill somebody next."

A week or so after Cooper moved into the Cummings house, Melody moved in with her two children, Billy, who would turn four in December, and Megan, who would be two in November. Cummings insisted that Melody move in for the same reason he had wanted Cooper to move in—more witnesses if they were ever needed.

Another woman in the house provided more fodder for the chaos Cummings thrived on.

Having more people living there meant sharing the same dirty bathwater over and over. Four children, Melody, Anita, Sherry and Cooper all had to bathe in the same water. No matter how rancid the water got, it was never emptied until it was Cummings's turn. He would get the fresh hot water, as always.

With each passing day, the search for Melissa intensified.

Several suspects were examined and reexamined as days went by, and there were still no signs of Melissa. Most of the officers involved knew in their hearts that the little girl was dead.

Cummings picked up three identical pocket notebooks at the five-and-dime. He called Anita and Sherry into the kitchen, where he dropped the notebooks on the table. He explained he would keep identical notes in all three, one for each of them. They were instructed to record every time the police talked to them and what they said. "That way when they come back later and asked us questions, he'd have the books to tell us what to answer," Anita explained. "Anytime we got questioned and weren't sure what we answered the first time [we were] to tell them we'd have to get back with them. Sometimes we'd ask them to come back later and then we were supposed to get with him [Jesse]. He would get the notebooks out and go over the answers of what we'd said."

The officers and agents could not believe it when they talked to Cummings and he pulled out the notebook. Before answering questions he'd say, "Wait a minute. Let me look at my notes." He didn't try to hide the notebooks when authorities were there.

But for Cummings, a creature of habit, the three notebooks were as logical as the notebooks he made the women use to keep their sexual activities and partners straight. It seemed a great way to him to keep them all on the same page. For Cummings, it wasn't much of a leap to apply the same logic to the activity of rape and murder.

Another favorite pastime of Cummings's after Judy's funeral was to speculate on where Melissa might be and who might have her.

The concerned uncle would tell all who would listen, "Well, she could still be alive. Maybe whoever took her is just holding her hostage."

Anita and Sherry's rehearsed remark to this line was, "Oh, my God. What is this person doing to her? She could be tortured or molested."

Cummings loved the game and followed up with his favorite line, "I'd like to be in a room alone with whoever done this." Anita would get a sick look on her face every time the sentence left his lips.

Cummings would take Anita off to the side and say, "Now you understand why I'm havin' to do this. 'Cause, if I'm saying this kind of stuff, they'll never think of us havin' anything to do with it. It's just a way of covering our own asses."

When he tossed out his "in a room alone with . . ." routine, Anita and Sherry would look at each other, both thinking, *Yeah, well so would we, buster.*

"The way he acted was sickening," Sherry has stated. "He knew if he talked about Melissa, me and Anita would start crying. He did it all for show."

Time only served to solidify Sheriff McCool and Deputy Head's belief that Jesse Cummings was the guilty party. The two officers worked endless hours on the case. McCool and Head traveled many miles with Agent Childers. The trio talked to people all over the countryside. They even ventured as far as Fort Smith, Arkansas. After the trip they were no closer to finding Melissa, or her body.

On Wednesday, October 16, 1991, just one day before Sherry's twenty-fourth birthday, Brian Wilkins found the skeletal remains of little Melissa Moody. The devastated man left the scene and called the Choctaw County Sheriff's Department.

Reanae Childers had put in hundreds of hours trying to find the little girl. She would miss this event, too. Because Michael St. Clair had escaped, she was called to Kentucky to help track the convict down.

In Childers's absence the call went to seasoned agent Chuck Jeffries. The middle-aged deputy inspector and his wife, Renee, a teacher, had two children. The dedicated and diligent agent worked out of the bureau's Antlers office, where the agency's only polygraph machine was kept. The expertly trained polygraph examiner possessed a keen perception and sensitivity, tools he relied on when his assigned task was ferreting truths from lies.

Pulling out of the Antlers parking lot, Jeffries traveled south to Highway 70, then west to Boswell, Oklahoma, to Highway 109A. Five miles down the highway he crossed the Twin Set Bridges over Clear Boggy River.

Parking the car, Jeffries climbed out and approached the

north side of the southern bridge. He climbed over the guardrail. His long face mirrored the dread of what he knew was waiting for him. The deputies on-site met the agent and led him carefully through the high grass and rocky terrain to a cement drainage culvert.

Jeffries observed the skeletal remains of what appeared to be a small female. The legs and torso were in the culvert. The head and shoulders were lying on the north side of the culvert twenty-two feet east of the guardrail. The body fat, muscles, and nerves were decomposed. The weather had leatherized the skin down to the bone.

The agent steadied himself as he took notes. The skeleton had been dragged about four feet north of where the remains now rested. The majority of the skeleton was intact except for one hand and both feet, which had been pulled off. Jeffries attributed the feet and hand torn from the body as the work of wild animals that inhabited the rural area as they scavenge for food.

The skull was the size of a child's, with a few strands of sunburned brownish long hair still attached. Jeffries noted the friendship bracelets encircling the left wrist. He recognized what they were immediately as he had two little girls. He took in a deep breath and shuddered as his mind recalled how his own little girls wore them. The sight struck way too close to home.

After a search by Boswell police officers and Choctaw County deputies yielded no clothing or further evidence, Jeffries began photographing the crime scene. After he clicked off the last roll of film, he steeled himself for his final task. Jeffries knelt in the dirt beside the remains of what was once a vibrant, loving child. Gently, he lifted the tiny hand, its fingers curled into a tight grip, and respectfully removed the four friendship bracelets that encircled the wrist bone. The last one removed and tagged as evidence was white with purple and gold twine interweaved.

On the drive home the agent felt suffocated, his lungs filled with sorrow, not air. An exhausted and emotionally spent Chuck Jeffries walked through his front door. He bent down as his children ran into his arms to welcome him home. The father's embrace lingered a few minutes longer than usual as he tightly held on to his own two daughters—daughters Melissa's age.

Fifteen

Late that Wednesday afternoon OSBI agents arrived at the Cummings house. When the car rolled to a stop, Jesse walked over to the agent's car. When he heard Melissa had been found, he bowed his head, took his hand, and covered his eyes to hide nonexistent tears.

Anita, Sherry, Melody, and Judy's son Henry wandered outside. Sherry sat down on the porch joining Mildred Tucker, who was already seated. Tucker, in an effort to comfort Sherry, told her, "Well, now it's all over with. We can bury her. We don't have to wonder if she's alive or dead." Sherry just looked at her.

Cummings got into the car as soon as the agents left and drove once more to the Atoka Funeral Home. A distraught Jesse Cummings, Sr., remained home. The arrangements were less bothersome this time. Cummings ordered the exact no-frills funeral he had given his sister.

Melissa's funeral was held the next day on Sherry's birthday. As the cheap casket lay under the green tent, Rev. Lester repeated the same simple ceremony he had for the child's mother. Most of the same people that had attended Judy's funeral were there for Melissa's—with one major exception. Lisa and Pat Cathy weren't there. No one had bothered to tell them. The next day they picked up the paper and in utter shock read that Melissa's body had been found. Lisa would never experience closure in her best friend's death because of the thoughtless disregard for her love for Melissa. Lisa placed the newspaper beside her on the couch she was sitting on and burst into tears.

The only time Jesse Cummings admitted to anyone what he did to Melissa that fateful night was about two weeks after her body was found. He ordered Sherry out of the bed to cook breakfast, then told Anita he wanted to play around. He took out the handcuffs and cuffed his wife to the bed, hands over her head, just as he had Melissa.

"Usually he had us spread-eagle and would tie our feet, but this time he had my hands cuffed way above my head," Anita recounted. "I was on my back and Jesse was on top of me. He started having sex with me, then he got real close to my right ear and whispered what he had done to Melissa the night she died. He told me about undressing her and playing with her, only he didn't put it that way. He used gutter language to describe his acts. This was such a rush for him and so exciting it overwhelmed him. The big boom for him came when he talked about slitting her throat. Usually Jesse had such an abnormal sex drive, he could keep climaxing during sex. But the violence drained him so much, he couldn't climax again."

When Anita heard the description of Melissa's murder, her first reaction, even knowing Jesse as well as she did, was to disbelieve him. He had told her that Sherry had killed Melissa. Anita fervently wanted to believe that story, because she was so relieved she wasn't in this thing alone. She had rationalized that it would be harder to make two wives disappear than one. There was always safety in numbers.

As night fell on Monday, November 4, 1991, Jesse, Sr., told the women good night and lay down on his fold-out bed in the living room. Anita remembered waking up, "Pop was having problems breathing, and Jesse wouldn't let me call an ambulance, saying he'd tend to him. So I went back to sleep."

"Jesse told us to leave him alone, he'd be okay," Sherry corroborated. The next morning when the women got up and started stirring around, they went in to see how Jesse, Sr., was feeling. Anita and Sherry jointly walked over to the cot. They broke down in sobs when the women saw that their father-in-law was dead. Jesse was sitting in a chair calmly rocking back and forth, staring straight ahead. He looked at the startled, crying women and simply offered, "He died in his sleep."

Anita and Sherry believed, as many other people did, that Cummings murdered his father by smothering him with a pillow in the middle of the night. Friends who had visited with Jesse, Sr., saw that he was clearly despondent over Judy and Melissa's murders. However, despite the depression and the cancer, he looked healthy and actually seemed to be improving some.

Sherry's reason for believing Cummings killed his father was insightful. "He wanted his dad dead because he hated him and just didn't care. I don't think at this point Jesse cared about anyone but himself. His dad and I had a very special bonding. Pops needed someone to talk to. Jesse knew we sat over morning coffee, just the two of us, and talked about everything in our lives. He was scared to death I'd tell his dad about the murders. He knew his dad well enough to know, scared or not, he'd go straight to the police. I think he was slowly eliminating the problems in his life, and me and Anita were next."

On Tuesday, November 5, less than three weeks after Melissa's funeral, Jesse Cummings was back at the Atoka Funeral Home to make arrangements to bury his father. He was becoming a regular customer for the burial business. His attitude toward his father's funeral was the opposite of when he buried his mother.

This was a hurry-up and let's-get-this-thing-over-with event. As with his mother, the day after his father's funeral, Cummings never brought up his name again. Both Anita and Sherry had grown attached to the old man and genuinely loved him. According to Sherry, "Anita and I would start reminiscing sometimes about Dad. When Jesse got tired of hearing it, he'd irritatingly say, 'Well, you can quit just about anytime now!' Jesse never showed any emotion over anything, other than anger."

On November 19, two weeks to the day after his father's death, Cummings celebrated his thirty-sixth birthday.

After Jesse, Sr., died, Jesse gave Sherry and Anita the order to find his father's estranged wife Joyce Denman and kill her. But Joyce, smart enough to know when to get lost, had gone into deep hiding with her daughter. A definite pattern was emerging for people around Jesse Cummings. There were a lot of people who knew a lot about his life, and they were dying. It appeared that Cummings was attempting to rid himself of those people whom he felt knew too much for their own good.

After the murders and following the death of Jesse's father, Anita and Sherry would suffer from almost unbearable guilt. Anita was the first of the two to try and take her life and end her pain. "I decided I can't do this stuff anymore. I can't live with this man. When everyone was gone, I took a handful of sleeping pills out of Jesse's black bag and downed 'em." Cummings got back before the pills could do any damage.

Sherry attempted suicide next. When Sherry returned home from work one afternoon, she was surprised to find the house empty. Not one to miss an opportunity, she decided now would be a good time to die. "I was just tired of living in those circumstances, and this was my opportunity to do what I needed to do with everyone gone."

She found Cummings's black bag and took out some nitroglycerin tablets. She held them under her tongue and let each one dissolve. "I started getting this really weird feeling. Then I heard a car door slam. I got scared and went onto the back porch and made myself vomit. Most of it came up, but I was sick the rest of the night." When Sherry ventured onto the front porch, no one was there. "I thought, heck, you could've been dead by now, you fool."

Despite Cummings having solicited donations to buy a headstone to identify his sister's resting place, Judy's grave was left unmarked. Right before Christmas, a concrete headstone was erected on Melissa's grave. Those who provided the marker preferred to remain anonymous. It is rumored that the volunteer firemen, who searched the woods relentlessly for the eleven-year-old, spending days away from their families, even searching on their days off, were responsible for the tribute to Melissa. The wooden plaque mounted on the front reads, "Melissa Marie Moody Born March 7 - 1980 Died October 16 - 1991." On any given day, visitors to Lehigh Cemetery can see the plentiful tributes to the little girl, where flowers and stuffed animals cover her grave.

Jesse Cummings was so successful in alienating and isolating the women, it would be years before they knew they were both thinking about killing their common husband. The strongest, lingering thoughts involved heavy consideration of ways to kill him. They just never realized each other wanted to kill him.

Sherry has talked about her various plots, "I thought about killing him a lot. I went as far as thinking which of the guns would kill someone quicker. At the time we had two .25s. We had a .22 which could switch from a regular .22 to a magnum .22. And we had a .38. One day I asked Jesse which gun would kill someone the fastest."

Cummings's sage advice to Sherry was that the best gun to kill somebody with was a .22 magnum. He told Sherry, "If you're gonna kill somebody, the best place to shoot 'em is in the kidney area or the heart." He never asked Sherry why she wanted the information. He volunteered she should never try using the .25.

Anita confirmed, "Yeah, he always preached to us that a .25 will stop somebody long enough for you to get away, and that's it."

According to Sherry, "I even convinced Jesse to let me carry the .22 magnum for a while, but I chickened out." For a while, Sherry fantasized about sliding the gun out from underneath his pillow and shooting him in the head. Or just reaching under the pillow. "I would lie beside him for hours and think about nothing but sticking my hand under there and blowing his brains out."

Unfortunately, both Anita and Sherry had seen Cummings get violently injured in a fight and still walk away barely scathed. He had been stabbed in the head, and shot in the back and leg with an exploding bullet. And still he walked home from the encounter. To his wives, Jesse appeared invincible.

"It was like no one could hurt this man." Anita paused in her recollection, then continued. "When I started thinking about killing him, I would stop myself and say, 'Okay, say you're actually lucky enough to hit him, what are you gonna do when it don't take him down and he's still standing there looking at you?' " Their fear assured Jesse's health.

Both women independently thought about putting poison in Cummings's food to kill him. He was prepared for that contingency. He started making the children eat from his plate before he took a bite, and take a sip from his glass before he drank.

. Anita explained, "If you made him something at night, he'd stand there and watch you make it. A lot of times he'd have you take a bite of the food before he would. He wouldn't eat any of it till we got the kids up to go to the bathroom. Then he would have one of them come in and take a bite of what we had fixed."

Jesse Cummings's abuse of the children in his care continued nonstop. One of his favorite punishments was to make the children stand in the corner. Sometimes the children would be allowed out of the corner to go to bed. The next morning they were promptly placed back in the same corner. Cummings sometimes would do this to a child for days.

If the children were being punished in the corner, and Cummings had to leave, the mother of the child being punished would rush over to the child and allow them to sit down and rest while the other kept a lookout for Cummings's return. If the mothers ever dared to interfere with the punishment or tried to get Cummings to stop, the children were hit twice as hard by him. He would tell them, "You're getting this one 'cause your mama butted in."

Cummings didn't allow pictures to be taken in the house, unless he was present. If anyone did, he or she would get in trouble. One reason he wanted to be around was to make sure no one was caught being punished. In the Cummings house somebody was always being punished.

If he ever caught Scottie, Billy, or Megan sleeping on their feet, they were in trouble. Scottie had been suffering devastating abuse at the hands of his stepfather ever since he was a one-year-old. He was made to stand in the corner so often that he mastered the art of falling asleep on his feet. Scottie became so good at it, he rarely got caught. Cummings began to watch the child like a lion in the brush waiting for his prey to make a mistake.

As Scottie started to slowly lean toward the wall, Cummings knew he had caught him. Cummings would jump up and whip the child across his back. At times he would actually wear himself out beating Scottie. The beatings were so frequent and so harsh it got to the point that Scottie could tolerate an enormous amount of pain.

But Billy was never able to accomplish that skill. The minute Billy fell asleep, he would start leaning toward the wall. Cummings would grab the tired child and spank him for falling asleep, then return him to the corner.

Anita has spoken about this. "If they couldn't stand in the corner right, he'd make them walk. If they couldn't walk right, he'd fill gallon jugs of water and make them carry it as they walked. We're talking little bitty kids. If they spilt the water, they got whupped. I'm not talking going in and take 'em over your knee and spank 'em. He would literally beat 'em, or he'd make us go in and spank 'em. And if we didn't spank 'em the way he thought they outta been spanked, then he'd go in and spank 'em and tell 'em they got the extra spanking 'cause we didn't do it right. Then he'd beat on us."

Other times Cummings would punish the little boys with the

water jugs by making them walk endlessly, but with an added twist. Sometimes he would sit on the bed with the bullwhip and pop them with it.

When Cummings was bored, he would sit down and watch the children eat. The bullwhip would be lying across his lap. He would tell the frightened children to hurry up and get through. He would also use the whip on the children if they didn't walk across the room fast enough to suit him. He would trail behind the offending child popping them on the feet and the back of their legs.

Cummings became a master at thinking up gruesome punishments for the children. Anita detailed a particularly horrible method of torture Jesse used on the children. "He used a cattle prod on 'em. You could see the little blue line go between the prongs when he touched 'em with it. If he thought they'd been lying to him, he'd make 'em stick their tongues out and shock 'em on it. He'd wet their hands or our hands because he said it shocked better. Jesse'd stick the kids with the cattle prod and then remove it a few seconds, then shock 'em again."

Their little bodies violently reacted to the cattle prod jerking with each shock.

Cummings liked to use medicine he had obtained from the veterinarian on the children. He would injure them, then spray "fly spray" on the injuries. The children would dance around and squeal as their skin burned severely from the ointment. The bright purple spray, designed to keep flies away from a horse's wounds, stung unbearably.

Cummings would also make the women and children scrub their arms raw. When he felt they were raw enough, he would pour straight bleach over the exposed wound. The children would scream with pain. Sherry remembered her reaction when he first did that to her, "I was gasping for breath, with tears running down my face, after he did it to me."

If one of the children accidentally wet themselves, they had to be taken outside, stripped, and hosed off with the water hose hooked to the kitchen sink. If there was snow on the ground and it was freezing, it still had to be done.

One night Scottie accidentally wet his bed. Cummings put him in a diaper and took his picture. He told the humiliated child that he was going to put the picture up. He promised Scottie that when he got in school, he was taking it to the school to show all his friends the big baby in a diaper. Then he would parade Scottie around in the diaper.

If visitors were in the house, he would make everybody talk about Scottie's terrible deed. Cummings would taunt him, "Well, don't Scottie look cute in that diaper?" The others present would go along with Cummings, agreeing with whatever he said. He would push the point, humiliating Scottie until the child was devastated and in tears. Scottie's face said everything. He wanted to scream and bash his fists into Cummings's face. His hatred for Cummings simmered like a volcano waiting to erupt.

One of Cummings's favorite pastimes involved abusing animals. The land he rented afforded the opportunity for him to keep various animals. The animals he abused the most were the horses that grazed the land. Anita and Sherry were trying to get a stubborn horse to go across a bridge one day. Anita recalled Cummings's solution to the situation. "He beat the daylights out of that horse and kept beating it till it went across the bridge. If he'd had to, he'd a killed that horse without giving it a second thought."

Sherry remembered a chilling scene between Cummings and a billy goat. He was keeping the animal as a favor for a friend. Sherry spied Cummings as he walked out of the house and headed to where the goat was tied up. She watched in horror as he aimed his pistol point-blank at the frightened animal's head and fired. He shot the animal simply to watch it die, then told his friend that the horse had stomped the billy goat to death.

Even mules didn't escape Cummings's cruelty. He would tie the helpless mules up with ropes secured high above their heads, leaving them with no way to reach food and water. They would stay that way until each of the mules had died. Their carcasses were taken down the road and thrown off the bridge one by one.

A mangy dog wandered onto the property late one afternoon obviously looking for food. The animal was pregnant and looked as though she would give birth any moment. Two days later she did deliver. Sherry and Anita both loved animals and convinced Cummings to let them stay. The women located a box and blanket and placed the puppies inside. Sherry located an eyedropper, and she and Anita took turns feeding the pups nightly with regular warm milk. Three nights after the pups were born, Sherry got up to feed them as she had the past two nights.

She noticed movement beside the box where they slept. As her eyes adjusted to the darkness, she saw that it was Cummings. She muffled a gasp when he took a knife from his pocket and slashed the pup's leg open. As soon as Cummings spotted Sherry in the shadows, he told her there was something on the pup's leg and he had cut it off. He then laid the injured pup down next to the mother instead of back in its box.

The next morning everyone searched tirelessly for the puppy Cummings had "doctored" in the night. When Cummings came out of the bedroom to find out what they were looking for, he coldly replied, "Oh, well, it was an injured pup, I 'magine the mother probably ate it."

By placing the pup next to its mother, who would be able to smell the blood, he had made sure the mother would devour her young pup that night. Cummings was an expert at devouring children.

Sixteen

Jesse Cummings liked to humiliate Jessica even more than Scottie. One day Jessica got in a fight with Billy, Melody Thompson's son. As the two went at each other in the yard, Cummings heard the commotion and ran outside. He started yelling at his daughter, who was losing the fight to a stronger, older boy. "If you don't whup his butt, little gal, I'll whup yours. Now get him," Jesse exhorted. Jessica tried until she was exhausted.

When she was knocked down for the final time, she sat in the dirt crying. Cummings walked over to her and spit out, "I don't like losers. Stay away from me the rest of the day." He looked disgusted as he left the sobbing child. After her daddy left, Jessica walked off crying and dejected. Thirty minutes later she came back up to Cummings and said, "Daddy, I'm ready to fight again. I'll beat him this time, just give me a chance." With an icy stare Cummings callously shot back, "You had your chance. Now get away from me."

Jessica shut her eyes as tears began to ooze in trickles down her cheeks. Then Cummings turned his back on the little girl as she sobbed for causing him such disappointment. But as his back turned on her, he smiled. He knew she would be a useful commodity for plans he had started formulating years before.

The various and sundry women continually rounded up and provided for Cummings were not enough to satisfy the unnatural lust in him. The man began devising a plan to kidnap an unsuspecting woman, perhaps a stranded motorist, and keep her chained in the cellar as a sex slave. He had been formulating the plan since the move to Phillips. A friend of Cummings's showed him a stun gun. He had never seen one before and was so fascinated by it, that the friend told him he could have it.

The stun gun seemed perfect to use on the unsuspecting woman to disable her. He could use it against her back, legs, or body in general. He would have to learn where it was most effective, how fast it brought the woman down, and how long she stayed out. The women in the Cummings household would do nicely for that purpose.

His voice dripping with evil, Cummings told Sherry and Anita he wanted to keep a woman in the cellar to use for his sexual entertainment. The plan was to use her for sex, any way and any time he wanted, until he impregnated her. When the woman came to term, Cummings would cut the baby out of her womb, then kill the woman and dispose of her body. He believed he could successfully remove the child without harming it. The baby would be claimed as his own.

The women in the Cummings household soon became unwilling guinea pigs. When Cummings got it into his mind to have a practice session with the stun gun, he would first select his victim. He walked over to her to catch her off guard and pressed the stun gun firmly against her body, zapping his victim with the powerful current. He did it so fast they rarely had time to see it coming. Then he timed how fast they went out, and how long they stayed that way.

Anita has described how the current felt. "It's like you got an electric wire and it's got a short in it and you don't know and it really hurts. Sometimes he'd just hold it there for a while. There was nothing you could do 'cause if you fought him, you'd just get it ten times worse. Eventually you just got used to the pain."

Once he used the gun on a naked-and-bound Anita. Out of curiosity he stuck the device on Anita's genitals and held it there. Anita thought she would die from the excruciating pain.

When she had to visit the doctor over the burn caused by the incident, the confused gynecologist asked Anita how in the world the injury occurred. Not knowing what to answer, Anita, embarrassed and humiliated once more, simply shrugged her shoulders.

Cummings also decided to practice cesarean sections. A lot of stray dogs hung around. Cummings encouraged them by supplying food. He would be needing them to practice on. The first time he operated on an animal, he chose a pregnant mixed-breed dog that had wandered onto the property.

Cooper was visiting the day Cummings decided to cut the puppies out of the mother. He ordered Anita, Sherry, and Cooper out of the house. Howling and yelping, the dog was laid on her back. Sherry was on the left of the dog's head, firmly holding down her paw. Anita was opposite, holding down the right paw. Cooper was instructed to hold the dog's head still so she would not bite Cummings in her kicking frenzy. Cummings straddled the distressed dog's back legs, with a knee firmly anchoring each hind leg. As Cummings flipped open his pocket, the women closed their eyes and turned their heads away.

He didn't bother to sterilize it before he plunged the blade into the animal and cut her stomach open. The poor helpless dog struggled and fought, bellowing from the atrocious pain. Cummings delivered four pups. After the delivery he used an ordinary needle and thread to sew the mother's stomach up. The dog got a bad infection from the unsterile conditions, but managed to survive the ordeal.

After the harrowing experience, if Cummings so much as looked at the animal, she snarled and bared her teeth poised to bite. It was clear she hated his guts. Other c-sections weren't so successful. Most of the time the animal died, either during the process of delivery or from an infection caused by the primitive and unsanitary conditions.

Cummings would hunt deer out of season. He would specifically search out every pregnant deer he could find. He would kill the mother, cut out the fawn, and take the newborn home.

Both Anita and Sherry were worried that Cummings was getting way too skilled at the deliveries.

When Melody Thompson moved in, Billy was used to saying anything he wanted. If he got mad, he would look at the women and declare, "Bitch, I don't have to do what you say." Cummings didn't allow the kids to cuss.

Billy's learned insolence was probably the reason he was punished so much. Billy had scars on his feet from where Cummings beat the little boy so much. He had ordered Billy to stand in the corner on his tiptoes as punishment from some perceived disobedience. If little Billy's feet or even his heel touched the floor, Cummings would flog the boy's feet without mercy. As a result, the child's feet formed blisters. Anita described the Cummings-inflicted injuries. "Billy had great, big blood blisters, and when they'd pop, they'd leave indentions in his foot. His little feet were permanently scarred."

Anita and Jesse's third wedding anniversary on June 14, 1992, was marked by the usual violence. Only this time Cummings was the target of the blows. He got into a vicious fight with another man.

According to Anita, here's what happened: "I'll never forget his name. Carl Sanders was the only man that Jesse wasn't able to whip. They started fighting over how Jesse had hurt Melody's kids. He stabbed Jesse in our front yard in the head with a knife, and Jesse was still getting up fighting. Jesse was wearing his head shaved at the time. The wound was deep enough that you could see his skull."

Sherry and Anita stood on the front porch and watched the fight as it progressed down the road. Sherry recalled, "I was sitting there telling Anita, 'I can't believe how he's getting beaten.' "

Anita picked up the story, "Jesse came running up to us and yelled to get his gun outta the bedroom. I calmly told him I didn't know where it was."

Sherry filled in what Cummings did next. "He came over to me asking where my gun was, and I told him in the bedroom somewhere. We were happy to watch him get the hell beat outta him. Finally Anita went in the house to pretend to look for the gun. He kept yelling at me to get the gun. I told him Anita was looking for it."

Anita finally came out with the gun and Cummings tried shooting the enemy, but the gun didn't work. He hadn't taken the safety off the gun. And both delighted women knew it.

Within ten minutes of getting nearly beaten to death, Cummings took twelve Percodan. He was feeling no pain. He grabbed Melody and beat her mercilessly.

Cummings's distorted reasoning figured it was her fault that he got beaten up. He had beaten Megan and Billy recently. Melody had shirked her motherly duties by not covering up the children's bruises properly.

When the kids got bruises from beatings, the women were instructed to put toothpaste on them to make them lighter, then cover the paste with baby powder to make it even lighter. Cummings always had them use a white toothpaste like Colgate. The women were instructed to put clothing over the injuries.

Every woman was to help—except for the injured child's mother. If a particular woman's child was beaten, she was not allowed to touch the child, dress him, or talk to him. If the mother was caught looking at or mouthing anything to the child, both would get beaten.

By now, Cummings had the welfare-agency drill down to a science. If someone was injured, he would send the child to spend the day at another house. If he got caught on short notice, he would make the mothers doctor up his victims to cover the bruises. If the children had bruises on the top part of their bodies, the women were instructed that when the welfare worker came over to check the child, they were to assist by pulling the child's shirt up or the child's pants down. The women were further instructed to pull the garment to the point where the bruises were not visible. Sherry remembered, "They never asked us to pull 'em any lower. Once in a while they would question the children."

Sherry and Anita started suffering severe anxiety attacks. During typical panic attacks the victims become frightened or overwhelmed, and their minds and bodies are forced to shut down. Their hearts pound wildly inside their chests, and they start sweating profusely. An attack can be totally debilitating to the people having it. Just hearing the sound of Cummings's car pulling into the driveway was enough to set off an anxiety attack for Anita. The intense feeling hit and felt like a hot spear tearing through her chest. For both women it was happening on a more frequent basis, keeping their bodies and their minds paralyzed by the fear.

Once when the women went in for a gynecological checkup, Cummings instructed the women to each steal a speculum. The women complied, placing the speculums into an extra large purse. Cummings would examine the women if he felt they had a problem, then he would announce his diagnosis and retrieve antibiotics from his black bag and order the patient to take them.

One time when he examined Anita, he decided that because she was red and inflamed, she should start a regular daily routine to help. He would make Anita fill a douche bottle with water mixed with horse liniment. "That was probably the worse thing I've ever done to my female organs, or that Jesse's done to them. You can't imagine the pain I felt. It burned ten times more than Ben-Gay. He'd watch me to make sure I did it, or have Sherry watch me if he couldn't. He'd get it from the pharmacy in the veterinarian department.

"He knew he was torturing me on purpose 'cause when I would put the liniment on his sore back, if just a little bit ran down and landed in the crack of his butt, he'd scream, holler, and throw a big fit." Anita would be forced to use the liniment at least once a month, sometimes more, until the day she was arrested. The only respite Anita would receive from this method of torture was when she became pregnant. Cummings stopped the forced treatments until after she gave birth. During this horrible experience, Anita perfected the art of blocking out pain.

She explained how she did it as such: "You dealt with the pain 'cause there was no way to stop it. I shut it out like when the murders happened."

Cummings's sexual games were extracting a heavy toll emotionally, as well as physically, on the women in his life, especially Anita. Anita started inflicting injuries on her own body to try to keep from turning tricks and to avoid sex with the man she now hated. She found by trial and error if she misused her birth-control pills, they would bring on uncontrollable and risky bleeding over a lengthy period of time. When Cummings sent Anita to the doctor, she "couldn't tell this doctor that I was making myself bleed so my husband wouldn't force me to prostitute. I just couldn't. I was so ashamed." It worked, but Anita would pay a terrible price for betraying her body.

Anita had once been a pretty, young woman, but the beatings had taken a toll on her. Once a lifetime ago, she had carefully done her hair and applied her makeup. Now those things were forbidden. After Anita's tooth was broken by Cummings, she became especially self-conscious. Every time a picture was taken of her, she would instinctively turn away from the camera or duck behind another person. With her beauty scarred and her spirit now broken, Anita showed no signs of the spunky, carefree girl from Arkansas. She had become a mere empty shell, with eyes that had slipped away from seeing anyone else's pain, even her own.

Seventeen

When Anita found herself pregnant in October 1992, she was beside herself. Nausea, having nothing to do with morning sickness, churned inside her stomach. She wept nonstop for hours. The last thing she wanted was another child brought into her disastrous marriage. When the familiar panic subsided, Anita would spend day after day trying to figure a way to get away from the monster she had married. Sherry was absolutely livid over it and blindly furious with Anita. A baby only meant it would be that much harder to leave Cummings. "I knew it was gonna take longer to get away, if ever." Jesse's ego misread Sherry's resentment and despair as jealousy over Anita being pregnant instead of her, and so did Anita. Sherry allowed both to believe what they wanted. Neither woman had the vaguest notion they were both thinking the same things throughout the bigamous marriage.

The further along Anita got in her pregnancy, the heavier Sherry became. "I's so miserable, and I knowed this baby would make it harder for us to get away. I thought long as I kept food in my mouth I couldn't say nothing and I wadn't gonna mess up and say something I'd get smacked over. When I ate, it let me feel like I was shutting it all out. I ate so much I couldn't fit in my clothes." Cummings warned Sherry to lose the weight, or else.

The abused women received no reprieves nor respites from Cummings's beatings. The battering took place even in front of company. He beat them in front of anyone who was in the house at the time he went into a rage. Terrified to interfere, the company would just stand there and watch, or turn around and leave.

Anita recounted an especially brutal beating she witnessed Sherry get. "We had some people over, and got angry over something and drug her by the hair into the bedroom."

Sherry continued the story, "This particular night Jesse kept beating me and beating me until I was crawling on the floor. I was bruised from my rib cage down to my knees. My arms was black and blue. When I was on the floor, Jesse'd kick me with his steel-toed cowboy boots."

One of his kicks landed on Sherry's knee tearing the ligaments and permanently damaging it. As Sherry cringed in pain, Cummings kicked her in the ribs again. "He told me to get my ass back up. It was either get up and take his fist or open hand, or stay on the floor and get kicked in the face."

Anita was terrified that night. "I was sitting in the living room hiding behind two of his friends. If Jesse came out of that bedroom, I didn't wanta be in the line of his eyesight. With Jesse, it didn't matter that I hadn't done nothing. Many times he'd come out of the bedroom from beating one of us and go to the other one and say, 'You stupid, fuckin' bitch!' And smack, you got backhanded across the face."

One of the men visiting told the other one to go in and do something. He rapidly replied, "Nope, don't think so. I'd rather it be Sherry getting the shit beat outta her than me." The beatings were so bad, and occurred in front of anyone, that the only time Anita or Sherry felt safe in anyone's company was when an agent from the OSBI was there to follow up on the investigation.

After a year of practice, Cummings became quite adept at doing c-sections on farm animals. He decided to go to the next step and have the women accompany him to hunt down a victim.

Practice runs in order to perfect his plan started. Anita and Sherry were ordered alternately to go along on the hunt. While driving around the countryside, Cummings would often brag about murders and rapes he had committed.

Whenever Cummings hollered for one of the women to go with him in the car, they shook from the time they got in the car until they arrived back home. His targets were women stranded along the highway with car problems or a flat tire. Once he spotted his prey, he would slowly drive by her, then pull up a ways. He would instruct whichever woman was with him, to walk back to where the stranded motorist was. If no other adult or child was with her, the women were to offer the victim a ride.

Knowing women would trust other women, Cummings reasoned Sherry or Anita would be much more successful in capturing a woman than he would. Sherry remembered the horrifying rides. "Every time we left, I'd get deathly scared 'cause I didn't know if today was the day he'd find a victim or not."

Many times Sherry and Anita would climb out of the car praying Cummings wouldn't back up as they approached the woman. Their assignment was to check out the victim, make small talk, then head back to the car.

Anita and Sherry would always lie when they returned from talking to a potential victim, telling Cummings the stranded woman had someone with her. They dreaded the day he saw through their lies.

In March 1993, less than five months after Anita learned she was expecting Jesse's child, Agent Childers, who had developed a good rapport with Anita, also found herself pregnant. It would be her first child and she was thrilled.

She made a point to stop by the Cummings house as often as possible. The rapport established between Anita and Childers strengthened with the common bond of motherhood. During and after the respective births, the mothers would chat and look at baby pictures. A slow but steady trust began to build between Anita and Reanae Childers.

On July 12, 1993, Jesse Cummings's second child was born. He demanded that the little girl be named Chelsea Marie. However, always the head strong one, Anita signed the birth certificate before Cummings had a chance to get to it. The new little girl's name was Chelsea LeAnn Cummings, and she was beautiful.

"After Chelsea was born, I started back taking the birth-control pills to make me bleed so Jesse couldn't put me on the street. And I kept my ass in the hospital having surgeries. At least for a few weeks after surgery, I didn't have to dread his sexual advances." Anita became an excellent opponent playing games with Cummings. "I breast-fed Chelsea, so I'd go to bed at ten o'clock 'cause I had to get up with the baby." As soon as the women got the children in bed, Anita would say she was going to bed, too.

Sherry, trying to accommodate the new mother, told her, "All right, go ahead. I guess I'm gonna have to stay up with Jesse." Anita would continue to disable herself to avoid sex with four major surgeries. "I had my tubes tied, I went in and had my tonsils taken out. Then I had bladder surgery and reconstructive surgery on my female organs."

While recuperating from the surgeries, Anita had no medication to help with the pain. "Jesse'd go pick up my pain pills and he took 'em himself. He wouldn't let me have a one." As soon as Anita started healing from one surgery, Cummings would say, "In a couple of weeks we can go back out on the streets."

Anita would rush back to the doctor's office getting the next thing taken care of.

For the past two years, Agent Childers had very little activity on the murders of Judy Moody Mayo and Melissa Moody. She had interviewed everyone possible. Reanae Childers knew if someone did not come forward, the murders had little chance of being solved.

Whenever she had a few extra minutes, she would go back over leads in the case file. She made a point to stop by the Cummings house as often as possible. Jesse Cummings hated it with a passion when the agent came to the house. Childers was confident and smart. Cummings did not intimidate her in the least.

Anita and Sherry liked her for the very same reasons Cummings did not. Perhaps, worst of all, he had absolutely no control over her whatsoever. He never saw fear in her dark eyes.

After the murders, the beatings accelerated more with each year that passed. It increased for the children, too. Immutable fear overwhelmed the lives in the Cummings household. They could not sleep, eat, or relax because of Cummings's unpredictable terroristic behavior. Sherry recounted the brutality that kept getting worse. "You get into a daily routine, and the beatings become such an everyday occurrence. There wadn't one day that went by I didn't get hit or Anita or the kids."

When one woman was getting battered, the other went off to another room as far away as possible. Sherry maintained, "I never did cry physically. I mean, I did inside, but I'd go like in the kitchen and stand there and say, 'God, if you're really here, don't let this happen.' "

By this point Anita had lost all faith in God. "I'd given up saying get me outta this. I'd say to myself, 'He ain't here. There ain't a God.' "

If there was a lot of screaming and hollering going on, the children would cry, sometimes they would pretend to be asleep and almost always they would clamp their hands tightly over their ears as a barrier to keep their mothers' screams from invading them.

At first young Scottie would scream at his stepfather, "Don't touch my mommy! Don't touch my mommy!" Eventually he stopped screaming. He stopped crying. He would sit and watch in silence as his mother was beaten senseless. Finally all expression in the little boy's eyes vanished, replaced by a cold, blank stare that became more distant each day, until one day the blank stare was replaced with pure hatred.

Eighteen

In the fall of 1993, Jesse Cummings began sexually molesting Melody Thompson's daughter, Megan. She was not yet four. Anita observed Megan playing with her doll. "She was complaining her boo-boo hurt, which was her word for her private parts. She was sitting with a doll and had taken her fingers and was hitting the doll through the legs. I picked up the doll and asked her where on earth she saw that. She told me, 'Daddy do it to me. That's why my boo-boo hurts.' I pulled down her shorts, and her little butt cheeks were bruised. Megan didn't know her real dad, so she called Jesse her daddy."

Megan's real father was Henry Moody, Judy's son and Jesse's nephew. Anita quizzed the child about when her daddy did this thing to her. Megan told her, "When you were gone."

The night before, Cummings woke Anita up around eleven o'clock. "I'd already went to bed and he told me to take Melody to the hospital in Coalgate. He said she had sprung her ankle somewhere around two o'clock that afternoon. Sherry was in the living room wide awake, yet he came in and woke me out of a dead sleep knowing I'm gonna be up with the baby in about an hour. I'm thinking, it's pouring down rain; the only vehicle we have is a standard; Sherry is in the living room awake and she don't have to feed a crying baby at three o'clock in the morning. What's wrong with this picture?"

Anita has asserted that he picked her to leave because she

would have caused him so much grief if she had found out what he was doing to the toddler.

Sherry already knew that Cummings was molesting Megan. "I caught him out in the barn with her. It was just a few weeks before this. There's a back room in the barn, where Jesse'd hang and skin illegal deer. There's no door there. He had Megan inside the barn. She was stripped naked and he was fooling around with her. He didn't realize at the time I'd seen him. Megan wasn't crying. She just stood there real quiet. Megan knew better than to cry 'cause she'd seen us beaten over it."

Cummings saw the back of a shirt as Sherry turned and left. Melody was the first one he confronted after the assault. He talked to her, and when she answered that she had not been outside, he went to Sherry. "Jesse told me I'd better keep my mouth shut. I told him I didn't know what he was talking about."

Anita sent Megan inside and went to confront Cummings, who was in the outhouse. "I jerked the door open and said, 'Jesse, I wanta ask you a question. Are you playing around with Megan?' You could see he was guilty as sin. At first Jesse tried to say it was her real dad who molested her. I said, 'She ain't around her dad.' Then he told me to go get Sherry. I don't know what he said to her, but she went back in and called Megan into the bedroom. Sherry asked the little girl why she was lying on her daddy. By the time Sherry was done, she had Megan telling me she'd lied on her daddy. Sherry told her, 'If you'll tell mama Anita the truth, you won't get in trouble. But if you keep lying, you're gonna get in trouble.' So, immediately Megan came to me and said she'd lied. I knew better, though. I'd done seen what he'd done to Melissa, heard what he wanted to do to other children. But I didn't bring it up no more 'cause I knew Megan would just be punished for it." When Melody walked up on the porch, an angry Cummings turned on her, shaking his finger in her face, and warned her, "Get your damn daughter's story straight. Right now!"

On December 23, 1993, Reanae Childers gave birth to a dark-haired boy, Zachary. After she returned from maternity leave, she stepped up her visits and dropped in to see Anita as frequently as she could.

Cummings told Anita he wanted to adopt Scottie so that if anything ever happened to her, Scottie would legally be his. The idea that Cummings would adopt out of love the little boy he had perfected acts of torture on was laughable. Anita knew his motive was solely to collect Scottie's SSI disability checks. Once the adoption was approved, he could eliminate her and continue to earn money off of the little boy.

Anita's suspicions that Cummings was planning her death grew even stronger once the adoption proceedings actually started. She knew the real reason he had started the adoption proceedings, and it scared her to death. When the adoption agency visited, they told Cummings there would be no way they would approve the adoption as long as he stayed in a house ready to be condemned.

Cummings liked to play mind games with his wives. He would watch for an opportunity and strike. Such an incident happened one night to Anita. The children were to be in bed by nine o'clock every night without fail. One time when it was Anita's turn to tuck the children in, she busied herself with the task. While she was in their room, Cummings turned the kitchen clock back an hour and ten minutes. Sherry watched him do it but was too scared to warn Anita.

By the time Anita emerged from the bedroom, it was in reality close to ten o'clock. Jesse flew into a rage saying, "Why in hell are the kids in bed? It's ten minutes till nine." Anita quickly glanced at the clock on the wall watching the second hand jerk silently as it worked its way around. She planted her foot firmly in a defiant stance, placed her hands on her hips, and told her husband the clock was wrong. The two began to argue. Anita rebelliously pointed to the television, which had just started to broadcast the ten o'clock evening news to prove her point.

Failing to consider the effect her words would have, she shouted, "You're crazy. The news wouldn't be on if it was ten minutes till nine, Jesse!" Cummings hated to be challenged, especially by a woman. Simultaneously the thought caught up with the effect, and Anita turned to run. Cummings quickly grabbed Anita by the hair, pulling her back to him, then violently pushed her backward over the couch. His left hand wrapped in a tight grip around Anita's throat cutting off her screams and denying her air as he choked her. He jammed a screwdriver he had been holding in his right hand deep into Anita's side. As the weapon was plunged in, she fought to keep from screaming. She knew it would prove to be another sleepless night for the troubled children in the next room.

Yanking the weapon out, and waving the bloody screwdriver in the air, Cummings admonished the weeping woman who was lying on the floor curled in a fetal position, with her arms wrapped around the injury, to never question him. Sherry observed that "Anita would mouth off, and Jesse had this tendency, he knocked you down 'cause he wanted you to be down and stay down." But the impertinent woman would get back up, and Cummings would hit her again. Anita's independence almost got her killed several times around Cummings.

Anita started working at a wood shop in March 1994. It was located in Atoka minutes away from Phillips. A woman named JoAnn and her little brother Mike befriended Anita not long after she started. When Anita came to work with visible bruises, they tried to talk her into leaving Cummings, promising her they would make sure she was safe. But, then, they didn't know Cummings.

Anita was accustomed to his constant spying. "When we'd go to Dairy Queen, I'd be totally scared to death that Jesse would see me with this girl going to lunch instead of driving my pickup by myself."

Joann asked Anita what she and Jesse did for fun. All they did was watch television. They never went out to eat. "The only time we ate out, we'd go to Taco Tico or McDonald's, but never to a restaurant."

Anita and Sherry would plead with Cummings to let them go to a movie. He said no. They begged him to let them go to the carnival when it came to town. He said no. They appealed to him to let them go to the skating rink. He still said no.

Cummings didn't like the changes he was seeing in Anita. He started sitting outside the building where Anita worked. He'd stay there all night watching Anita's every move with a pair of binoculars. Then he would tell Anita everything she did at work. He kept Anita under surveillance because she was talking about leaving him. Sherry had been working for a while, too, at the local Pizza Hut. "Every day Jesse was there watching me. He'd come in and tell my boss he needed to talk to me. He'd stand behind the 'Please wait to be seated' sign. I'd go over there and he'd say, 'Who you talking to?' I said, 'Jesse, I'm just doing my job.' He said, 'Well, that better be all you're doing.' Then he'd demand to know who I was talking to when he came in. I said, 'Jesse, he's just a customer.' He'd say, 'Yeah. I know what kind of customer you want him to be.' Then he'd turn around and leave."

Cummings started looking for a second house after he was informed by the adoption agency that the Phillips house was unacceptable. He started looking for a house with more modern facilities.

By the end of May he had located a house that would do in nearby Lehigh. It was run-down, too, but was a palace compared to the Phillips house. The rent was one hundred twenty-five dollars a month, five times as much as he paid for the house in Phillips.

As required by law, a formal announcement of the adoption proceedings was printed in the local newspapers to serve notice of the event to any and all interested parties. People who knew Jesse Cummings had two wives promptly reported the fact to the agency. The agency called Cummings to tell him that reliable sources had informed them he had two wives. He was issued a choice. He could drop the proceedings or obtain a divorce from Sherry. He told Sherry he would be filing a sixty-five-dollar uncontested divorce the next day. Infuriated over the additional cost he was forced to incur, he angrily made it very clear the divorce was a mere technicality. He had no intention of letting her go anywhere. Freedom would elude Sherry. Things would remain as they always had.

Cummings's willingness to spend money and jump through bureaucratic hoops served to fortify Anita's growing fear regarding the adoption.

Before a particular visit from Child Welfare, Cummings had savagely beaten Billy's feet. The child was exhausted from standing in the corner on his tiptoes for hours. Because he did not stand on his toes just the right way to suit Cummings, Jesse continued to beat the child.

His mother, Melody, didn't bother to check the child's injuries nor treat them. They got infected and his foot started decaying from the neglect. By the time Sherry and Anita realized how bad the injury was, it was too late to hide Billy from the prying eyes of Child Welfare. Billy was propped up in bed with his foot on a pillow when Cummings learned of Child Welfare's impromptu visit. He had to hustle, but in less than twelve hours he had relocated Billy to another town, with Anita to take care of the injured boy. Melody took a horrible beating because she had not properly attended to Billy's foot. This particular flogging took place in the Lehigh house. Child Welfare had barely pulled out of the driveway when Cummings started beating Melody. He was so enraged, he almost killed her during this assault. He slammed Melody's head through a kitchen window and viciously kicked her in the ribs which were severely damaged. After he threw Melody through the window, she went down to her knees. In a mindless frenzy, he kept kicking her with his boots over and over. He wound up accidentally kicking her into Sherry. "I was trying to clean a pig for dinner, and he's slapping and kicking her all over the place and right into me. He just kept on kicking her until finally she stopped moving. It took her a long time to recover from that beating." At least six people witnessed the horrible scene.

Cummings's part-time girlfriend Vivian and her male companion stayed in a small trailer parked in the yard of the house in Lehigh. He had a second trailer out back that Cooper used. A third thirty-six-foot travel trailer was parked around the back.

Depending on his mood, Cummings would sometimes make Melody and her kids stay in it. Since he still was paying rent on the Phillips place, he would have different people switch from the trailers to the Phillips house.

Cummings was letting Anita keep forty dollars a week out of her check. "This is the first money I'd ever kept out of any of the money I've earned to put gas in my truck and buy supper and stuff. This was the first place I'd worked that didn't supply my meals for lunch and supper. All the other places I worked, like Wal-Mart, it'd all been fast food. So there was no need for me to have money. Jesse'd put gas in the car and I'd go to work." It was so bad around Cummings, that Anita spent almost eighty dollars in a three-week period on bottles of Mini-Thins. "They only cost five dollars a bottle. I was taking a lot."

By mid-July, Anita was at the end of her rope. "At that point I was ready to be killed. I couldn't take anymore. Jesse was either gonna just kill me and get it over with, or I was leaving. When I started thinking about dying, I started thinking about Scottie and if he kills me he's gonna have Scottie, and you ain't gonna be able to protect him at all." The internal battle that had raged so furiously, for so long, inside Anita would be settled soon.

PART THREE

Nineteen

On July 22, 1994, Anita accompanied Jesse Cummings to Durant to pick up groceries. During the silent drive she thought hard about her life and the tunnel of wasted years filled with emptiness, regret, pain, and the terrible guilt she felt over what she had done to Scottie. Anita decided she was living a life she had long ceased to care about. As Cummings pulled into the store parking lot, Anita reached a decision. She would take her children and leave Cummings. There would be no turning back this time. She would tell him as soon as they began the drive back home. Her heart pounded so fast and furious at the thought, it felt as though it might explode inside Anita's chest at any moment.

As they started traveling the forty-minute journey home, Anita somberly told Cummings she was leaving him. In her voice a finality existed that she thought had been lost forever.

They fought about the point all the way home. He kept telling her it wasn't going to ever happen. She kept insisting it was. The car pulled into the driveway. He turned off the ignition. There was no movement—just stony silence that was broken with him finally screaming at her she was not going, and her screaming back oh, yes, she was.

Voices irritated from the tirade that had been going on almost nonstop all the way home fell silent again. Cummings calmly turned to Anita and issued a final ultimatum, "Well, what's it gonna be?"

Anita reflected back. "He always threatened me about hurting other people if I left him. He'd threatened my family, I don't know how many times."

This time he threatened more. "I'm gonna go down to that job of yours and waste every person at that shop."

Anita looked at Cummings as if she hadn't even heard him and replied matter-of-factly, "Well, when we get these groceries unloaded, I'm packing my shit and leaving."

Voices mute, they unloaded the groceries. Anita started gathering up her things to show Cummings she meant it this time.

As fast as she gathered up an armful of her belongings, Cummings would jerk them out and fling them across the room. The two argued back and forth the rest of that afternoon and into the night, with Anita finally saying, "You told me if I was unhappy I could leave. I want to leave and I'm leaving."

Cummings countered, "Oh, no, you're not. You're not getting outta my sight!"

With those words, he hurled the telephone at Sherry. She was instructed to call Anita's boss and tell him she wasn't going to be able to work the next night due to personal reasons.

Anita spent a restless night lying next to Cummings. Her mind was in such turmoil. Perhaps she had gotten two hours' sleep before the sun started shining through the windows.

Monday was spent in silence, with Cummings and Anita virtually ignoring each other. Around noon a desperate Anita mustered enough courage to talk about leaving once more. She'd had all she could take. More and more women were coming into the home with their children. The chaos around Cummings kept swirling faster and faster, sucking Anita farther and farther down. But it was the adoption papers that Cummings had filed on Scottie that had Anita so desperate and determined for them to escape this time. She tried reasoning with him, begging him, lying to him. Nothing worked. He was just as adamant no one was going anywhere.

Anita had tried everything. Her nerves, already severely frayed, began unraveling at record pace as she continued to listen to Cummings's threats. With a different certitude Anita came to a decision. She, Scottie, and Chelsea were leaving one way or another. Anita had decided she had nothing to lose by taking Scottie and Chelsea and fleeing. If they were all gunned down before making it to the car, she consoled herself that they would be freed from their life of utter despair, hopelessness, and resignation. It would no longer exist. The horrible, physical agony and suffering would no longer exist. Dead people feel no pain. The three of them would be out of this living hell and in a heaven that is real with an all-powerful God, who would strike the mighty Jesse Cummings down, protecting them eternally. There would be no backing down this time, for any reason.

But as always, Cummings's diabolical mind was way ahead of Anita.

As Anita headed out of the door with an armful of clothes, steeled with a new and unyielding resolve, she came to a dead halt. Putting one foot over the doorway, she froze in her tracks as Cummings yelled out, "It's 'bout twenty-five feet to your car. I tell you what, if you can make it there before I shoot you, I'll let you leave." Oh, my God, Anita thought, he's not gonna give me the chance to get Scottie and Chelsea before he kills me. With those words Cummings had taken away any hope of Anita and her children escaping, dead or alive.

If he killed her when she took another step, as she knew he surely would, she would be free, but she would leave behind what mattered more than life itself, her babies. Scottie and Chelsea would be there existing in a life full of indescribable pain. Cummings wasn't about to kill Scottie because the adoption would assure him an income from her son's SSI and disability checks. Alive, Scottie was worth money, and that thought scared Anita more now than all the years put together that she had spent afraid Cummings would kill Scottie. The thought that his continued torture without her around to afford him some measure of protection forced her to do what she had vowed never again to do. She turned around, walked back in the house, headed straight to the bedroom and, feeling helpless to ever escape the madman, threw herself on the bed and wept all the way down to her gut.

Monday night she did not sleep, even though she cried herself into a complete state of exhaustion. When she heard the door open, she knew Cummings was coming to bed. The rest of the night would be spent quelling her cries so she wouldn't wake him up, and brainstorming to think of a way out.

Most of the next morning was spent with Sherry and a couple of the other women in the kitchen. A couple of Cummings's friends were working on cars outside.

Anita sat on the couch starting to cry again, and still trying to think of a way out of her situation alive. When Cummings came out of the bedroom, he headed outside to talk to his friends and avoided looking at Anita's sullen face. He heard Anita make a remark as his hand touched the screen to go out. He turned around and stared at the insolent woman. Anita and Cummings immediately starting arguing like a ping pong ball back and forth, "I'm leaving!" "Oh, no, you're not!" "I'll call for help!" "Oh, no, you won't!" Furious, Cummings picked up the telephone and hurled it at Anita, telling her to go ahead and call someone for help. He would kill them when they got there, make her watch, and then kill her. He exploded. He'd had enough of this shit! He jerked Anita to her feet and dragged her into the bedroom, where he raped her as she fought to keep him off.

After the rape Cummings called Sherry into the bedroom where he had Anita sequestered. He told her to take all adults to the house in Phillips to spend the night. The reason Sherry was to give was that Welfare was coming out the next day, and Cummings didn't need a bunch of women and kids around. When everyone was gone, Cummings approached the terrified Anita. He got his gun from under the mattress, and the terror began.

He shoved Anita down on the bed. He held both her hands together above her head with one of his. Then he placed the gun against her temple and threatened, "I ought to just take everybody here out. Take you out, the kids out, Sherry out, all of 'em." Anita knew without doubt the man was crazy enough to do just what he said he would.

The ordeal continued to escalate. Sometimes his violent behavior would escalate, and then he would settle back down for a while. But then he would start terrorizing Anita more. He laid his head up against Anita's. Her heart started pounding as he told her, "This .38 is so fuckin' powerful I could lay my head right here by yours, side by side, pull the trigger, and it'll go through your brain and mine, too."

Anita was ready to let him get it over with. The flesh was weak, but the spirit stayed strong. Scottie and his safety kept her holding on by a very slender thread. "When I thought of my baby, that's when I started begging Jesse not to kill me. I tried to calm myself by thinking, Okay, you stay and you'll figure out something sooner or later, and you'll be able to get yourself, Scottie, and Chelsea outta here. I told myself this over and over while Jesse was holding a gun to my head."

Sherry got back from taking everyone to the house in Phillips. She walked into the scene and saw the gun held to the head of the panic-stricken, sobbing Anita. Self-preservation came first in the Cummings family, so Sherry slowly backed out of the room and retreated into the living room.

Sherry rounded up the kids, fed them, bathed them, and then sent them off to their rooms, where Anita's screams, which were terrifying them, might not be heard as easily.

At one point Cummings tried to drag Anita out of the bedroom. Her body was numb, but her mind heard him say, "We're gonna go for a ride and neither of us is coming back from it." Terrified he was going to take her out, kill her, and dump her body, Anita, who thought she had no strength left in her body, fought so hard to hold onto the mattress she broke almost every fingernail.

Cummings raped Anita again.

For hours Anita begged for her life unrelentingly, while the gun was constantly being held to her head, and Cummings lay on top of her.

While Anita screamed and begged for her life, Sherry tried to just stay out of the way. "I was all over. Just nervous, walking, cleaning. I done the cleaning. I dumped the coffee out of the pot. I cleaned it, filled it up, made new coffee. I was shaking. There was some kind of stuff stuck on the counter, and I was shaking and digging at it with a knife. I almost cut myself. I was sick to my stomach with nerves. I dropped a couple of plates and shook as I picked up the pieces. I was shaking so hard I almost dropped 'em again. I was terrified that Jesse heard the racket and would beat me. I thought that night would never end."

Anita did not expect intervention from Sherry. She was doing exactly what Anita would have done if the roles had been reversed.

But they weren't. She was the one being held hostage at gunpoint by this lunatic, while the kids were in their beds asleep or pretending to be. They loved their mommies but they knew the self-preservation rule, too. Both women had known that the majority of the time they checked on their kids in the past, they were pretending to sleep. The children were too scared to sleep, and the noise coming from their mothers was sometimes horrific. They had playing possum down pat.

Anita completely understood the concept of pretend sleep. "I have faked sleep more in the last five years when I was married to him [Jesse] than I did in my whole life."

After holding his horrified wife hostage for hours, Cummings got off her and stood up, the gun positioned at his side. Anita's throat was raw from screaming and begging for hours for her life. She promised him anything and everything.

He told Anita to get up and go into the living room. He instructed her to lie down on the couch. Because he hadn't put the gun down, Anita still didn't feel safe.

Sherry disappeared into the bedroom with Cummings and surfaced in only a few minutes. She told Anita that he wanted her to sleep in the kids' room on the extra mattress kept there. Melody usually slept on it and Sherry or Anita would sleep on it if Melody was in Cummings's bed for the night. Anita, happy to be alive, obeyed and immediately went to the kids' room. Chelsea, only one year old, was curled up sleeping soundly on another mattress. As Anita pulled the covers around her, Scottie rolled over and reached down to hold his mother's hand. He asked her if she was okay. The terrified boy had heard the whole thing. Worst of all, Scottie knew he could do nothing to save his mother's life.

Scottie, now almost six-years-old, could no longer be protected from serious abuse. Anita whispered to her son, "If I was ever to leave Jesse, who would you want to go with?"

Scottie quietly answered without hesitation, "I wanta go with you."

"Don't say anything to your daddy," Anita whispered to her son.

Scottie looked at his mother sadly and whispered back, "Mama, when I get older, I'll take care of you. I'll never let him hit on you no more."

The light shining in the hall gave Anita a glimpse at Scottie's eyes as he spoke. "It was a look like—I hate to say this, but it was like looking in Jesse's eyes 'cause Scottie had that cold, blank stare.

"I told him I was okay. Then I told him, 'If your daddy catches us talking, we're gonna be in big trouble. So you need to roll over and go to sleep and be real quiet 'cause you don't wanta get in trouble.' " Scottie rolled over and closed his eyes.

Anita turned over and thought to herself, I gotta get these babies out of here.

Sherry came into the room. Cummings stood in the doorway. Sherry picked up Chelsea, now lying by her mother. Anita asked what was going on. Sherry responded, "Jesse wants Chelsea." Anita, not seeing Cummings in the doorway, asked Sherry where he was.

She was shocked to hear his voice respond, "I'm right here.

Whada you want?" Anita nervously explained she was just wondering, that was all.

Sarcastically he advised her, "Don't worry about where I'm at. You better worry 'bout yourself."

Chelsea was taken and placed in her playpen in the living room to sleep. Cummings deliberately placed himself between the baby and the front door. There would be no way Anita could get in there, get the baby, and leave. He had made sure of that.

Anita didn't sleep that night, either.

On Wednesday morning Cummings roughly hauled Anita up from the mattress on the floor and took her to their bedroom. She could hear Sherry preparing breakfast. He threw Anita on the bed and raped her again. When he was through with her, he told her to get dressed. He informed her he was taking her to McAlester to a place called Scrap Corp. Cars that have been junked are taken there for scrap money. He would drive Anita's pickup. She was instructed to drive an old, beat-up bus, which was to be scrapped.

Before they left, he directed and watched Anita as she took all the guns out of the house and put them in the trailer. He had already unloaded them before she awoke. There were several rifles, one or two pistols, Anita's .25 and Cummings's .38. One weapon had a scope on it. Anita referred to the cache as Jesse's own mini-arsenal. He had a large toolbox that stored a large variety of knives. Cummings was always well armed.

After locking the guns up, Cummings followed Anita to Scrap Corp. Money exchanged hands and he told Anita to get in the truck. The unpredictable Cummings began to frighten Anita as he drove farther into the country. The petrified woman finally worked up the nerve to ask, "Where are we going?"

Cummings responded, "I'm just looking around." He finally pulled up beside a creek bed in the middle of nowhere, deep in the woods. He ordered Anita out of the car. She got out, sure that this was where he intended to kill her. Another car pulled up with fishing gear in tow. Visibly agitated, Cummings told her to get back in, they were leaving. He drove farther down the road and stopped at a pond and ordered her out again.

The terrified woman got out. Cummings told her he was going to try to find a baby deer he had seen run across the road. Anita managed to choke out that she hadn't seen the deer. He assured her he had seen one and told Anita to help him find it. Anita's gun was stuck down in Cummings's back pocket. They walked deeper into the woods. He kept urging her to walk in front of him. As she hesitated, not wanting her back to him, he angrily pushed her in front of him and told her to move.

According to Anita, "About that time, he looked over to one side of him and there was a man in hunter's orange walking across the field by the pond. Jesse said we were gonna have to leave, that there was somebody out here. So we left. If there was ever a time I didn't believe in guardian angels, I do now."

The two went home. Anita was faced with a painful but imminent decision that afternoon. She knew Cummings was plotting her death. She steadied herself for what she was about to do. Years later, Anita's voice still quivered as she told of her plan. "I decided the only way I was ever gonna get out of that house, was I'd have to make him believe we was fine. You know, make Jesse believe after all this that I wasn't ever gonna leave and everything was fine between us. It took everything I had to convince him of that. *Everything* I had. We was standing in the bathroom, and I approached him for sex. I knew that afternoon, that Wednesday, I had to make him think everything was fine. That was just something I knew."

During her marriage to Cummings, the hope he had offered her had become utter despair; love had become absolute hatred; and lovemaking was just sex, and it had been since the first time he prostituted her.

"The only thing I could think of to make him think everything was okay with me was to make him think I wanted sex, 'cause I'd been avoiding having it with him for some time. I figured the only way I'd get the babies and me away from him was with sex. And that's what I did. And it worked. That's the only reason we're still sitting here alive. I mean, I felt so dirty. But I used everything the man taught me about being a prostitute to be able to stomach it."

Sherry remembered talking to Anita that day. "Before she made up with Jesse, I was in the kitchen with her telling her she was gonna have to do something to keep our family together. I knew that if things kept on going the way they was going, Jesse'd wind up killing one of us or both of us, and maybe the kids, but I didn't tell that." Cummings had successfully been able to keep the women completely distrusting of each other.

Anita's instincts were right. Fooled by the impromptu sex, Cummings did something he rarely ever did. He let his guard down. He informed Anita a few hours after the encounter that he had decided to let her go back to work. She could start back tonight he told her. Finally someone had managed to outscheme Cummings.

The ruse worked well, but Cummings was not completely convinced Anita wouldn't leave. He instructed Sherry to go with Anita to work and ask for a job. If they wouldn't let her start that night, she was to return home.

Sherry got in her car and pulled off after Anita. "We took off and went up to the highway by Mable's Bar and Al's grocery store in Lehigh. I pulled out on the highway and my speed was about twenty or twenty-five miles an hour. Suddenly the whole axle wheel came off the car. I started to panic. I remembered Jesse telling me if anything happened how to steer the car off the road. I managed to get my car off the road without wrecking it. Anita was right behind me. She pulled next to me and I was shaking inside out. I grabbed my purse and keys. She told me to get in the truck and we'd go back to the house."

Jesse had managed to keep the women so estranged that when the axle wheel fell off, Anita thought she was the one that was going to be killed by Sherry. As Sherry shook getting into the truck, Anita shook just as badly behind the wheel, they mistrusted each other that strongly.

"Jesse was sitting on the porch with a couple of friends, and we got out of the truck and told Jesse what had happened. He had this smirk on his face. I felt they'd rigged it up for me to wreck and kill myself. Then Anita and Jesse'd go to the police and say I did the murders and they'd go free. It took me a long time to convince myself Anita had nothing to do with the wheel falling off."

Anita's luck was still holding. Cummings, pissed off about the axle, shrugged off his earlier condition that Sherry go to work with Anita and keep an eye on her.

That night at work Anita finally broke, and for the first time told an outsider about Cummings's abusive behavior. She told her friend JoAnn about her night of terror. JoAnn ranted to her little brother, Mike, "That idiot held a gun to her head for three and a half hours." They both told Anita she wasn't going home.

Anita told them they didn't know what they were getting into. "They thought this was a case of Jesse beating on his wife, trying to make her stay. Nobody knew the extent of the murders, and I'm, like, 'People, you don't know what y'all are dealing with here.'" Mike told Anita she needed to go in the office and talk to Eddie. Rev. Eddie Fields owned the shop and had pastored his own church for years.

Anita initially refused. Fields was a friend of Cummings's, and that put him in the category of a potential threat.

At the meal break Fields came back and told Anita, "I know something's wrong. Do you want to talk to me? You know I'm a preacher. I know you weren't at work last night for personal problems. Is it something I can help with?" But Anita was still on her guard.

Fields pursued the matter. "If you two wanta talk or get counseling, I'm a marriage counselor."

Anita thought, Yeah, right. She told him Cummings would never agree to counseling.

Fields walked off, and JoAnn approached her friend. "Anita, you're gonna have to trust someone." Anita was so dejected she just shrugged her shoulders and walked away. None of them understood what kind of man she was dealing with.

Fields approached her again. "Anita, we can take you to Dallas tonight. I know people who'll hide you out, and then we'll worry about getting your kids later."

Anita quickly responded, "Oh, no! I've got to get my kids out tonight before he knows what's going on."

Anita, who hadn't had a cigarette in five years, except for the one she smoked after killing Judy, smoked one pack in thirty minutes to try and calm her nerves. As they talked, Anita's heart pounded in her chest. She told her coworkers, "You don't understand. He'll kill them kids."

"What makes you think he'll kill 'em, 'Nita?" JoAnn questioned.

"Y'all don't know everything. He'll kill those kids, and I know it!"

At the end of the meal hour, JoAnn assured her friend if she needed a place to stay she was welcome to stay with her. JoAnn shared with Anita her own personal experience with battering.

Shortly after the break, Fields called Anita into his office. "Anita, what makes you so sure Jesse won't let you leave, and leave alive?"

"Because he's got stuff on me, and I know stuff on him, and he's not gonna let me go."

Fields softly asked, "Well, I have just one question, Anita. Does it have anything to do with his sister and his niece's murders?"

Anita's heart was racing as she took a deep breath and exhaled the word, "Yes." At this point Anita knew she had gone too far to back out. "If I'd not left that night and went home and he'd gotten wind of me talking to them, I can assure you we'd all be dead."

Fields called his wife, Diane, into the office. She started calling around in the middle of the night trying to locate Agent Childers. Anita felt she could trust Childers only. "She was a woman, first of all, so I felt I could trust her. And we'd formed a friendship during the investigation. We'd both been pregnant at the same time and talked a lot about our pregnancy. I didn't trust no man, period. Well, I trusted Eddie 'cause he was a preacher. When I answered his question about the murders, I thought, well, it's now or never. You can trust him and you might get out alive, or you can not trust him and you know you're gonna die. Or you can trust him and he'll tell Jesse and you will definitely die. All this stuff was going through my head with that one question."

Diane began intensely searching for Reanae Childers. Continuing her streak of unfortunate luck, the agent had left for vacation only a couple of days before. The Childers recreational vehicle loaded down with her son, her husband, and her parents, was on its way to New Mexico.

When Diane proved unsuccessful in locating the agent, her call was routed to an agent by the name of Perry Unruh. Agent Unruh detested homicide work and all it entailed. He had transferred to car theft to avoid it.

It was almost three o'clock Thursday morning when the phone rang. After the fourth ring Unruh stirred and then grumbled in the direction of the incessant ringing. Forced out of bed, he snatched the offending receiver from its cradle. Thoroughly irritated at the early-morning intrusion, he muttered, "What?"

The police officer on the other end of the line caught the ire in Unruh's voice. "Sorry to bother you so late, but we got a woman here who says she's gotta get her kids away from her husband tonight."

Unruh stretched the sore ligaments in his bum leg and barely managed a polite, "OSBI doesn't do domestics." An impulsive thought raced through Unruh's mind before he could sit back down on the bed, *You idiots!*

The officer on the other end answered apologetically, "Well, really that's all I got."

Perturbed at the totally unnecessary invasion into his sleep, Unruh responded as nicely as he could manage, given the hour, "Well, you can handle it, so just handle it."

As the agent placed the receiver down, he thought, Geez, the woman just needs a damn escort. This is ridiculous.

Agent Unruh chuckled when reminded of the incident. "Reanae gave me holy hell over it when she got back. And I do mean—holy hell!"

Failing to reach Agent Childers, Diane Fields started calling the surrounding police agencies, except for Cole County, where Anita lived and Sheriff Bill Ward was in charge. Every agency she talked to said the same thing, Anita would have to go to Coalgate. Anita told Rev. and Mrs. Field that wasn't happening.

Frustrated, Diane Fields woke judges up throughout the county that night. They told her there was nothing they could do. Anita would have to go to Coalgate because proper jurisdiction was where the kids were.

Diane Fields told Anita, who was now in tears, that Sheriff Ward would be called into the office to come talk to her. Anita balked emphatically, "No! Y'all get Bill Ward in this and I ain't coming in!"

After hours of bargaining, Anita was eventually worn down and said she would go to Sheriff Ward's office. But she was not happy about it. A police escort was arranged to take Anita on the twenty-minute drive from Atoka County into Cole County.

Anita was terrified during the drive. None of the police agencies had been told they were dealing with a double homicide. All they thought was that they had a simple domestic matter.

When Anita arrived at the sheriff's office, Undersheriff Tom Griffin greeted her. Still, Anita did not mention the murders, continuing to let them believe this was a domestic matter. Griffin told Anita, "Look, we'll just send Welfare out there with you and an officer."

Anita panicked and yelled, "No! I ain't going out there!"

Griffin pursued the matter, "You gotta go out there. We can't get anything done unless you do."

Anita was standing at the booking counter. She vehemently repeated, "I'm not going out there!"

Griffin reiterated, "All we know to tell you is you're gonna have to go out there with us. We'll send Deputy Norman Cummins. There's no other way."

She kept pleading with them that she couldn't go back to the house.

Marcie Lambert, Coalgate's police chief, walked over to the hallway, where she stood and lit her cigarette. Anita was relieved that a woman was there. Finally, after much inner debate, Anita turned to Diane Fields and whispered, "Well, the only way anybody's gonna get those kids out of the house and all of us, even half of us get out alive, is if they know the whole story."

Diane nodded her head in agreement.

Anita walked over to the bench in the hallway near Lambert and sat down. Tom Griffin was leaning on the wall across from her. Anita took a deep breath to quell the storm roaring in her stomach, then blurted out, "Jesse made me kill Judy. I'm confessing to Judy Mayo's murder, and I'm telling you right now Jesse was behind all of it. He made me do it. He was behind Melissa getting killed and he raped her, too." Startled at the speed with which the words tumbled out of her mouth, Anita took a breath, then said, "Now, will y'all go get my kids before that crazy motherfucker kills 'em?"

Lambert and Griffin looked at Anita. Both were in shock. They knew the case Anita was talking about, and knew it well. They were also aware the double homicide had remained unsolved for three years. Griffin walked to the doorway and hollered at the dispatcher, "Call Bill Ward and tell him to get down here right now. We just got a murder confession."

Because Cummings never had a time schedule, and no one ever knew where he was, Anita worried all the way into town. She was keenly aware that Cummings had sat across the street only a couple of nights ago with a pair of binoculars and spied on her. Anita never knew where he might be at any given moment.

The very next statement out of Anita's mouth concerned her false accusation three years ago. "I told 'em that I lied about the policeman beating me up and asked if they would find him and tell him how sorry I was, and that Jesse made me."

From there, the story is picked up by Sherry. "Jesse'd left earlier that morning between four and four-thirty. I had no idea where he went. He didn't say nothing, just got up and left. And you didn't dare ask Jesse where he was going."

Sherry had gotten little sleep the last two nights because of Jesse and Anita's constant fighting, trying to delicately balance staying out of his way and finding out what was going on.

Cummings returned shortly before five. Sherry had developed the gift, or curse, of knowing every time Cummings moved and every time he left and returned home. Sherry had the tendency to stir at any kind of movement, inside or outside. "I was terrified of Jesse. He slept with a gun under the pillow that laid on top of his stomach, and another one under the pillow his head was on. I knew anytime he could wake up and shoot us and it wouldn't faze him one bit. Whenever I closed my eyes, I knew it could be for the last time, too terrified to go to sleep. I lost so much sleep that I couldn't get in a car without dozing off. That's why I fell asleep when Jesse was driving Melissa into the woods. The only reason I think I didn't have a nervous breakdown was 'cause I knew if I did flip out, there'd be nobody there to take care of the kids."

It was six o'clock when Deputy Norman Cummins and Deputy Rick Dunkin stepped up on the Cummings porch. Jesse Cummings was lying on the couch with his gun. The children were in their room. Chelsea was in the playpen in the living room. Cummings whispered for Sherry to get out there. "Jesse told me there were cops outside and it freaked my mind." Sure enough, as she crouched beside Cummings, Sherry saw the beam of a flashlight shining through the windows unobscured by curtains.

Cummings looked at Sherry and asked, "What the fuck did you do? You got on that fuckin' phone while I was gone. Didn't you?" He pointed his gun straight at her. "You stupid, fuckin' bitch."

Sherry was confused and terrified. She figured if they were coming to arrest Jesse, he'd probably shoot her before they even made it through the front door. Sherry realized that Anita had not made it home, and Anita was always home no later than five-thirty in the morning. Cummings made sure of that. He would set the alarm for six o'clock each morning, and if Anita wasn't home, he would go looking for her.

The moment Sherry was thinking it, she heard Cummings's voice stating the thought out loud. "Well, maybe Anita's had a wreck."

Cummings wasn't worried about Anita going to the police because he reminded her daily that if she turned him in, she would fry, too. After all, she pulled the trigger. Sherry worried him much more than Anita because she was the least culpable of the three.

Deputy Cummins tapped on the window with the flashlight in his hand. Although Anita had forewarned them about Cummings's arsenal of weapons, both officers' guns remained holstered.

Cummings opened the door. Cummins and Dunkin stepped inside. As Deputy Cummins put it, "I put on the 'good-ole-boy shuffle,' telling Jesse, 'Hell, I don't know what's going on, Jesse. Anita had a nervous breakdown or somethin' and was screaming for them to come get her kids. She was crazier than hell, hollering about her kids, not making a licka sense.'"

Dunkin retrieved Chelsea from the playpen while Cummins went into the back room and got Scottie. As they carried the sleeping children away, Cummins turned back to Cummings and told him to come down to the sheriff's office later that morning, and he was sure by then the whole thing would be straightened out.

A few hours later, Cummings and Sherry dressed. They put Jessica in between them and pulled around back. Cummings let his daughter out and told Melody Thompson, who was staying for the moment in the trailer to mind her. Then he headed toward the Cole County Sheriff's Department.

On the drive into town Cummings turned to Sherry and said, "You know what's going to happen today." Sherry shook her head. Cummings yelled, "You stupid bitch!"

Nervous and antsy, Sherry misunderstanding him sheepishly replied, "Jesse, I can't help it if I didn't get an education."

He scolded, "You don't think about nothing."

Sherry surprised herself when she shot back, "Well, I've got you to do that for me. Don't I?"

He looked at her and announced, "We're going to jail 'cause you and that conniving little bitch told."

They bickered all the way into town, him accusing and her steadfastly denying.

"He knew he was going to jail and he drove himself right there," Sherry said astonished at the thought. "I'll never know why Jesse didn't run."

As they pulled into the parking lot, Cummings warned his wife, "You might as well just get ready, 'cause when we walk in that door, they're gonna handcuff you. They're gonna stick a gun in your mouth." He got the response he wanted. Sherry looked terrified.

While waiting in the parking lot for Cummings, the sawed-off shotgun clutched in Norman Cummins's hands was discreetly held at his side. Cummings pulled up to Cummins and asked what was going on. The deputy replied, "Hell, if I know, Jesse. Go down and ask the sheriff. I'm backing you all the way, partner."

Cummins walked behind the pair, and two deputies joined them. One walked on Sherry's side and one on Cummings's as they entered the back door of the sheriff's office. Cummings placed his hands on the counter and asked the sheriff what was going on.

Deputy Dunkin was behind Sherry. Sheriff Ward just looked at Cummings. Norman Cummins broke the silence, "Jesse Cummings, you're under arrest for the murder of your sister, Judy Moody Mayo."

By the time Cummings got out the words, "You gotta be kidding me," Tom Griffin had taken his gun from his holster, stuck the Beretta in the small of Cummings's back, and commanded him to get down on the floor.

Dunkin pulled his gun and held it on Sherry. One of the deputies continued to hold his gun to Cummings's head. The other officer placed his knee in the small of Cummings's back, and both quickly took him to the floor. Up until now, Cummings had been the one who placed handcuffs on his victims. This time, a metal pair was quickly snapped around his wrists as they were held behind his back.

Sherry stared down at her husband. The only thing she felt was enormous relief. Sherry was politely asked to lie on the floor. Two deputies eased the compliant woman down. A female officer present asked Sherry if she could take her glasses off so they wouldn't get broken. Sherry nodded and they were removed. They seized Sherry's purse.

Deputy Dunkin has stated, "As soon as she heard the words, 'Jesse Cummings, you're under arrest,' this look of tremendous relief flooded her face."

Anita, Sherry, and Jesse Cummings were immediately separated upon the arrests. Anita, for the time being, was to remain in Coalgate in Cole County Jail. When she was told a few hours later about the arrests, she asked the officer to tell her exactly how Cummings's arrest went. When she heard her nemesis was taken to the floor, and a gun held to his head, Anita savored the image.

Remembering her foray with Cummings holding the gun to her head only a day before, Anita slapped her hand against her knee and told the deputy, "Damn, I'd like to seen that. I swear, I'd a dropped to my knees, gotten right down in his face, and asked, 'Well, Jesse, how does it *feel* to have a gun to your head? How-does-it-feel?' " As the officer walked away, Anita felt the clamor of a foreign sound swelling within her as it ascended the dark place it had been deeply buried and rushed to the surface, spewing from her mouth. Laughter raced down the hall after the deputy as he headed back to his station. It swiftly caught up with him, and he smiled.

Twenty

By that Thursday afternoon Jesse Cummings had been transferred to the Atoka County Jail in nearby Atoka, where he was booked for capital murder.

Sherry was delivered to McAlester in Pittsburgh County by OSBI agent Charlie Mackey. Mackey was a tall man in his forties, a fact betrayed only by the scattering of a few gray streaks throughout his dark hair. A longtime member and high-ranking officer of the Army National Guard, Mackey had a rare ability. He was the type of guy who exuded an empathy that people around him found endearing. Additionally, his laid-back attitude was conducive to creating an atmosphere where anyone felt comfortable enough to let their hair down. Conversely, his empathetic nature could be instantly extinguished, replaced by a cold, stiff, harsh, regimented one, most likely fostered by his extensive military training.

An excellent illustration of this dual ability was demonstrated when Mackey escorted Sherry to the jail in McAlester to be booked. Sherry was reserved, trembling as if she were chilled during the lengthy drive. Mackey made small talk during the trip to settle the frightened woman's nerves. She never spoke during the ride. Once they arrived at the McAlester jail, Mackey escorted his prisoner to the booking room. The empathetic agent stood beside Sherry as support, while she was Mirandized a second time. When the reading of her rights was completed, a caustic Sherry defiantly and sarcastically spoke for the first time, "I'm not saying a damn thing." The empathy the agent had felt for her seconds earlier instantly vanished. Austerely turning toward Sherry Cummings, who he had so delicately handled moments earlier, Mackey stared straight into Sherry's eyes and, with a voice as cold as ice, declared, "Book her on capital murder!"

A female deputy dumped the contents of Sherry's purse on the counter and began to log its contents. Property item number 8 was Sherry's key ring. Sherry identified each key on the ring for the deputy, except one. She remembered seizing the lost key and quickly slipping it back onto the key ring, escaping a beating like Anita had received a day later when she could not account for a missing key from her ring. The key Sherry could not identify belonged to Anita.

David Cathey, the young, good-looking trooper who had been present during the investigation of the Cummings shoot-out with a pimp at the end of 1990, became an OSBI field agent a couple of months before Anita turned herself in. Agent Cathey worked closely with Agent Childers from the moment he started working for the bureau.

Childers remembered their initial pairing. "We don't have partners, per se. It's just that David and I knew each other and had been friends before he came to work as an agent. We basically partnered ourselves off." Assimilation in part for new agents consists of them reading other agents' case files to observe how reports should read and learn to effectively write their own. Cathey immediately took a real interest in this case, partly because a little child had been brutally murdered. Although the agent did not have children, he loved being around them.

Childers took the neophyte agent around, allowing him to watch her do interviews, and letting him do interviews, as well.

Cathey can well remember his introduction to the Cummings case. "The file was massive. There were so many examples of reports in there. It was perfect for me to study well-written reports because there were so many in the file. In the process

I'd read the complete case file and I became pretty familiar with it." The agent continued, "It got my attention for several reasons. It was interesting, unsolved, and I could tell it had weighed heavily on Reanae for a long time."

Cathey, described by Childers as a quick study, soon knew the file better than anyone, with the exception of herself. The intelligent agent was enthusiastic and possessed all the energy that being so entailed. Cathey was devoted to his new job and to his partner, who recognized the perceptive agent as a natural and an asset to her on this case.

According to Childers, "He knew all the players. So he could actually call and inquire about something for me and it'd click. In fact, David had done several interviews for me. Together we tracked down various leads. I wasn't worried about David holding his own."

Whenever Cathey had some free time, he would holler in Childers's direction, "Hey, let's do something on Judy and Melissa."

It was David Cathey who overheard a statement that someone had been desperately searching for Reanae Childers. "I stopped by the sheriff's office in Durant, Friday morning, and said, 'Hey, what's this about someone trying to call for an OSBI agent.' The dispatcher looked up and said, 'Diane Fields called and left this number. Wouldn't tell us exactly what they wanted, but were sure anxious to talk to y' all.' "

Cathey immediately recognized it as an Atoka phone number. "I don't know, there was just something that said, 'You need to call this lady.' I went back to Reanae's office and called Mrs. Fields. I told her I understood she had been looking for an agent last night. Then I apologized that we hadn't been able to respond and I told her I was ready to help her today. She was real hesitant to talk to me. She was saying, 'Well, I don't know you.' I asked if she could give me some clue what this was about. She said, 'Do you know the name of Judy Moody?' I said, 'Yes, I do.' Diane then said, 'Well, my friend killed her.' I was like, Oh, wow! Stop! I took a second, then asked where she was right then. She told me and I said, 'I'll be there in thirty minutes or less.' I immediately went to Atoka and found Diane and Eddie Fields at the Final Harvest Ministry they run and began the interview."

Diane Fields told Cathey how the murders occurred. She explained that Anita had turned herself in at the Cole County Jail, but she didn't know what had happened after that. The agent told her that made two of them.

Cathey continued his story, "I called Cole County and spoke briefly to Agent Mackey. I said, 'Charlie, you know what's going on with this Judy Moody thing?' He said, 'Well, not entirely. Get on over here and we'll try to piece it together.' " Although Mackey had escorted Sherry to McAlester, lately he had been working more in a supervisory capacity. He would wait for Cathey and talk with him before he claimed to know things he didn't.

Criminalist Chris Dill, who had originally worked the crime scene where Judy's body was found, had switched to field agent in March 1994 and worked out of the bureau's Durant office. Childers, Dill, and Cathey had all been longtime friends. Dill and Cathey went back sixteen years, when the two had served in the Army Reserve together.

Agent Dale Birchfield also operated out of the same office as Dill. They were both the same age. Birchfield had sandy-brown hair, was clean shaven, and was always meticulously groomed. His slight smile hinted at the jovial person hiding underneath a no-nonsense attitude that he relied on when he was on the job. Birchfield had been a part of the initial crime scene back in 1991 when Judy Moody Mayo was found. He'd also spent hours searching for Melissa and helping canvass the area interviewing people.

While David Cathey was on his way to put heads together with Charlie Mackey, Dill and Birchfield were spending a fairly routine day when the bureau's proficient and pretty secretary Lela Richardson stuck her head in the office and announced, "Hey, you guys. I hope this is a good call. Y'all need to go to

Cole County. It looks like the Judy Moody Mayo case is coming unraveled."

Both men, who had been sitting in one of the offices chatting, sat straight up. Dill looked at Lela and said, "No way!"

Though the agency received a lot of this type of call, most of them were strikeouts. Usually the caller turned out to be a prank or a drunk. Nevertheless, both agents' hearts pounded a little faster at the message. At this point they couldn't afford to treat the call as anything but deadly serious.

The men grabbed their coats, told Lela they were on their way, and exited the building. They headed straight to Agent Birchfield's car. The men talked excitedly as they drove toward Cole County.

Per Dill's recollections, "We were trying to get there fast as we could. This was a double murder. A two-year-old homicide at that. We all love Reanae, she's like a big sister. I knew, gosh dang, this was Reanae's case. If we get a chance to solve it and we don't, she's gonna kill us."

Birchfield's state car was low on gas. He pulled into a station to fill the tank. Dill started pumping the gas as Birchfield filled out the obligatory paperwork using the top of the car as a writing surface. Pumping the handle to squeeze out the last drop of gas, Dill looked over at his partner coaxing him, "Hurry, hurry, hurry." The words rolled out of his mouth so fast they stumbled over each other on their way out.

Birchfield finished his report and got behind the wheel. Out of nowhere a car pulled in, drove right past the agent's vehicle, hit the still opened driver's door bending it back.

Both men looked at each other like they couldn't believe what had just happened. The timing couldn't have been worse for the anxious men. A trooper was called to the scene. When he finally got there, he said, "Nope. I can't work this because it's on the store's property." Birchfield and Dill collectively moaned. The anxious agents had to wait yet again for another police officer to arrive on the scene. It was now three o'clock in the afternoon.

Dill described the action as bedlam. "By now, we're going nuts! It was getting later into the afternoon, and being a Friday we couldn't find anyone to okay the paperwork." The police officer finally arrived and to the agents' dismay informed Birchfield and Dill he really shouldn't work the accident because it was on private property. "We were hectically looking for someone to approve what was going on and we couldn't find anyone. Not anyone!" Agent Dill smiled and continued, "Not for the homicide, you understand, we're big boys. We can solve homicides on our own, but not little bitty fender-benders." He chuckled and continued, "It was unbelievable."

The two agents eventually got back on the road toward Cole County in their wounded vehicle. They pulled into the parking lot and went inside, where they briefly talked to Sheriff Ward. A quick discussion took place between the agents on how to proceed while the sheriff fetched the prisoner. Since Agent Dill had worked the crime scene in 1991, it was decided that he would be the one to interview Anita. They knew they had to tie what Anita had to tell them into that crime scene. That decided, the men headed toward the back door of the sheriff's office.

As Dill and Birchfield entered Sheriff Ward's office, they were greeted by Cathey and Agent Jeffries. After talking to Mackey, and with the knowledge he possessed on the case, Cathey had hotfooted it to the county jail. Agent Chuck Jeffries, who had worked Melissa's crime scene, had been called to the jail as the regional supervisor.

Chris Dill has reflected about that day, "Man, Anita was the one to turn this whole thing around by turning herself in. It had to be the toughest thing she'd ever done 'cause Jesse had convinced her if she turned him in, she would fry."

Anita Cummings was taken out of her tiny cell and introduced to Agent Dill. He told Anita they were going to step into Sheriff Ward's office to talk.

The sheriff accompanied Dill and Anita inside. Relief flooded Anita's face as she stood in the small office. Finally someone was going to listen to her. As the agent closed the door to the sheriff's office, she blurted out, "Thank God some-body believes me! Thank God the OSBI's here, y'all believe me." Dill quieted the excited woman down and asked her to have a seat to answer some questions. Anita immediately de-manded to talk to Reanae Childers. Anita had seen the agent as a good and decent person she trusted. She was a mother that exchanged baby pictures with her, and it was Childers she was talking to, or she wasn't talking. Anita added an exclamation to her point by sitting down and defiantly crossing her arms in front of her.

Dill looked into the worried woman's eyes and, with the boy-ish charm that was so appealing and direct, implored Anita. "I'm sorry. I'm all you got, girl. You're just gonna have to tell me." The concerned look didn't fade; Anita's arms didn't un-cross; and her mouth remained unopened. Dill decided to take another run at it. In a voice possessing the same consideration and understanding, brooked by no-nonsense, Dill took another shot. "Look, I was there when Judy's body was recovered. I worked the lab. I'm gonna know what you're talking about, if what you're saying is true, okay?"

Anita uncrossed her arms and this time she spoke. Anita went on and on for more than an hour, barely stopping to catch her breath. Dill was patiently trying to listen, yet he knew they had to get down to business. Anita was going all over the place, from as far back as the truck hauls she had accompanied Jesse Cummings on in Arkansas. The agent gently interrupted her from time to time to nudge her back on track. The passive woman, who had hardly uttered a word in over a year, was baring her soul in the safety of Sheriff Ward's office.

Dill was beginning to know Anita's life story, but wasn't getting any closer to what he was there to talk about. A lot of verification would be needed to corroborate what Anita had claimed happened when she was arrested to justify the arrests of Cummings and Sherry. Time and time again, the anxious agent patiently steered Anita back in the direction of the time zone he was concerned about.

The tiny one-story courthouse had closed for the weekend, and the air conditioner had been turned off. Stifling heat pervaded the building. Cathey and Mackey waited patiently outside the sheriff's office. Craning their necks, they listened at the door as the interview droned on. The duo's legs began to cramp from their squatting position. When the two periodically caught Dill's eye through the office window, the two agents would give him the universal signal to wind it up.

Finally Anita began to describe Judy's murder, saying she just pointed the gun in her sister-in-law's direction and pulled the trigger until the cylinder of the gun was empty. Dill's interest piqued. The agent knew the condition of Judy's body from working the crime scene in 1991, and Anita's description of the bullet holes in the body matched perfectly the reality of what he'd seen.

But the clincher for Dill was when Anita started describing what they had wrapped and dragged Judy's body to the cellar in. Being so familiar with the lab work he had conducted, Dill immediately knew she was describing the mattress pad. The same pad with the hospital stamp on it that he had recovered still cloaking a portion of Judy's body in the murky pond.

It was extremely fortunate that the agent sitting and listening to Anita had worked the scene years before and completed the lab work. "The whole time she was talking I just kept thinking to myself, She's got to give me something at that crime scene 'cause she couldn't be making all this up. When she perfectly described that mattress pad, I was like, 'That's it!' It corroborated what she was telling me."

There was a sense of urgency in getting the corroboration. "When the sheriff goes out and arrests these folks, the clock starts running. Once you go out and arrest somebody, you're gonna have an initial arraignment or an appearance before the judge. You got forty-eight hours to put your case together. Here they were sitting in jail for twenty-four hours and we didn't even know it." Dill knew time was of utmost importance. He had to get enough probable cause to detain Jesse Cummings in jail. He knew if Cummings was released, that was it.

"One of Anita's big things that she kept talking about that afternoon, was her little boy, Scottie. She told me, 'I did it. I shot her. Jesse told me to shoot her and I shot her.' I needed her to tell me she did it because Jesse made her. She went on and on about that little boy, how Jesse would've run away with him and harmed him. You could tell she really cared about that little boy. It was Scottie. Scottie was Jesse's strongest weapon against her."

When the interview was over, Dill offered his apologies to the men as they limped and stretched their legs, while pulling their soaked shirts away from their backs. Dill's rebuttal was a sincere, "Guys, there is no winding that girl up."

With the precision of a well-oiled machine, the agents immediately decided who would go where and do what, the clock had not stopped ticking and wasn't about to stop now.

Dill turned to Birchfield, slapped his partner on the back, and announced, "I think we have enough to have us a friendly chat with ole Jesse."

While Birchfield and Dill headed to the Atoka County Jail, where Cummings had been transferred earlier, Cathey remained behind to introduce himself to Anita and talk to her about obtaining her permission for a search warrant. Cathey asked Anita, "Does everyone have common access, or are there any portions of the house that are exclusively Jesse's?" The agent was attempting to ascertain if Anita really had the standing to give consent.

Anita didn't hesitate in her answer, "Well, I pay the damn rent. Is that good enough?"

It was. Since she lived there and they had a common bedroom, her permission was all that was needed for Cathey to obtain a search warrant.

After obtaining the search warrant, David Cathey entered the house in Lehigh and began a tedious search for evidence. Surrounded by total disarray, Cathey would spend hours rummaging among the filth and squalor, logging and bagging items of possible evidence. He quickly located specific items Anita had mentioned: the handcuffs, the three notebooks that had been used by Cummings, Anita, and Sherry to keep their stories straight, the badge Cummings used to intimidate people, and a picture album which contained photographs of Cummings, his friends, and the women who had loved him, all naked in different sexual positions with different partners. The women's faces stared up at the agent with vacant eyes and plastic smiles.

Cathey talked about some of the items he confiscated, "Out of everything I gathered there, probably the most important items I located were the three identical notebooks in Jesse's handwriting all with the same story." The agent shook his head and continued, "Those notebooks were like little scripts for the girls and himself. I think somehow, in Jesse's mind, he thought those written records of his alibi would somehow lend them credibility."

The unusual idea most likely stemmed from Cummings's practice of keeping meticulous recordings of the sexual activities that went on in the Cummings house.

Dill's and Birchfield's emotions surged as they sat parked outside the city jail. They briefly discussed how they would approach Cummings. With time running, it was critical to get him to implicate himself in the murders.

When the agents went inside, Cummings was pulled out of lockup and placed in the sheriff's office. Neither agent was in a good mood about being in the same room with the man, and they briefly discussed that they damn well better follow procedure in the critical interview.

Cummings seemed totally unaffected by the presence of the two agents standing in front of him accusing him of murder. In an effort to get a reaction, they told him what they thought had happened. Cummings's demeanor was cool, detached, and rather arrogant. He denied the charges as they were hurled at him by each agent. "He'd cross his arms, sit back, and chant a litany of, 'Prove it. Prove it. Prove it.' " Dill felt biting anger well inside him as he listened to the arrogant man before him.

Cummings wouldn't make eye contact with either of the agents. It was driving Dill nuts. "When you look me in the eye, I know I'm getting something in there [suspect's mind]. If I got in Jesse's face, he'd shift and look at the floor or the ceiling. I never got him to look me in the eye."

Cummings was not talking, and looked like he had no intention to begin. The agents knew they had to at least engage him in some conversation, or he would never admit anything to them. Dill recalled, "He didn't even acknowledge our presence in the room. We could've been saying, 'Holy smokes, Jesse, it's snowing outside!' He'd just sit there with his arms crossed and just look at us and say, 'You can't prove that.' He wouldn't even deny it. Just kept saying 'Prove it, if that's what y'all think.' He was one of the most pompous men I've ever known. And boy, was he cocky. We couldn't rattle his cage at all."

Disappointed with the way the interview was going, Dill finally threw his hands up in exasperation and told the deputies to lock Cummings back up.

The second interrogation took place later that same day. It lasted about an hour and took place upstairs in a witness room. This time Cummings just kept saying he was in Oklahoma City with his dad and he had the phone records to prove it.

Dill remembered how "he'd never just say 'I didn't kill Melissa, I didn't rape Melissa. I didn't kill Judy.' He just kept saying 'Prove it.' "

The agents approached Cummings every way they could think of that was legal, and still he had little to say. Sometimes he would pipe up with, "That's not right. I don't know why she's [Anita] telling you this. What does Sherry say?"

At this point Sherry had nothing to say. Dill and Birchfield tried to bluff around the last question. Reading the agents pretty accurately, Cummings looked at the men in disgust and spouted off, "Y' all ain't got nothin'." Disappointed at the lack of progress, the defeated agents sent Cummings back to his cell again.

Later that night a final attempt was made to get Cummings to talk. Each time Dill and Birchfield talked to him, they repeated the Miranda ritual of reading Cummings his rights and requiring him to sign the form indicating so. He never asked for a lawyer. If an attorney had entered the picture, he would have given Cummings the standard advice, "Shut your mouth and keep it shut," and that would have been that. But Cummings was so sure of himself, so sure of his superiority, that he never asked for one.

This time the interrogation took place in Sheriff Gary McCool's office and wasn't truly a structured interrogation. Cummings behaved at this one as he had at the others, telling the agents to prove what they thought he had done.

This time, however, the clever leverage was turned against him. Chris Dill was tired of Cummings's less than cooperative nature. The men were burning their collective candles at both ends, and the flame was about to die out. They were exhausted and had had enough of Cummings's bullshit for one day.

Dill, who had conducted the bulk of the interrogation, was especially tired. He wanted to go home and see his wife, who was only two months away from giving birth to the couple's second child. He wanted to see Chrissy, his delightful five-year-old. He missed them both. He wanted to be there, not here, not with Cummings. The exhausted agent massaged his temples. His head felt like it would explode if he heard the words "prove it" come out of Cummings's mouth one more damn time.

The next time Cummings looked at the frustrated agent and said "prove it," Dill turned on him. "No, *you* prove it, Jesse!" Controlled anger pervading his dark eyes, Dill issued a challenge, *"You* take a polygraph test for us and *you* prove you're innocent! Take a polygraph, pass it, and we'll back away and never question you again, Jesse."

Cummings, looking even more sure of himself than ever, spit out, "I'll take your damn polygraph." Everyone in the room was stunned that he'd foolishly accepted the challenge. The interrogation was immediately halted.

Dill swallowed a grin as the word "yes" slipped out from Cummings's lips. He stepped out of the room and headed for a phone. Chris Dill allowed his emotions some much needed release, and the smile spread across his face. It was the slow smile of a cat who had just cornered a mouse, only in Cummings's case, a rat.

Dill placed a call to the home of Agent Jeffries, the polygraph examiner for the OSBI and the agent who had been recruited on that steaming October day to work Melissa's crime scene. Dill began, "Chuck, I know tomorrow is Saturday, but will you do Jesse tomorrow?"

He could hear the disbelief in Jeffries's strong and clear voice. "You're telling me Jesse Cummings wants to do a polygraph? You bet, I'll be there. Bring him to the Antlers office around eight o'clock in the morning."

As Jeffries hung up the phone, the horrible memory of examining Melissa's body roared back. He would forego just about anything for the chance to question the man responsible for the carnage he had seen and had been unable to shake, a vision he knew would forever haunt him.

Chris Dill and David Cathey rose early the next morning and headed to pick Cummings up and transport him to Antlers, where the OSBI's only polygraph machine was. Cathey remembered the drive over as "two rookie agents [going] to pick Jesse up, and, well, we wanted to go anyway."

Interrupting his friend, Dill's observations matched. "You couldn't of kept me and David off this one with a gun."

Cathey continued, "We picked Jesse up, shackled him and put him in the car to go to Antlers. He wasn't very friendly to either of us. Driving over to the polygraph, we were as nice as we could be to him, treating him with professional courtesy. Put him in the car and be as nice to him as we could be, without creating a safety hazard for us."

"Yeah, we handcuffed him like 'Jesse, you know we gotta do this.' We treat him with kid gloves 'cause we don't want him to back out of the polygraph," Dill explained. "Because we know failure of a poly is an excellent end to a good interrogation. I mean, here he is agreeing to the test. We weren't gonna mess with him; kinda like hands off."

The rapist, torturer, and killer of women and children was completely docile in the company of the two men.

Escorted by Dill and Cathey, a confident Jesse Cummings sauntered into Chuck Jeffries's office. As Jeffries introduced himself to Cummings and shook his hand, Jeffries used every ounce of his well-honed skills of perception and sensitivity just to enable himself to talk to the monster responsible for what he had witnessed in the woods of Choctaw County. Jeffries ushered the prisoner into the polygraph room. Carefully he explained to Cummings the procedure they would be going through.

The agents already had Anita's statement and the fruit of the search conducted in Lehigh, so Jeffries knew to pattern his questions to her statement, especially about Cummings helping move Judy's body. As Jeffries placed Cummings in the chair and began strapping on the apparatus, he patiently explained each step. When Cummings said he had no questions, the crucial exam began.

With butterflies hovering in their stomachs, Dill and Cathey sat outside the examining room wringing their hands and sweating. Cummings and Jeffries were in the room for almost an hour. When the test was over, Jeffries unstrapped Cummings and told him that he had to examine and score the test results. Dill and Cathey anxiously got to their feet as their coworker shut the door behind him. Agent Cathey went in to stay with Cummings.

Jeffries retired to another room, where he carefully examined and scored the test. When he had finished, he stepped out of his office, waved Dill toward him, then walked to the examination room to motion for Cathey to join them in the hall. Cathey told Cummings they would be with him in a minute. The agent closed the door behind him and stepped into the hall. No one else was in the building, Cummings wasn't going anywhere without one of them seeing him.

Chuck Jeffries broke the nervous silence, "Man, he knocked the top off this thing. It's kinda strange, guys, some of the questions he passed, some he failed."

The three agents began to discuss the results of the test. Leaning against a wall, they talked in low whispers to figure out a game plan before confronting the suspect. Cummings had passed the question "Did you kill Judy Moody Mayo?" because he had told the truth. He had not actually killed his sister.

Chris Dill has revealed, "If this doesn't make you a believer in polygraphs, nothing will. Your examiner is so important. He's got to know what he's doing [and] how to ask a question correctly. And Jeffries was brilliant. He asked Jesse, 'Did you cause the death of Judy?' and Jesse miserably failed the question. When we got to Melissa's death, and Jesse said he didn't kill her, he knocked the top right off the chart."

The men brainstormed and concurred that, because of Cummings's failure on some questions, they would have to reinterrogate him. Their obligations could easily become secondary in the excitement, but the outstanding agents would not allow that to happen. This was a job. But it had become personal, very personal. The men fought to keep in check the overpowering emotions they were feeling at the moment because they knew, without a doubt, they were dealing with a child killer.

The three mutually agreed it would be best that Jeffries be the one to tell Cummings that the polygraph showed deception. Dill mused, "Chuck was gonna tell him he failed the test, but he wasn't gonna just go in and say, 'Jesse, you flunked this test, you lying son-of-a-gun.' "

It was all in knowing the right approach, and Jeffries knew exactly how to do his job. Jeffries walked into the room carrying the polygraph papers containing lines similar to the ones found on an EKG sheet. He carefully spread the papers across his desk. Cummings was sitting in a chair across from the agent. A proven technique to interrogation often involves invading the suspect's space. Dill was on Cummings's right-hand side, with Cathey on the left.

Cummings listened intently to Jeffries as the agent started to explain the test results. Jeffries had the confrontation orchestrated down to the finest detail. The agent began, "Jesse, do you remember the question, 'Did you kill Judy Moody Mayo?' "

Feeling quite sure of himself, Cummings rocked back in his chair, his fingers laced behind his head, and cavalierly answered, "Yeah, I remember."

Jeffries continued, "Well, here, see on my sheet, that's question number twenty-six. This test says you told the truth. You said you didn't kill Judy and the machine says you told the truth. Now everyone in this room believes this test, right?"

Cummings, fully imperious and relaxed, readily agreed, "Yeah, this test is right. It says I didn't kill Judy. I told ya I was telling the truth." The men watched the air fill in Cummings's chest as he smugly puffed it out.

Dill recalled, "He's like 'I passed man' and he's all arrogant. It's like he's fixing to get up and walk out of that room a free man. He was completely pleased with himself."

Jeffries carefully proceeded. "Let me show you this, Jesse. Here's a question, 'Did you help move Judy's body?' and the test says you failed on this one. That's what the machine says, and you already agreed with me awhile ago that this is a good machine. So why do you think this machine told us you lied?"

Cummings was just about to open his mouth when Jeffries interrupted. "Now, wait a minute, wait a minute. If we believe the machine over here when it says you passed, we gotta believe the machine over here when it says you failed. And the test says you failed, Jesse, big change—huge change! Now, you agreed with me awhile ago that this machine is a good machine. I mean, everyone in the room has agreed this is a valid test, and we can believe it, right?" Jeffries let the question dangle in the tense air.

Cummings shifted uncomfortably in his seat, then breaking the silence, the jittery man managed to mumble, "Yeah, I guess."

According to Dill, "Chuck was brilliant. He back-doored this guy, like 'Come follow me, my little child.' "

David Cathey and Chris Dill took the signal and began tossing dialogue back and forth between them and the suspect, saying, "Well, those crazy women must of killed Judy while you were in Oklahoma City. Those silly bitches. What were they thinking killing her like that while you were away?"

Cummings nibbled on the bait. After a second he answered, "Yeah, that's right." With those three words, Cummings was busted. He had just painted himself into a corner he couldn't get out of.

Cathey and Dill took turns speaking, voices alternating, sometimes blending into one. "We believe you didn't kill Judy, but you helped move the body, didn't you? You took your daddy to Oklahoma City. You don't know what went on in that house. You walk in tired and you're confronted with what happened. We can't blame you for wanting to help your wives out. Hell, any man would want to. You come home and your wife has done something stupid, you're gonna want to help her out, you know. We understand that."

Cummings underwent a complete transformation in the span of ten seconds as the starch seemed to melt right out of him. "It was pure textbook body language," Dill, still amused with the memory, went on. "He literally went from his closed stance of, 'You ain't got nothing on me' attitude. His shoulders slumped. His arms uncrossed. And, his head dropped down."

The soft, low-keyed interview was working. Cathey verbally empathized with Cummings. "Well, Jesse, you were just trying to help your wife out. We understand." He had just given Cummings an out, expressing that anybody would've done the same thing.

Dill recalled, "Jesse bit on it like a big dog. I'll *never* forget it in my life 'cause me and David are like face-to-face. Jesse said, 'Whew,' just letting the air come out of him like that, just this big sigh. Then Jesse said, 'Yeah, you're right. I helped move Judy's body.' That's all we needed. Just that one sentence. But now, we needed it on tape to make the case. We didn't have it till we got it on tape."

At the startling admission Cathey and Dill looked straight at each other and locked eyes once more. The iron clamp that had held the agents' emotions in check slipped a notch, and they desperately fought to keep it from showing. Cathey vividly remembered the moment, "It was one of those moments where time just stood still. It was like, oh, my God! He just admitted being tied to this thing."

Dill clearly remembered the scene, too. "It was like, Gosh dang, he just gave it up! Of course, you gotta be cool. We said, 'That's right, Jesse,' and the whole time your guts are bursting inside and you wanta just scream. He repeated, 'Yeah, you guys are right. I helped move Judy's body.' "

The agents looked at each other after the additional admission. They silently pled with their inner emotions to stay calm, just stay calm.

Dill smiled. "You can't jump up and down and say 'We're sending Jesse to jail!' but that's what you wanta do." Cathey and Dill had been agents only a short while, but they knew in that one moment when Cummings uttered the small confession to moving Judy's body, that the case had gone from shaky to hitting a home run in the ballpark in less than five seconds.

Dill remembered how he "had interrogated that guy twice and he hardly even admitted to me his name was Jesse. We throw the polygraph out all the time to suspects like a politician throws out taxes. 'I'll have someone here in an hour.' "

Cathey continued the synopsis. "We chose not to talk about Melissa. We got him hooked, but just barely. Let's not yank it out yet. So, he tells us, 'Yeah, I helped move her.' And we say, 'Well, tell us your story.' Jesse was like, 'I don't know what happened and I didn't ask. Hey, that's my sister. I don't wanta know. We put her in the truck, rolled her in the grass and put her truck up there by the lake.' "

Solicitously the agents counseled Cummings to let them record his statement so they could play it for the district attorney and show his cooperation. When Cummings agreed, the agents told him they needed to step outside for a moment. They had to. Their emotions were ready to blast out from where they were shoved during the interrogation. The men left the room for a moment to compose themselves. With the door separating the cops from the criminal now shut, the three grown men stood in the hall high-fiving each other like high school football players after scoring a touchdown. Quickly getting it out of their systems, the agents got back down to business.

When they reentered the room, the tape recorder was started, and the interrogation of Jesse Cummings by all three agents began. "On the transcript, we were sugarcoating everything. It was kinda sickening. Here, he'd killed this little girl, and we're talking to him like he's a Catholic minister or something," Dill recalled with a disgusted shake of his head.

Cummings peppered his statement with a lot of "I don't remember's and "I don't recall's. The agents pressed on as they carefully questioned him. A paragon in contradiction, Cummings stumbled through some parts. But throughout the tape he consistently blamed his betrayer, Anita, and Anita alone, clearing the loyal and obedient Sherry of any wrongdoing. When Cummings was asked if he knew if Judy had been shot or had her neck or throat cut, he conveniently lost his memory, again saying he didn't know. Patience running out, an irritated Chris Dill let out a sigh and leveled an accusation, "We've *told* you she was shot, Jesse."

At one point during the statement, questions were asked about Melissa. On the taped statement Cummings pled, "Melissa was already gone when I come in."

Cathey interrupted, "She [Anita] said she'd done away with Melissa?"

Cummings replied nonchalantly in a voice disconnected from his soul, "Yeah."

Dill remembered Cummings's temerity with disdain. "He wanted us to believe he didn't even ask where Melissa was. I thought, Okay, if you want to sit there and tell those twelve men and women you didn't even ask where this little girl was—if that's the stupid story you're gonna tell, well, we just let him tell it. 'Cause we knew it was hanging him just as bad showing such callousness for that little girl."

The interview finally came to a close. Jeffries reached over and hit the stop button on the recorder. This would be the last time Cummings would publicly utter a statement about the murders other than to plead not guilty.

Cummings was returned to his cell. David Cathey, Chris Dill, and Chuck Jeffries relaxed for the first time in a long time. They had done a superb job. No one could have done it any better.

"You know Jesse was such an arrogant fuck, he thought he could beat us. Funny thing is, he did for a while," Cathey reminisced. "If he'd just kept Anita close to him and been good to her, she would've never talked. But, he finally made her afraid for her own life."

The lies that had rolled over Cummings's tongue as smoothly as the truth had served him well all his life. This time no one was buying it.

When the dust finally settled, the agents bantered about the reason why Cummings had agreed to take a polygraph in the first place. Perhaps it was as simple as his own arrogance, or maybe it stretched all the way back to August 3, 1991, the day after Anita's twenty-second birthday. After all, that was when Cummings met the authorities' challenge and told Anita, "You go down there and tell 'em you'll take their damn polygraph." The cops backed down. Cummings gambled and won that time. This time he had lost, and lost big.

Twenty-one

Agent Reanae Childers had set out on her trip just a couple of days before Agent Perry Unruh's rude awakening. It seemed like every time Childers was away, something major happened on the case. Childers's untimely vacation kept her from personally being there to see her three years of labor come to fruition.

Agents Dill and Jeffries took off for McAlester to interview Sherry. Agent Cathey started trying furiously to reach Childers through her pager. The relentless Cathey had to find her and tell her about the confession: "Reanae had put her heart and soul in this case, and she wound up missing almost everything except all the hard work." Cathey's persistence paid off and the pager finally picked up enough signal to reach Childers one state away. Unable to imagine why in the world somebody would be paging her now, Childers's curiosity was piqued as she pulled into a McDonald's and went straight to the pay phone.

When David Cathey heard his partner's voice, he couldn't get the words out fast enough. Excitedly he told her that Anita had confessed, and Cummings had partially confessed to Judy and Melissa's murders. Then he quickly added that all three of them were behind bars.

After Reanae Childers heard Cathey relate how Anita had tried to reach her for hours before turning herself in, the agent felt justified in the hours she had spent stopping by and talking to the new mother. Anita had told her many times that she did not trust the local officials and she never divulged her belief that Cummings had control over Cole County law enforcement officers.

"Here, I hadn't had a vacation in over two years. As soon as I'm out of town, we get a confession. Can you believe that?" Childers laughed at the improbability that she could miss so many key points in a case she had exhaustively and tediously worked for the last three years. The murders had weighed heavily on Childers. She had been unable to shake the memory of Melissa that dogged her like a relentless shadow and had been responsible for uncountable hours of her time.

Childers was delighted the confession finally came. As she hung up the phone, she sighed with relief. When she returned home, there would be plenty of time to worry about beginning the tedious work of putting the case together and preparing for trial. For now, Childers was going to enjoy the rest of her hard-earned vacation and time with her family.

On the drive to McAlester, Chris Dill and Chuck Jeffries came up with a plan. Dill was fiddling with the tape recording of Cummings, rewinding and playing certain parts of the conversation. The two men selected a portion of the tape where Anita was implicated in moving Judy's body with Cummings. On the tape, Cummings did not name the participant. The men decided to play those ten seconds for Sherry, hoping she would think Jesse was talking about her instead of Anita.

When they pulled into the parking lot, Dill played several times the portion of the tape that they intended for Sherry to hear, to get the cue just right. The agents also made sure they brought a copy of the Miranda form that Cummings had signed. Dill knew Sherry would recognize her husband's signature.

When Dill and Jeffries went in to interview Sherry, she had little to say. Sherry has discussed that day. "At first when they came in, I wouldn't say a word. Then they told me Jesse was blaming it all on Anita and me. Well, that kinda blew my mind. At this point I didn't know that Anita'd confessed. They kept on telling me what Jesse was trying to do. Finally one of 'em said, 'Well, let me play you something.' And they put the tape in and I could tell it was Jesse talking. I listened to that voice to make absolutely sure it was Jesse's 'cause I thought it was a fixed-up deal." Sherry concentrated as the recorder played the short piece the agents wanted her to hear:

Dill: "Okay, you . . . you turn left and you're in
    your pickup, in Judy's truck."
Cummings: "Right."
Dill: "Now, what . . . what happened. Tell me . . ."
Cummings: "We just pulled straight up to it. We
    got her out of the pickup and we's right
    there at the pond."
Dill: "Okay, you both got her out of the pickup.
    How did you get her? From which side of
    the pickup did you take her out of, left or
    right? Passenger or driver's side?"
Cummings: "From the passenger side."

When the recorder was shut off, Sherry's face showed a look of betrayal, followed by a heavy sigh of recognition. She couldn't believe that Jesse was actually blaming Judy's death on her. Her lips started to quiver and she burst into uncontrollable sobs. Her shoulders heaved. Dill went and fetched Sherry some Kleenex. She used every one, and he went back for more, until the tears that just kept raining down stopped because she was too exhausted to cry anymore.

After Sherry pulled herself together, the agents quietly asked the distraught woman if she would like to tell her side of the story. She nodded and was Mirandized. Sherry's statement was succinct and recited woodenly. It was obvious she wanted it out and over with. Using the minicassette tactic had been a brilliant idea. More importantly, it had worked.

As Sherry told Dill and Jeffries what had happened, one moment caught both men emotionally off guard. Sherry told them that Melissa was put in the car by Cummings. Then she added that Melissa looked really scared. Both men's eyes looked into the other's as they shared a common thought. Agent Dill verbalized it later. "When I heard that—that Melissa was really scared, it absolutely broke my heart in two." It made Jeffries hate Cummings even more.

When Anita was arraigned with Sherry, it was the first time since Anita had turned herself in, and Sherry had subsequently been arrested, that the two women, who had been bitter enemies for so long, saw each other. Anita looked at Sherry and had only one question. "I said, 'Sherry, do you hate me because I turned us in?' "

Sherry answered slow and deliberate, "No, I don't hate you, Anita. I'm just glad it's finally all over with." The two women, who had shared so much heartache, pain, and torture, turned and briefly hugged one another. Sherry continued, "For once, I'm gonna enjoy going to sleep knowing Jesse's not in the other room just waiting for me to fall asleep."

Anita understood exactly what she meant.

Sherry remained at McAlester for the next three days. Food brought in was left untouched. Both women were terrified Cummings would escape and hunt them down. Anita explained why. "He had always told us, it didn't matter where we'd go, he'd find us, even if he was in jail, he could get to us. And if he couldn't do it hisself, he had people who could get to us."

The first few months in jail, Anita and Sherry panicked that they would have to leave their private cocoons.

Both experienced major problems making simple everyday decisions. They had been told for so long by Cummings when to eat, when to dress, when to take a bath that they were incapable of making a decision on their own.

Sherry's cellmates would have to tell her when to take a shower. "When one of them asked, 'Sherry, aren't you gonna take a shower tonight?', then it would click, that I needed to make a decision. I'd sit on my top bunk and I'd just sit there. I wouldn't come down, unless I literally had to, like to go to the bathroom."

During the two years in jail awaiting Cummings's trial, Anita came to trust a man, the first that she had in over a decade. She trusted Agent Cathey. Anita had been quickly transferred from Coalgate to Durant in Bryan County after her arrest for several reasons. The Coalgate jail was so small, there was no real easy way to keep a female prisoner. Childers wanted to keep the friendly witness nearby as they prepared to go to trial. When asked to talk about his relationship with Anita, Cathey downplayed his role. "Sometimes I would transport her from jail in Durant to a hearing in Coalgate. Sherry was right there in jail in Atoka, and I would occasionally transfer her. I made a lot of trips to Bryan County jail. I spent a lot of hours building trust between us, and just going through the case preparing for trial."

Anita's wicked sense of humor would serve a vital role in helping her to cope with the tragedy in her life and her time in jail. "When the women in my cell'd get a little too rowdy, the jailer'd lightheartedly say, 'Don't y'all ladies make me get my handcuffs out.' I popped off before I could stop myself and answered back, 'Gee, that's foreplay for me, as far as I know.' I had to learn to laugh to keep from crying."

Sherry had been transferred to Atoka County Jail. She, too, would be needed close by. She would be a witness for the state, but certainly not as friendly as Anita. But she would need to be close as trial preparations got closer, and from the Bryan County jail, Atoka County was less than thirty minutes away. But the main reason she was transferred was because Cummings, who had been transferred after the polygraph examination to Coalgate under Sheriff Ward's supervision, was rumored to be planning an escape from the rustic jail. For security reasons Sheriff Ward transferred Cummings to the much more secure facility in McAlester, where he would remain until his trial.

On September 13, 1994, Chris Dill and his wife had a little boy. David Dill joined the family. He was born five years after his sister, Chrissy, almost to the day. Chrissy celebrated her fifth birthday five days later with her favorite present being her little brother. Chris Dill had worked exhaustively the few months prior to the birth. He had been gone a lot, and Cheryl had tolerated it good-naturedly, even with her condition. She wanted him home to enjoy his son. He was.

Agent Cathey's empathetic manner made people from all walks of life comfortable around him. He would now face the monumental task of gaining Anita's and Sherry's trust after years of abuse at the hands of a man. It was easy for the people he encountered to like and remember the agent. It didn't hurt that he had incredible, oceanic blue eyes—not at all.

Several times Anita became suicidal. When David Cathey and Reanae Childers came to visit her one day, she warned Cathey, "Y'all are gonna carry me out in a body bag. The first chance I get, I'm dead. I'm outta here. I just can't do this no more. My kids are safe, Jesse's in jail, and I can just quit fighting."

Anita had felt Cummings had swallowed her up forever.

The two agents called a pastor in to talk and counsel Anita's troubled soul. The pastor's church would furnish the only decent clothes Anita would have for the trial: a two-piece blue suit trimmed in black.

Sarah Yaws's silence about Cummings raping her that spring day in 1991 remained unbroken. Finally, on a cold February day in 1995, Sarah told her secret to Reanae Childers.

In August 1995, Childers found out she was expecting her second child. Staying true to form from the day she was appointed case agent in Melissa's murder, the birth would coincide with Cummings's trial for capital murder.

Childers knew there was little chance she would be able to attend the trial. Nevertheless, she worked as long as she comfortably could. Childers approached Cathey and asked him to join in the trial preparation. She had made up her mind that he would be the one she would ask to take her place at the prosecutor's table assisting in the trial.

Cathey recounted their joint preparation. "We spent hours going over physical evidence and marking the different exhibits. We put together the large hardbacked boards for the exhibits. And we painstakingly chose which photographs would be presented. Then we prepared in the eventuality that none of our photos would be [used]. We had alternates standing by with Velcro on the back to go on the boards if it became necessary. We went through witness testimony to make sure where they were going to be during the trial."

Childers was not out beating the streets, because she was so far along in her pregnancy. Instead, she would call Cathey and tell him what she needed, and he would take care of it.

Anita had managed so successfully to block out the horrible memories, that she was still unable to tell the only two people in the world she trusted what had happened the day she shot Judy. A week before the trial, Childers and Cathey arrived at the jail and showed Anita the clothing that Judy had on the day she was murdered. This was the agents' one final attempt to prompt Anita's repressed memory to open up. "When they showed me the shirt, it came back, the entire shooting. I mean, I knew when I walked in that room Judy was alive, and when I left, she was dead, but I had no memory of what happened in between."

When the agents left, Anita sat on her bunk and pulled her legs toward her chest. She bowed her head and thanked God for allowing herself redemption for the terrible act she committed September 5, 1991. Anita had retreated so deeply into a protective cocoon of denial she had not known if she had the strength to will herself out of it long enough to see that all of them were punished for the despicable things each had been responsible for.

Reanae Childers had one last thing to do before she could abandon her heart's work into the more than capable hands of her partner, and she knew she couldn't put it off any longer. She had to tell Anita that she would not be at the trial. The very pregnant agent paid one last visit to Anita before the trial started.

Although Anita trusted and was comfortable with David

Cathey, when Chiders told her that Cathey would be taking over for her because of the baby, Anita threw a fit.

Childers reassured Anita that she and Agent Cathey were total counterparts. Whatever one does, the other can do. "Anita, we're completely interchangeable, I promise you."

Anita, calling her bluff, blurted out, "Well, send *him* to have the baby, then!"

Childers laughed softly at the recollection. "I told her, maybe interchangeable was not exactly the right word I was looking for. I said, 'Anita, there's a couple of things that David can't do, and that happens to be one of 'em. Believe me, if he could do that for me, I'd sure let him.' "

Childers had not realized that as far back as Zach's birth, and her subsequent visits with Anita, that every time Anita looked into the agent's decent eyes, she felt a small piece of her heal. Reanae Childers had become Anita's center, her rock. It was Anita's personal strength and courage that enabled her to turn herself in that morning in July. But it was the strength and courage she had derived from the agent that enabled her to take the stand and testify about the terrible thing she had done in her world gone-so-wrong.

Twenty-two

Jesse Cummings's trial would take place on May 6, 1996, in the Cole County Courthouse situated in Coalgate, Oklahoma, population steadily inching toward two thousand. Ironically, it was the same town where his grandfather had served as marshal. It had been decided that both capital murder trials be tried together, in order for the jury to be able to cohesively understand exactly what took place. Since Judy Moody Mayo was murdered in Cole County, jurisdiction remained there.

Fittingly, the children whose parents elected Garrett as their top law enforcement officer would now determine if the well-respected lawman's grandson had committed the unimaginable murders of Garrett's own granddaughter and great-granddaughter. And if so, whether he should die for it. Marshal Garrett had respected and followed the letter of the law all of his life, and he loved his family. Jesse had done neither.

Judge Douglas Gabbard II was the presiding judge in several of the counties in Oklahoma. Cole County happened to be one of them. Gabbard, swathed in a billowing black robe, was impressive-looking, with intelligent eyes revealing a mixture of dedication and extreme judicial diligence. He is considered by the attorneys who present cases before him to be a fair and equitable judge. He would be the presiding judge at Cummings's trial.

James Thornley, who was elected district attorney in January 1995, would be the lead prosecutor in the trial. Thornley is a soft-spoken man who possesses a keen mind. Though he prefers to keep a low profile, in the courtroom he is a powerful, dynamic man and a formidable adversary for defense lawyers who find themselves in trial with him. His fervor is fueled even more by defendants such as Jesse Cummings. He would bring commitment, intensity, and superb prosecutorial skills with him to the counsel table.

Assistant District Attorney John McPhail, young but experienced, sat next to his boss. McPhail, who meticulously prepared his cases for presentation, was untiring, incredibly organized, and fastidious—attributes that would be critical for presenting cohesively the complicated facts of the two murders to a jury. The attorney had taken a personal interest in the case as soon as he read the file, and had spent hours talking with the principals at the OSBI agency, and campaigning to be assigned as second chair to the district attorney when Cummings went to trial.

Next to McPhail, OSBI agent David Cathey sat as a substitute for Reanae Childers, his partner and friend, who was nervously sitting at home ready to go into labor at any moment, and anxiously waiting for two major events in her life to come to a culmination.

Agent Cathey brought to the prosecution table passion to see justice done, and the tireless energy that had been so necessary preparing to go to trial, and that would be even more necessary as the trial commenced.

Cathey, who had assisted Reanae Childers in trial preparations, had arrived early. One of his responsibilities would be to assist the prosecutors with all the exhibits that he had tediously helped prepare. He set up a large easel that would support mounted crime-scene photographs, which were leaning against the wall for quick retrieval, photos so gruesome no one should have to view them. The full weight of the agency's responsibilities and duties during the trial now rested squarely on his shoulders. He had lived and breathed the case along with his partner.

As Thornley busied himself reviewing notes, and McPhail

flipped through the pages of the voluminous file checking and rechecking, Cathey stared long and hard at the man responsible for everyone being there, and equally responsible for the irrevocable and permanent absence of two others, Judy Moody Mayo and her little girl, Melissa. He stared at Cummings a few more minutes, then turned his attention from Cummings when Judge Gabbard entered the courtroom. The time to see if a jury would give Jesse James Cummings the ultimate punishment for the rape and murder of a child had finally come.

Jody Minter and Paul Faulk, Cummings's court-appointed attorneys, sat at the defense table directly across from the state. At the very end of the table sat Cummings. The two attorneys seemed to be strange bedfellows. Faulk was a clean-cut, fair-haired, all-American boy, while Minter looked like an aging hippie, with his hair neatly pulled back in a long ponytail.

Situating himself behind the oak bench, Gabbard asked if the state was ready to proceed. Thornley answered in the affirmative, as did the defense when the same question was asked of them.

The state presented testimony from Steven Lee, who found Judy Moody Mayo's body. Agent Chris Dill was called to testify that he was working for the OSBI as a criminalist when the murders happened, and had processed the crime scene and told what he had found. Further into his testimony, Dill told the jury about Cummings's taped confession that he had been present for in his capacity as an agent for the agency.

Dr. Robert Hemphill, who performed Judy's autopsy and ascertained the cause of death, testified next. After Dr. Hemphill stepped off the stand, additional testimony was presented as to the tool markings on the murder weapon. Agent Chuck Jeffries testified to finding Melissa Moody's decomposed body and processing her crime scene.

The defense team was unable to make a dent in the professionals' testimony.

Tim Chancellor was called to establish that on June 5, 1990, Cummings traded a .22 rifle and a goat to Chancellor for his

.38 pistol, the weapon believed to have been used to kill Judy Moody Mayo.

When asked if the defendant had made any remarks after the murders about where the .38 pistol was, Chancellor answered frankly, "He said it was a gone son of a bitch."

Dr. Ronald Distefano was called to testify as the medical examiner who examined the remains of Melissa. He explained to the jury that severe decomposition of her body made it difficult to establish the exact cause of death. He testified further that Melissa's body was exhumed in 1994, shortly after Cummings's arrest. The injuries from a second examination were determined from Melissa's bones, since the state of decomposition left no tissue to examine and indicated damage had been done to the second, third, and fifth ribs. The doctor stated in his opinion those injuries were most likely the result of a sharp object such as a knife.

The jury stared for a long time at the mounted pictures of Melissa's hand, some turning away from the sight.

Sherry Cummings was called as the state's next witness. Cummings's eyes locked onto Sherry's eyes, where they stayed until she stepped from the witness stand. Sherry appeared scared to death. After the oath was administered, she brought her right hand down and clasped the other one that was shaking in an effort to steady them. In a trembling voice that seldom rose above a whisper, she told the jury what she had said when Jesse approached her about killing Judy. She described hearing the shots fired by Anita, helping Anita move Judy's body to the cellar, then cleaning up the blood.

When asked what Cummings had done immediately upon returning home, she answered, "He asked me if it was done. 'Nita looked at him and nodded."

Thornley wanted to know what happened next.

"He turned around and slapped me."

Sherry testified that she accompanied Cummings when he ordered her to go with him to dispose of Judy's body, and described how it was dumped in the pond near Atoka Lake. Finally

Sherry testified to Melissa's rape and the long ride in the car with Cummings and Melissa into Choctaw County and her wait in the car as she watched the two disappear into the woods with only Jesse returning. The testimony was rendered in an emotional, shaking voice. Sherry softly cried during the entire time she testified about Melissa's rape and the trip to Boswell.

Sherry was only asked a few questions regarding the beatings administered by Cummings and the terror surrounding the family. But the answers she gave to the ones that were asked made it clear that violence went on daily in the Cummings house. It appeared evident to those watching her testify she was either mind-bogglingly terrified of the man sitting only a few feet away from her, or she was an exceptional actress.

In final testimony she described Cummings as so controlling, that his years of tyranny had left her incapable of making a decision on her own.

Jody Minter's voice maintained a sharp edge as he cross-examined Sherry at length about inconsistencies in her prior testimony and statements she had given to the police. During questioning Minter's tone occasionally bordered on contemptuous. The defense attorney made noises about the plea-bargain agreement that Sherry had secured. She never hesitated in talking about it, and the sinister note hinted at by the defense when it was brought up soon diminished.

The woman who had shared Sherry's life of abuse, Anita Cummings, was called by the state next. Once situated in the witness-box, Anita, whose hands also were tightly clasped together, stared down at her lap, only raising her head when she was administered the oath to tell the truth. Anita was visibly nervous as she waited for the first question. As he had done with Sherry, Jesse Cummings locked eyes with the witness, but this time the stare turned colder, harder, sometimes lapsing into a scowl.

During her testimony Anita detailed for the jury her part in the terrible tragedy. Several times Anita, looking drained, would lift her right hand and press it to her temple and rub in a circular

motion for a few minutes. She appeared to be fatigued and
under extreme stress. Most of her testimony was rendered in a
flat, monotone voice interrupted occasionally by an effort to
choke back tears, even when she graphically described Melissa's
rape. When her efforts failed, Anita would quit talking until the
tears she had momentarily lapsed into were extinguished. The
briefly interrupted testimony was once more rendered in a dull,
flat cadence.

Defense attorney Paul Faulk accused Anita of lying regarding
Cummings's physical abuse, and as proof offered into evidence
a love letter she had written to Cummings not long after their
marriage. Handing Anita the marked exhibit, Faulk asked her
to read the letter to herself during a brief recess the court was
about to take.

During the break Anita attempted to attract Prosecutor John
McPhail's attention. When she was unable to, she called out
lightly, "John." The two quietly talked for a moment, and the
prosecutor returned to his seat.

The defense seized on the incident immediately after court
resumed, when Faulk levied an accusation at the frightened witness.

"I was at the bench and you were reading this letter to yourself when you looked up and called Prosecutor John McPhail
over to speak to him. You referred to him as John, didn't you?"

Anita, confusion written across her face, meekly answered,
"Yes, sir."

Faulk hurled his next accusation. "So, you're on a first-name
basis with Assistant District Attorney John McPhail, are you?"

Before an objection could be raised, Anita politely answered,
"No, sir. I just can't pronounce his last name."

Laughter trickled through the courtroom as Faulk flushed a
bright red, which began at the base of his neck and surged up
the all-American face. The attorney immediately turned the
jury's attention back to the love letter and away from his blunder,
asking her to read the contents of the letter to the jury, which

Anita did. The letter spoke of a young wife's love and devotion to her husband and a desire to work their problems out.

When she had finished reading the letter, Faulk inquired, "If Jesse Cummings was the abusive man you testified to earlier that beat you within weeks of your marriage and also beat your infant son, why would you write that letter expressing your love and devotion toward your husband?"

Anita's explanation was simply that she was fighting for the survival of a marriage that she had made a commitment to before God. She said she felt an obligation to try despite all the terrible things her husband had done.

The defense team quickly went on to another topic. They chose not to emphasize Anita's life-sentence plea bargain. It was the stiffest punishment other than death, and the subject was wisely left alone. As with Sherry, the topics of inconsistencies were discussed. Anita's ordeal finally came to an end. With one deep sigh that seemed to bear the weight of the world, Anita left the witness-box and was returned to her holding cell.

The women's testimony had been critical for the prosecution, and severely damaging for the defense.

At the defense table Jesse Cummings listened to his wives testify against him, defying him. He was angry. It would be the only emotion shown by the defendant through the rest of the trial. More than anything, Cummings appeared bored by the banality of the words coming from the witness-box, no matter how shocking, lifting his glasses from time to time to rub his eyes, and occasionally lifting his right hand to his mouth in an effort to stifle a yawn brought on by the tedious testimony.

Agent David Cathey, who had been present in the courtroom throughout the testimony, was called to the stand next. He was questioned extensively by defense attorney Jody Minter about the consent and the warrant the agent had gotten to search the house in Lehigh, and the validity of the evidence seized during the search. The judge, after listening to Cathey's testimony, ruled that the search warrant was valid, and his testimony continued as he explained to the jury his part in the case. When Agent Cathey stepped down, the state rested its case.

The defense began by immediately calling Cathey back to the stand. Questions were raised once more about the search conducted. On cross-examination, the state had only a few questions of their witness. The final question by the state revolved around Cathey's partner, Reanae Childers. The name had been heard several times in the courtroom, but the jurors had no idea who Childers was.

"I understand that the original case agent is Agent Reanae Childers. Is that correct?"

"Yes, sir."

"And she is now awaiting to give birth at this time."

"Any minute now. I've been associated with the case for a while. Reanae had been expecting that her childbirth might interfere with the trial. So I've been preparing with her to try and fill her role here this week." With that point cleared up for the jury, Cathey was allowed to return to the chair he had been occupying at the state's table.

Cummings's sister Debra Smith was the next witness called by the defense. Debra had very little testimony to impart to the jury about her brother, since she possessed no personal knowledge of the murders. She was on the stand to tell the twelve people as heartfelt as she could just how much she loved her brother.

Up to this point all they had known of the defendant was what the state's witnesses told them, and it was pretty bad. In an effort to bring human characteristics to Cummings, his sister was called. While Debra was in the witness-box, it was obvious she loved her brother. However, she divulged to the jury an incident she had failed to tell anyone during interviews.

Debra testified that Anita had gotten into "a knockdown, drag-out fight with Judy a couple of days 'fore she was missing. Anita told me 'bout it and said she'd 'told the bitch off.' "

The prosecutor, angry at what he felt was blatant perjury

right before his eyes, took little time demolishing the accusation.

He reminded the witness she had spoken to the case agent David Cathey on many occasions and never mentioned this fact until now. She answered she couldn't remember if she had told him or not.

"If Agent Cathey were to say that you had not told him about this incident, would you have any reason to doubt that?"

"No."

An inmate from Anita's jail testified next in her jailhouse orange. The testimony elicited by the defense consisted of the fact that the inmate found Anita to be an aggressive and hostile person who could never be influenced, whipped down, or cowed down.

On cross-examination Prosecutor McPhail established the inmate's lengthy history involving felonies where she had been convicted of intentionally and habitually lying. He posed one final question for the woman.

"You've done this kind of dishonesty thing a whole bunch, haven't you?"

Her lengthy criminal record spoke for itself. The inmate answered the only way she could. The implication was clear.

Rev. Edward Fields was called by defense attorney Jody Minter. Testimony was elicited about the things Anita had told him the night she turned herself in. When questioned, Rev. Fields answered that Anita was very upset and crying, and that after the confession she looked like a terrible weight had been lifted off her shoulders. The witness managed to get in that Anita continually watched the door to the shop, like she was watching her back. Minter's objective had been to bring to the jury's attention that some of the facts remembered by the witness were not the same as given by Anita in her statements.

The state deftly cleared up the allegation. The witness explained to the jury that he had been in shock, and had come in and out of the room as Anita told her story to his wife.

The defense then rested.

The rebuttal stage of the trial began.

The state recalled Agent Cathey once more. He was asked if Debra Smith had told him about the remark she attributed to Anita. He testified that as recently as April he had given her his card with his office number and told her if she thought of anything that might be important, to please contact him. He told the jury that he had heard Debra's allegation for the first time in the courtroom.

Both sides rested, and final argument in the guilt or innocence phase of the trial began.

James Thornley, who appeared calm and kept a low profile during most of the testimony, stood up and approached the jury. When he opened his mouth, the booming voice accused, "If we didn't do what Jesse wanted, we got in trouble!" Then he continued speaking barely above a whisper, as the gallery, startled by the sudden change of tone, strained to catch his next words: "Anita told you that. When asked about what type of relationship they had with Jesse, she told you she was beaten, sometimes daily. When asked how she dealt with that, do you remember her answer, folks?" Thornley's voice took rise again as he shouted, "She said, 'I learned to do what Jesse said!' "

Thornley lashed out at the defendant again. "Eleven years old! Only eleven years old! He rapes her and takes her to Choctaw County, where he kills her!"

The prosecutor then addressed Judy's death. "Just because this man didn't pull the trigger doesn't mean he's not guilty of her murder." In a more sedate voice, Thornley began the task of educating the jury regarding the charge.

Thornley's unrestrained voice picked up pace. "In the household of fear conducted by Jesse, you learn to do what Jesse tells you to! Thank you."

Because of the state's burden of proof, Thornley would have one more chance to address the jury.

Jody Minter rose and walked to the center of the courtroom. He talked long and low until he got to one issue. "Is this defendant guilty of bigamy? Probably. But that's for another jury, another time. Is this defendant guilty of committing an accessory after the fact by helping to move his sister's body? Almost certainly. But again, that's for another jury, another time."

Minter reduced the emotional facts of the case to a quick, sterile, and cold summation. "Basically, in 1991 about all anybody knows is that Judy is shot, her body dumped in a small pond by Atoka Lake. Melissa was stabbed in the chest and her body was dumped plumb off in a different county thirty or forty miles away.

"They can't be scared of Jesse 'cause he can't be there all the time. They claim they were so terrified of him they got a gun and killed another human being, instead of doing the right thing and certainly the more satisfying thing of shooting the SOB as he walks in the door!

"Sherry, thinking that Jesse burned her after listening to a portion of his tape, talks and gets thirty-five years, not too bad.

"They have a motive for blaming this on Jesse. It's called a plea bargain." Minter closed his final argument with a rather macabre analogy that had nothing to do with the murders. "The evidence the State of Oklahoma has to give you, metaphorically, is like a banana split. It's gorgeous. But when you look closely at it, it has maggots in it. What the state is telling you, folks, is, if you pick out the maggots, what remains is the truth and you can eat that. I'm saying if you have maggots in your food, throw it out."

When the defense attorney finished the unappetizing statement, he rested his case, sat down, and glanced over at the clock. It was closing in on noon. Unfortunately, appetites in the courtroom took a nosedive after Minter's allegory, which hopefully would be forgotten about before Judge Gabbard dismissed them and the jury started deliberating Jesse Cummings's fate.

James Thornley stood once more. "All you have to do is look at the trained professionals, the OSBI people who did such a wonderful job here. Chris Dill, Chuck Jeffries, David Cathey. They didn't try to deceive you. If they couldn't remember, they simply told you that they couldn't remember. Isn't that normal?

"Yes, there are inconsistencies in these ladies' testimony. I don't mean to be flippant, but when you look at the inconsistencies in Anita's and Sherry's testimony, I ask you to remember an old song by Maurice Chevalier, in which he and his wife are reminiscing about their younger days. He says, 'Oh, yes. I remember it well. You were wearing blue.' She replies, 'I was wearing pink.' The song goes on where the couple remember events, and both remember it differently. Folks, that's a very common thing!

"Jesse knew Melissa was dead. He knew Judy was dead. And what does he do? He takes their pictures and fills out a missing person report. He even takes a friend to go out and look for Melissa when he knows exactly where she is and exactly what condition she's in!"

Thornley picked up the three identical notebooks that Agent Cathey recovered in his search of the home, and as he addressed each one, he placed it on the jury rail to emphasize his point. "He writes in these books, one for Sherry, one for Anita, and one for himself. This is a man who handcuffs people in his house, and he is a man who wants to keep his story straight when he is questioned.

"Do you believe for one minute that a man who terrorizes his family for small infractions, would do nothing when he returns and finds out his sister was killed? Does he punch them? No! Think about what he does do. He hides the body. In that household with handcuffs, bullwhips and beatings, you don't dare do something unless Jesse tells you to do it!

"If you get in trouble for not eating, how much trouble do you think you would have gotten into for killing his sister, unless he wanted it done? Folks, the only one who got in trouble that night was Sherry, and he slapped her because she didn't do what he had ordered her to! I ask that you return a verdict of guilty. God bless you."

On that accusation the jury was sent to deliberate.

The deliberations were short. By the time the twelve men and women, along with the two alternates, retired, there was no doubt in their minds what they would do. Both sides studied the faces of the jury as they filed back into the courtroom and took their seats. The jury found Jesse James Cummings guilty of two counts of murder, one for the murder of Judy Moody Mayo, and the other for the murder of Melissa Marie Moody.

Witnesses were rounded up for the punishment phase of the trial, but not before Cathey made it to the nearest phone to inform Reanae Childers, who was anxiously sitting at home with her portable telephone at her side. Ready to go into labor at any moment, she nervously waited as both major events in her life were coming to a culmination at the same time.

Sarah Yaws, Sherry's sister, was the only witness called by the state in the punishment phase. Her testimony was dramatic and devastating to the defense. Sarah, eight months pregnant, was escorted into the courtroom by a bailiff. She took her oath and settled into the witness-box. The young woman was visibly distressed the moment she took the stand. Her heart began to race as her body trembled.

Thornley proceeded to question her with care.

The witness testified how she knew Cummings and why she was spending the night over at his house when the rape occurred. Sarah struggled for composure as she explained how Cummings had propositioned her and she had refused him.

When she began to testify about the rape that had occurred that night, short gasps for breath punctuated her anxiety over telling the details to a courtroom of complete strangers.

"When you woke up, Ms. Yaws, what occurred?"

"Jesse was sitting on the edge of the bed and I started getting scared because I'd never really trusted him anyway."

Thornley knew to proceed from this point forward gently and cautiously.

"When you woke up and he was on the side of the bed, what occurred after that?"

"He sat down beside me."

"And after he did that, what occurred?"

"He tried to force himself on me."

"And can you tell us how he did that?"

"He was lying down and forced himself."

Thornley was afraid this would happen. It was a natural re-action women had when asked to give personal and embarrass-ing details concerning a sexual act. The witnesses almost always hedged at this point, not wanting to say out loud what sexual acts had occurred. With that in mind, the attorney proceeded with due vigilance.

"And I realize this is difficult, but when you say forced him-self, please tell the jury what you're referring to?"

"He forced himself to have sex."

It was like pulling teeth. The fact that the young teenager was pregnant and ready to deliver any moment was not helping her mounting anxiety.

"And can you describe that for the jury, please?"

"I was lying there . . ."

As Sarah started shaking and gasping for breath, Thornley rushed to help her.

"Do you need some water?" he offered, trying urgently to help the young, expectant mother through the terrible trauma.

Sarah started mildly gagging and whispered she would take a drink.

The seconds ticked into agonizing minutes as Sarah contin-ued to gasp for air, would pause, then moan. Everyone in the courtroom thought she was going to pass out at any moment.

Paul Faulk quickly rose and offered, "Your Honor, we have no objection to a short recess."

Thornley approached his witness and asked, "Do you need a break?"

Sarah timidly nodded yes. Thornley helped the pregnant teen-ager off the stand. She had just taken a few steps toward the door when a bailiff walked up to escort her to the bathroom. Shocking everyone, Sarah's knees gave way and she collapsed into the bailiff's arms, which broke her fall to the floor. Judge Gabbard announced that there would be a brief recess.

When the recess was over, the fragile witness was gingerly helped back to the stand and asked the questions she so dreaded.

Tremulously she recounted for the jury what had happened to her that night. She fought choking on tears and words as she gave her last statement before being turned over to the defense side for questions. Sarah testified that the rape had resulted in a pregnancy that ended with a miscarriage four months later.

Jody Minter had the unenviable task of questioning the delicate witness. Handling her with kid gloves, he got her on and off the stand as soon as possible.

The state rested with their only rebuttal witness being Sarah. But she had been a powerful one.

The defense attorney called family and friends to speak of their love for Jesse Cummings, and their willingness to support the defendant emotionally and financially in prison if the jurors gave him a life sentence. Each predictably said they would.

The state would cross-examine them, asking if their opinion of Cummings, which was always glowing, had changed now that they knew he had killed two people. Their answers predictably were that they didn't think he had done it.

Mildred Tucker was called to the stand. Dressed in a green pair of stretch pants and overblouse, the sad, young woman waddled slowly toward the witness chair and eased her considerable girth into it. Breaths were held in the gallery as the sturdy oak chair creaked loudly, moaning from the burden of her three hundred fifty pounds. But the chair stood firm and did not break. Mildred fidgeted and looked distinctly uncomfortable as she kept her head down. She tearfully spoke of her undying love for Jesse Cummings, and informed the jury that the two were now engaged.

On cross-examination the state made the point that after eight or nine years together, the engagement conveniently occurred just a few days after Cummings's arrest. Sheriff Bill Ward was called to testify that Cummings had been a model prisoner. Cummings's frail aunt Edna testified that Jesse came from a loving home, and that she never saw him receive any spankings, much less a beating. Other relatives testified to basically the same things, that they loved Jesse and would support him always. The last witness was Rev. Joe Lester, the family minister, who had married Sherry and Jesse, and had conducted the funerals of every Cummings family member that had died. The pastor testified that he never saw Cummings mistreat any child or woman. When James Thornley asked the elderly gentleman if he knew that Cummings had two wives, the witness was taken aback for a second, then answered he did not, but the fact did not change his opinion of Cummings.

Thornley asked the pastor if he was aware that Cummings placed the children in handcuffs. The reverend hesitated, then answered, "No. I didn't know about that."

He was queried if the information would change his opinion. Reverend Lester cautiously answered, "I wouldn't have agreed with that, no."

Trying to salvage their witness on redirect, Jody Minter asked the reverend, "Even after what the district attorney asked you about, and what you know this jury convicted him of, do you think Jesse's worth saving?" The good reverend didn't hedge, he promptly answered that yes, he was.

Thornley stood with only one question for the preacher, but it was the perfect one.

"Do you think everyone's worth saving, sir?"

Without hesitation the preacher answered, "Yes, sir. I think everybody's worth saving."

Thornley had made his point and made it extremely well.

In final arguments regarding the life or death sentence, the jury would decide what Jesse Cummings deserved for his despicable acts. James Thornley went on the warpath immediately. "You just heard testimony that this man, right here, who was responsible for both deaths, also raped a fourteen-year-old girl! You heard her. She pleaded with Jesse. Told him no! But remember Jesse gets what Jesse wants!"

Thornley stepped forward into the well of the courtroom and told the jury their patience was appreciated by the state, that he knew they had been through a long and tiring day, but that they were almost finished. Then he advised them, "I'm not going to go through all the testimony in the last couple of days, but I want you to remember the evidence when you go back to deliberate in this phase and take it into consideration as well as what you heard today. And what you heard today, ladies and gentlemen, was approximately six months prior to the death of Judy and the death of Melissa . . ." Thornley paused, then startled everyone when the next words where delivered in a voice that shook with rage and indignation. "That this same man, right here, who was responsible for both their deaths, raped a fourteen-year-old!" Thornley raised his left arm and jabbed a stiffened finger in the direction of the defendant. He continued in a voice now quieted, "And when he did so, he put his hand over her mouth and nose until she passed out. She told Jesse no." His voice thundered again, "Jesse gets what Jesse wants!"

Thornley took a moment from the emotional diatribe to explain to the jury what special circumstances meant in applying them to the death penalty. With that task completed, Thornley's emotions took control again. "I suggest he is a continuing threat to society. He rapes a fourteen-year-old girl. He directs two women to kill his sister, he rapes an eleven-year-old girl and then he takes her out and he kills her, as well! If that's not a continuing threat to society, then I don't know what is. As to the other element of the charge, remember he threw her little jumpsuit in Atoka Lake, then tried to hide her down in Choctaw County. What did he tell Sarah Yaws after he raped her? I'll kill your mother. I'll get your family. He couldn't do that with Melissa 'cause she didn't have anyone to tell. We believe we've presented the evidence to support a verdict of death. Thank you."

The district attorney ended his passionate plea by asking the jury to return a verdict of death on both counts of murder.

Minter was up on his feet and raring to go. "They raped a fourteen-year-old! They killed his sister! They killed his niece! They raped that same niece! They were right in the middle of this thing! And, they are now doing one life sentence, and they are now doing thirty-five years." Every time Minter would say "they," he placed strong emphasis on the word. "All we're asking you for is to proportion it out. We brought you folks that testified that there *is* a good side to Jesse, and they love him.

"This is a man's life. We're not talking about a stretch in jail. We're talking about a man's life here. I ain't telling you he ain't done wrong. I ain't telling you that he is anything other than what he is, but I'm telling you that they did every one of those crimes, so no matter what you think about whether Jesse was controlling 'em or threatening 'em, they did it! I'm not telling you to set the man free. I'm telling you not to kill him.

"You're the ones that'll have to live with your decision the rest of your lives. Folks, when I'm through with this case, I'm gonna go fishing. No matter what the outcome. But I don't have to live with the thought that I've sent a man to his death. You do. I ask you to give him life. Thank you."

Thornley kept his final statement short, but right on course.

" 'They did it' just won't cut it, folks! They are not the continuing threat to society!" Raising his voice, Thornley pivoted, and once more squarely facing the defendant, jabbed his finger at him. In a voice that blazed disgust, he continued, "This man right here is! They were not out there when Melissa, a helpless, little eleven-year-old girl, was in the woods being stabbed to death! They weren't anywhere near! He took her out in the woods and he came back alone, covered in her blood! He is the cold-blooded killer! It's not them! It's him! He is the one, ladies and gentlemen, that deserves the death penalty! He's the one on trial. He's the one that's a continuing threat to society. He is the one, ladies and gentlemen, that actually does deserve the death penalty, and I ask that you give to him exactly what he deserves!"

James Thornley returned to the prosecutor's table and sat down, spent by the emotions that overwhelmed him throughout this trial. He was glad it was almost over.

The jury members retired to make one of the hardest decisions of their lives. By the time they retired to consider their verdict, it was 4:30 in the afternoon. Aside from Judge Gabbard and his court staff, the prosecutors, and defense attorneys, less than twenty people remained in the courtroom. Although it was now late in the day, no one left. They were all determined to ride out the wait for the verdicts, regardless of how long it took. It would be a long wait.

Quickly the assembly separated into two groups. The first one was made up of various people, for various reasons, who patiently and anxiously waited the jury's verdict bound together with one common goal. They adamantly wanted Jesse Cummings to go down for the murders and receive the death penalty for Melissa's murder.

Part of that gathering consisted of the OSBI agents, who had worked so hard in various stages since the murders to get to this point. Childers started her second vigil, where she had the first. The officers and deputies who had doggedly worked on the murders for years in an attempt to solve the crime, and bring the murderer to trial, were there, too. Scattered among the small crowd were a couple of spouses and several journalists.

Anita and Sherry Cummings were sweating out their wait locked in a small cell in the courthouse. Occasionally various officers in the Sheriff's Department and the OSBI would give Anita a short reprieve from her tiny cell. When out of her cell, she would be sequestered in Sheriff Ward's office. Ward was thoughtful enough to allow the journalists access to his prisoner for short periods of time. Anita was a complete wreck. She kept thinking, if the jury lets him off, I'm dead. He had told both women years earlier that he could get to anyone if he wanted to kill them, even when they were locked up.

The second group assembled consisted of Jesse Cummings, who spent his wait locked up. His sister Debra stayed for a while, and then would come and go throughout the long wait. Jesse's aunt Edna stayed until her frail bones made her go home. Mildred Tucker's father was there off and on, but he, too, had left early. Melody Thompson occasionally popped in and out.

Only one person was determined to stay the entire course for Cummings—Mildred Tucker. The sad, young woman spent most of her time just sitting and praying or staring off into space, terrified that Jesse would be locked away where she would not have access to him. Jesse's future wife would sit on that hard bench until hell froze over before she deserted the man she desperately loved.

Noticeably absent from the proceedings were Sherry and Anita's families. The women knew testifying about their deviant personal lives was going to be hard enough. Both families were asked to please stay home. The Lewis and Yaws family members respected the request. Two other absentees were Pat and Lisa Cathy, who both felt they were not prepared emotionally to listen to the testimony given in their respective best friends' murder trial.

Several hours into deliberations a knock was heard from the inside of the jury room. Hungry, tired, and ready for the ordeal to be over with, the crowd eagerly took their seats hoping the jury had reached a verdict. The bailiff responded to the knock and was handed a note. Instead of the verdict everyone had hoped for, a troubling note was sent out. It read, "If there are different sentences handed down on two crimes, will the greater sentence be served?"

Judge Gabbard sent back the only reply he was legally allowed. "It is your duty to set punishment and follow your instructions."

The confused jurors continued their deliberations, and the waiting resumed. Milling around the gallery, everyone speculated on the meaning of the question. The ones experienced in criminal trials all agreed it probably meant the jury wanted to give Cummings life for Judy's murder and death for Melissa's and did not know how to rectify the situation. As time dragged on, the agents and officers who had lived and breathed the case since 1991, and the prosecutors who had immersed themselves into trial preparations for the past year, began to express concern that the unschooled jury would solve the dilemma by giving

Cummings two life sentences. Finally as the hour was closing in on midnight, a loud rap on the door holding the twelve people captive startled everyone.

The jury's dilemma had indeed concerned the assessment of different sentences. When the jury began their deliberation on punishment, they had quickly and unanimously agreed Cummings should be sentenced to death for Melissa's murder. After a short discussion, the decision was made that Cummings receive a life sentence for Judy's murder.

The jurors had spent the rest of its lengthy deliberations attempting to answer the question they had sought the court's guidance on. With Judge Gabbard legally helpless to counsel them, the emotionally and physically drained jury, incensed at what Cummings had done and afraid that the lesser sentence would prevail, decided finally to take no chances.

People scurried to their seats as Jesse Cummings was being retrieved from his cell and brought back to the courtroom and seated. The three men at the prosecutor's table fidgeted in their chairs. Thornley and McPhail took deep breaths to quell the butterflies taking flight within their stomachs. Agent Cathey felt the cold knot that had occupied his stomach during the lengthy deliberations begin to tighten again. The gallery soberly settled back against the hard benches. When everyone was seated, the jury filed in, their faces blank.

With the indication from the judge that he was ready to proceed, Cummings rose to his feet. His stomach, once washboard flat, was now soft and flabby. The thick hair of his youth was thinning. Projecting the image of a harmless, middle-aged nobody, Jesse Cummings looked more like a Walter Mitty than a Charles Manson as he waited to hear his fate in the hushed courtroom.

The clerk stood to read the verdict. "Having found Jesse James Cummings guilty of first degree murder in the death of Judy Moody Mayo, we hereby fix his punishment at death." Cummings's knees buckled. The yellow jailhouse pallor, which colored his face, changed into a pasty white. Thornley shut his eyes for a full minute. A collective expulsion of air could be slightly heard from those who had held their breaths when the clerk started reading. Mildred Tucker, at first paralyzed, buried her face in her hands and softly cried. The clerk's shaking hands gripped the verdict form tighter as her voice, trembling from the gravity of the words she had just spoken, read that Cummings would also die for murdering Melissa Moody.

The jury's eyes were hard, cold, and barren as they waited for the judge to begin his pronouncement. Leveling his gaze at the defendant, Judge Gabbard began solemnly reading, "Mr. Cummings, on May 9, 1996, having been tried by a jury of your peers. . . ."

The tension in the air began to dissipate as the judge's voice slowly faded. Detached from the voice speaking in his direction, just as he had been from the sobs and pleas of Melissa as she stood terrified in the isolated woods, Jesse Cummings stared blankly ahead.

The gallery listened as Cummings was advised that he would be allowed to have a minister and five family members or friends present to comfort him on the day of execution.

The murderer and rapist of women and children was unable to keep the judge's voice at bay long enough to escape his final words, ". . . you will be strapped to a gurney and given a continuous intravenous injection of a lethal quantity of an ultrashort-acting barbiturate in combination with a chemical paralytic agent until such time as you are dead." The grave words hovered in the air of the silent courtroom.

The coldhearted killer, who had embraced death by deriving pleasure killing others, would now have to deal with his own at the hands of the state.

Cummings's prescribed method of death would be antiseptic compared to the atrocious one he had inflicted on Melissa. No doubt she would have preferred to lie down on a white cushion, comforted by the presence of those she loved, and painlessly drift off into a peaceful sleep. Instead the terrified child had walked with a quiet dignity into the isolated woods, where she was savagely raped and murdered, her lifeless body abandoned and crumpled in the dirt, surrounded only by darkness.

Jesse Cummings had once taken from Melissa the thing she wanted most in the world, now she had done the same to him.

The final sound in the courtroom was the judge's gavel sounding like a clap of thunder as it collided with the oak bench.

Sadly, the only people who attended the trial on Melissa's behalf were the agents and officers who had worked tirelessly to hold her killer accountable. They came seeking justice in a child's name, determined to find it. And they did.

Strengthened in the knowledge Jesse Cummings would kill and rape no more, Agent Cathey walked out of the courthouse into the spring night, renewed. Glancing at the breathtaking stars scattered around him, he momentarily paused, allowing the fresh breeze to wash the stench of Jesse Cummings from him. The verdict came as cold comfort when one considered the fact that Melissa would never again feel the wind filter gently through her hair..

Adults were supposed to protect the children of the world from harm and the monsters in it. The shawl of regret that was wrapped tightly around David Cathey's shoulders pulled a little tighter as he somberly stood in the crisp night air reflecting on this truism. With nothing more to be done, the agent got into his car and disappeared into the darkness. His thoughts lingered on the sweet, innocent child that no one had been able to protect from a monster named Jesse Cummings.

Author's Note

Anita caught a lot of flak because she received a life sentence instead of death. Extreme mitigating circumstances existed in this case like none I have ever seen. It is only through Anita's strength, courage, and willingness to accept whatever punishment she would be given, that Jesse Cummings sits on Death Row and can never hurt anyone else again. Agent Childers explained it best, "Because she came forward, I don't think she should pay for it with her life."

People who knew of Jesse Cummings's fascination with Charles Manson suspect Melissa was a "thrill kill," a way to be closer to his idol. Killing Judy accomplished two things. Cummings was cleaning house of those who knew too much, and it allowed him to get her out of the way so he could rape and murder Melissa. His father's suspicious death and Cummings's eagerness to adopt Scottie seem to echo the "cleaning house" theory. Charles Manson effectively and often used the technique of murder to rid himself of potential problems.

The research for this book was extensive and took me to various places. However, the most interesting place I ended up was in lockup in the Cole County jail. Time was precious and Anita and Sherry had so much valuable information to relay that Sheriff Ward graciously allowed me to interview and record Anita and Sherry while they were in his custody. He also was nice enough to tell his deputies as he left each day, throwing in a chuckle, "Let that nice, little writer lady out if she wants."

For a period of ten to twelve hours for over a four-day period, I remained sequestered in Sherry and Anita's tiny cell with them. The toilet was situated to the immediate right as I entered the cell, and right behind was a shower barely big enough to stand in. On the days I couldn't choke down the starchy diet, I went hungry.

By nightfall, exhausted and claustrophobic from being locked in a cell the size of my master bathroom, I quickly gathered my things and rushed to the hotel room an hour's drive away, which now looked like a penthouse suite to me. There, I lingered in an actual bathtub of hot water and climbed into a soft bed that got softer every night I was there. I enjoyed living like decent, law-abiding people get to. Each morning I would steel myself for another day of incarceration made even worse by listening to the horrible stories pent up for so long. Buried inside Anita and Sherry were deeds unshared even between the two, and now being shared for the first time.

The experience made an indelible impression on me. So much so, that driving home to Texas from Oklahoma, I set the cruise control on my little red Mustang and diligently watched for speed-limit changes. With the string of little towns from Oklahoma to Texas, there are many. Even now, I stop at red lights on deserted streets at three o'clock in the morning, with no prospect of anyone seeing, or caring, if I had slipped past it.

In jail privacy is nonexistent. It is a horrible place to be for even one day. It must be an agonizing way to live out the rest of your life. But steep prices have to be paid for the choices and decisions that destroy the lives of others.

After careful study and analysis of Jesse Cummings, I have reached the conclusion that he is a "serial, antisocial, lust killer with a disorganized personality." The sixteen basic characteristics that fit this type of killer match Cummings perfectly, and all were verified as traits he exhibited:

Lust killers fantasize a lot over a period of years; violently abuse animals; are usually loners; have negative personality traits; use drugs, alcohol or both; are very mobile, frequently changing jobs, towns or experiencing work problems; like to set fires; have a strong hatred toward society and against women in particular; have average to low intelligence; are socially immature; were harshly disciplined as a child; are usually bed wetters; and are sexually dysfunctional. Jesse Cummings was a dangerous man. Thank God, he was stopped before his sex-slave plan actually came to fruition.

When I asked Anita how she felt about her life sentence, she told me, "I'm not throwing a big fit over it 'cause despite the fact that Jesse was threatening me and my child, I still pulled that trigger. I can *never* change that." When I asked her if she could go back and change one moment in her life, which would it be, without hesitation Anita answered, "The five seconds I walked in that room and pulled the trigger."

When I asked the same questions of Sherry, regarding her prison sentence, she replied, "I don't have a problem with it. I deserve to be here.[Jesse was given the death penalty] I'm happy, but at the same time, I'm sad 'cause I know that it ain't gonna be long before my little girl asks me where's her daddy. I'm gonna have to lie to her and I've done enough lying in my lifetime for Jesse. I'm gonna have to tell her something. I just don't know what."

When I asked Sherry if she could go back and change one moment in her life, which would hers be, she hung her head and in a voice slightly above a whisper, said, "The day I said, 'I do.' "

Epilogue

James Thornley is still one of the finest district attorneys in Oklahoma.

The Cummings case was the last one John McPhail tried before he left the District Attorney's Office after being a prosecutor for ten years. He moved his family to Texas, where he conducts administrative hearings regarding illegal aliens.

Agent Reanae Childers had a beautiful, dark-haired daughter, Rachel. She is still a top-notch agent with the OSBI.

Agent David Cathey is now married. He and his wife, Dusty, recently had a baby boy, Michael David Cathey. Like his friends Reanae Childers and Chris Dill, he remains an excellent representative of the OSBI.

Agent Chris Dill continues to use the knowledge garnered in his days as a criminalist. He remains an excellent and diversified agent.

OSBI agents awarded commendations for their exceptional efforts in this case were Agents Reanae Childers, Chris Dill, Charlie Mackey, Chuck Jeffries, David Cathey, and Dale Birchfield.

Jessica Cummings is in foster care. She failed the third grade and still bangs her head against the nearest hard surface when she hears her father's name. Sherry is sporadically permitted to see her only child.

Custody of Scottie and Chelsea was given to Anita's parents. Anita sees her children every six months, and is attempting to get a transfer to an Arkansas facility so she can see them more often. Scottie is a troubled soul, the invention of Jesse Cummings. He is undergoing intensive counseling. Chelsea has no memory of her father and is doing excellent. Jesse Cummings's parental rights to Chelsea and Jessica were permanently terminated.

Anita, sentenced to life in prison, is working on a college degree in theology and mythology. In order to attend college classes, she has to pay her tuition, which she does with her parents' help. She is an education tutor for other inmates, teaching them how to read and write. Because of the severe physical trauma Cummings caused through torturing her, she bears permanent scars over her body and face. She suffers from high blood pressure, hypoglycemia, chronic pelvic inflammation disease, and chronic ceratitis. She is only twenty-nine years old. She will be eligible for parole when she turns sixty.

Sherry, sentenced to thirty-five years in prison, is working on her GED, a requirement of all inmates. Her physical and emotional scars are as prolific as Anita's. Sherry, who is thirty-one years old, will not be eligible for parole until she is almost fifty.

Despite the almost impervious wall Jesse Cummings built between the two women, Anita and Sherry weathered the storm together. Both women, undergoing extensive counseling, are housed in separate units at the Mable Bassett Correctional Facility in Oklahoma and rarely see each other.

The house where so much torture took place and sheltered too many demons was burned to the ground. I've been told some of the townspeople did it to erase the hideous memory. However the blaze started, no one was sorry and no one was ever charged with the crime. People are just happy that the monument to Cummings's sick, evil heart no longer stands.

It is not known where Melody Thompson, Megan, or Billy are today and if the children are safe. Hopefully, they are.

Mildred Tucker continues her wait to marry Jesse Cummings. Shortly after the trial, Judge Gabbard was approached by

Mildred to marry her and Jesse. He refused, and no other judge has been found who will agree to, either. She is the one person Cummings is now dependent on.

To the slain police officer's family in California, take what comfort you can in knowing what the State of California failed to do, the State of Oklahoma will set right the day Jesse Cummings is executed. The fact that Cummings sits on Death Row as a weak, unimportant, impotent little man, powerless to do anything but take the orders he is given, must make his life unbearable. That thought alone illustrates the reality and wonderful power of karma.

Jesse Cummings, unlike Charles Manson, who escaped being put to death when California temporarily outlawed the death penalty, won't be as lucky as his hero. And unlike Manson, no one comes down to do television interviews with the forty-three-year-old. Instead, Cummings sits on Death Row in the state penitentiary known as "Big Mac" in McAlester, Oklahoma. The man who could not stand to be alone, now is. He stares at four walls awaiting his destiny with the executioner.

Melissa would have been nineteen years old on March 7, 1999, but Jesse Cummings chose to rob the promising young girl of a lifetime of special moments. She will never experience her first kiss, high school prom, a marriage, or children. Instead, Melissa Marie Moody will remain forever in our hearts, forever frozen in time—forever eleven.

ACKNOWLEDGMENTS

I would like to thank the following people who made the writing of this book possible.

Debra Souka, the court reporter, who was of invaluable help to me.

Judge Douglas Gabbard II, an outstanding member of the bench, whose wonderful sense of humor kept me laughing instead of crying, along with his beautiful wife, Robyn, who graciously extended their home to me. The many courtesies Judge Gabbard extended to me were a tremendous benefit to this book.

Granny, for helping me maintain a sense of humor during devastating, chilling testimony. And, the "granny pillows" she provided me that literally saved my butt.

Wanda Utterback, my pal and fellow journalist. Whenever we were together, what she didn't think of to do, I did. We were both fortunate that she was friends with every officer on the police force in Coalgate.

Sheriff Bill Ward and his deputies, whose cooperation and many courtesies extended to me made it possible to get the in-depth interviews with Anita and Sherry.

District Attorney James Thornley, who effectively and chillingly brought home to the jury the horror of Melissa's last day on earth.

Assistant District Attorney John McPhail, whose organizational skills brought the cohesiveness this case needed.

Sheriff Gary McCool and Deputy Junior Head, who worked tirelessly in the background, on this case. The time you took to go over the case made the story more cohesive in writing.

Agent Chuck Jeffries, whose talent and skill led to a confession from Jesse Cummings.

Agent Chris Dill, whose skills as a criminalist played an important role in bringing this case to a close, whose talents as an interrogator resulted in Cummings's confession, and whose heartbreaking compassion for Melissa never failed her. As the only person who was consistently involved and present during all key moments, your invaluable help allowed me to create as closely as possible the events as they happened.

Agent Reanae Childers, who devotedly and tirelessly sought justice in a child's name, refusing to give up as years passed with Melissa's killer still free. And for maintaining a wonderful sense of humor when life's twists and turns prevented her from being present as the case she worked so hard on began to fall into place. Your input was invaluable to me also.

Agents Charlie Mackey and Dale Birchfield, both dedicated agents who contributed significantly to this case.

Most of all, my gratitude goes to OSBI agent David Cathey for his dedication and persistence in assisting Agent Childers on this case. His invaluable friendship to this author and the priceless information he entrusted to me made telling this story a reality. Little did this writer know, that on a spring day while covering a very boring trial in another Oklahoma courtroom, Agent Cathey would pop into my life and bring my attention to this heartbreaking story that so desperately needed to be told.

Janet Wilkins Manus, without question the best and most loyal agent that exists. Her encouragement and belief in me keep me strong.

Justin Manus, whose invaluable counsel throughout my research in this case, is just the best. I don't know what I would do without either of you, and hope to never find out.

My editor, Karen Haas, whose strong support, belief in me, and patience helped see this project to fruition. She is a treasure to work with.

Always my children, Lisa and Troy, and my parents, Thelma

and Bill McNabb, whose unwavering support keeps me healthy, sane, and focused.

Lisa and Pat Cathy, for sharing and reliving painful memories of their best friends, who knew them best. They gave me insight into the victims' personalities making them come alive for me. Because of them, Melissa and Judy lived once more to tell their story.

Anita and Sherry, for their candor. They never tried to shirk the heavy responsibility or culpability in this matter. They relayed the horrible truth in all its ugliness while reliving the most terrifying events in their lives. They did not do it to convince anyone of their innocence, but in hopes that other women might learn from their mistakes and escape the horror they were unable to. For making the precarious decision to trust me when all trust had been taken from them.

The Yaws and Lewis families, for cooperating and entrusting me with valued family photographs.

And finally to someone who holds a special place in my heart, and always will, "Even if I were blind, I'd know you are beautiful."